COMMUNICATION, COGNITION, AND ANXIETY

COMMUNICATION, COGNITION, AND ANXIETY

edited by
MELANIE BOOTH-BUTTERFIELD

Originally published as a special issue of the
Journal of Social Behavior and Personality

SAGE PUBLICATIONS
The International Professional Publishers
Newbury Park London New Delhi

Copyright © 1991 by Select Press

All rights reserved. No part of this book may be reproduced or utilized in any form or by any means, electronic or mechanical, including photocopying, recording, or by any information storage and retrieval system, without permission in writing from the publisher.

For information address:

SAGE Publications, Inc.
2455 Teller Road
Newbury Park, California 91320

SAGE Publications Ltd.
6 Bonhill Street
London EC2A 4PU
United Kingdom

SAGE Publications India Pvt. Ltd.
M-32 Market
Greater Kailash I
New Delhi 110 048 India

Printed in the United States of America

Library of Congress Cataloging-in-Publication Data

Main entry under title:

Communication, cognition & anxiety / edited by Melanie Booth-Butterfield.
    p. cm.
  "Originally published as a special issue of the Journal of social behavior and personality, 1990, vol. 5, no. 2."
  Includes bibliographical references and indexes.
  ISBN 0-8039-4087-4. — ISBN 0-8039-4088-2 (pbk.)
    1. Interpersonal communication. 2. Anxiety. 3. Cognition.
I. Booth-Butterfield, Melanie. II. Title: Communication, cognition, and anxiety.
BF637.C45C646   1991
152.4'6 — dc20   90-23793
                                                                         CIP

FIRST SAGE PRINTING, 1991

Sage Production Editor: Astrid Virding

Contents

The Interrelationship of Communication, Cognition, and Anxiety
Melanie Booth-Butterfield   vii

SECTION I:
PERSPECTIVES ON COMMUNICATION, COGNITION, AND ANXIETY

Anxiety, Cognitive Interference, and Performance
Irwin G. Sarason, Barbara R. Sarason, and Gregory R. Pierce   1

Willingness to Communicate: A Cognitive View
James C. McCroskey and Virginia P. Richmond   19

Anxiety, Cognition, and Behavior: In Search of a Broader Perspective
Mark R. Leary   39

SECTION II:
INTERNAL PROCESSES ASSOCIATED WITH ANXIETY AND COMMUNICATION

Toward a Hemispheric Processing Approach To Communication Competence
Daniel E. Sellers and Don W. Stacks   45

Chronic Issue-Specific Fear Inhibits Systematic Processing Of Persuasive Communications
Christopher Jepson and Shelly Chaiken   61

Public Speaking Anxiety Qua Performance Anxiety: A Revised Model and an Alternative Therapy
Michael T. Motley   85

SECTION III:
OUTCOMES ASSOCIATED WITH ANXIETY AND INFORMATION PROCESSING

Decision Rule Orientation and Public Speaking Apprehension
Michael J. Beatty and Robyn P. Clair   105

Shyness and Anxious Self-Preoccupation During a Social Interaction
Lisa A. Melchior and Jonathan M. Cheek   117

Self-Disclosure and Social Perception: The Impact of Private, Negative, and Extreme Communications
Linda E. Lazowski and Susan M. Andersen   131

SECTION IV:
ADDITIONAL PERSPECTIVES ON ANXIETY-RELATED COMMUNICATION AND ITS MEASUREMENT

Potential Cognitive Processes and Consequences of Receiver Apprehension: A Meta-analytic Review
Raymond W. Preiss, Lawrence R. Wheeless, and Mike Allen   155

The Development and Validation of a Measure of Negative Affectivity
Joseph P. Stokes and Ira M. Levin   173

Cognitive Components of Test Anxiety: A Comparison of Assessment and Scoring Methods
Kirk B. Blankstein and Gordon L. Flett   187

Communication Apprehension and Rational Emotive Therapy: An Interview with Dr. Albert Ellis
Arden K. Watson and Carly H. Dodd   203

Index of Names   211

Subject Index   219

About the Authors   223

The Interrelationship of Communication, Cognition, and Anxiety

Melanie Booth-Butterfield
Department of Communication Studies
West Virginia University

Researchers from a variety of social science disciplines have long been interested in the general effects of anxiety on both performance and observers' perceptions of the source. However, more recent questions are addressing underlying or attendent processes within the phenomenon of anxious arousal. Current research is aimed both at understanding antecedents and the mediating, subtle role anxiety plays in how anxious communicators process information. One major issue appears to be the extent to which biases in cognitive processing are induced or exacerbated by the anxious arousal leading to potentially dysfunctional communication patterns (cf. Carver & Scheier, 1986; Norem & Cantor, 1986). This volume focuses on two major aspects: (1) how anxiety influences thinking and perceptual/interpretative processes, and (2) how cognitions or thoughts function to moderate felt anxiety. Both processes are internal and yet have significant impact on subsequent communication production — thus, the interrelationship of communication, cognition, and anxiety.

One of the goals of this book is presentation of an eclectic approach. It offers ground-breaking and unique views of how anxiety and cognition impact communication. Based on an understanding of the foundations of anxiety-related research, these chapters present information or interpretations not generally found in more traditional collections. The researchers have employed widely divergent research and analytical procedures from both the fields of social psychology and communication in their attempts to explain the processes involved with cognition, anxiety, and communication.

Methods employed in these chapters range from experimental manipulation of communication variables such as type of self-disclosure (Lazowski & Anderson) or the quality of messages designed to elicit fear and anxiety about cancer (Jepson & Chaiken), to meta-analysis of studies of receiver-based anxieties (Preiss, Wheeless,

& Allen), to in-depth interviews with experts (Watson & Dodd), to the more clinical approach employed by Motley as he analyzes high public speaking anxious individuals' cognitive orientations toward public speaking events. However, all are unified in their investigation of communicative thought processes, emotional arousal, and the implications these have for human interactions.

Conceptual Perspectives

In the initial section, prominent researchers from the fields of communication and psychology present their perspectives on how cognition and anxiety intertwine to influence communication. Sarason, Sarason, and Pierce adopt a different, although not contradictory, stance compared to the statement developed by McCroskey and Richmond. Whereas Sarason and his colleagues contend that anxiety functions to interfere with cognitive processes and distract communicators, McCroskey and Richmond propose that communication is a volitional act, and anxiety is but one motivating factor in an individual's overall willingness to engage in communication. Leary's subsequent chapter discusses how these perspectives can be integrated and usefully understood in order to guide further research.

Research Perspectives

Several authors have pointed out that because anxiety and fear influence information processing, and because our cognitive orientations or attitudes also affect anxious arousal, a reciprocal relationship is created (e.g., Booth-Butterfield & Booth-Butterfield, in press; Cheek, Melchior, & Carpentieri, 1986).

Such mutual impact constitutes a "vicious cycle" in that when we experience the aversive state of anxiety, it leads to negative thoughts and attributions about the subject and situation. Conversely, as communicators cognitively identify and then ruminate about difficult or evaluative situations, anticipating negative consequences, heightened anxiety and worry is the outcome. In their chapter, Sellers and Stacks suggest that we develop trait fear or anxiety when brain modules are not functioning "normally" in the environment (i.e., inappropriate inter-modular communication). Hence, communication apprehension could be either cognitively-induced or affectively driven depending upon which brain hemisphere dominates.

The issue of whether the anxiety or the cognition originates the other is not the primary focus for the chapters in this volume. Rather, researchers focus either on how cognition and communication are altered by anxious arousal, *or* how the cognitive thought process acts to enhance or diminish anxiety. For example, Motley's work follows the latter line contending that whether speakers label a speech as a "presentation" or a "communication event" influences their felt anxiety. People who conceptualize communication as a "presentation" rather than an opportunity to interact tend to feel more negative arousal. Similarly in Watson and Dodd's chapter, they interview Albert Ellis, who emphasizes the importance of changing thinking and beliefs about communication in order to alleviate anxiety.

In contrast, several chapters in this collection begin with the presumption that anxiety motivates, influences, and changes our cognitive processes. Beatty and Clair, for instance, report that trait anxiety is systematically related to style of decision-making, with low anxious people tending to be more "optimistic" in their choices than either moderate or high anxious individuals.

Anxiety also seems to play a significant role in dyadic, interpersonal interactions. Melchior and Cheek's shyness study follows directly from Sarason's perspective that anxious self pre-occupation interferes not only with internal, cognitive tasks (e.g., test anxiety), but also can be debilitative in interpersonal encounters. They note that shy communicators are more negatively self pre-occupied and anxious during a dyad, receive more negative evaluations, and tend to take a relatively passive communication role by not directing topics of conversation.

Lazowski and Andersen also study dyads in their investigation of the ways in which types of disclosures (particularly about negative thoughts and behaviors) may elicit negative responses and attributions. Such messages seem to arouse anxiety in the listener and tend to lead to more negative evaluations and expectations of discomfort in subsequent encounters.

The Jepson and Chaiken chapter examines the influence of chronic fear on message processing. They found that higher anxiety, in this case chronic cancer fear, produced more habitual avoidance patterns. As a result, high fear subjects processed messages less carefully (i.e., found fewer errors and had fewer thoughts about the message) but were more persuaded by it than low fear subjects. Thus the anxiety mitigated careful information-processing.

Preiss, Wheeless, and Allen employ a different method, but still approach the problem beginning with the anxiety component. Their meta-analysis of receiver apprehension not only provides a useful review of 14 years of research on anxiety associated with decoding information, but also organizes these findings into a coherent framework. They find that trait receiver apprehension is consistently associated with outcomes such as poorer listening and attentional skills, preferences for simple, easily-processed information, and more disrupted information processing.

Finally, two chapters deal specifically with measurement issues by examining components involved in predispositionally anxious reactions. Stokes and Levin examine how negative affectivity—the tendency to experience and dwell upon aversive emotional states—may be the personality basis of more specific anxiety responses. For example, they find that general anxiety and negative affectivity are substantially correlated ($r = .64$.)

Blankstein and Flett analyze test anxious individuals' cognitive responses to difficult tasks. They find that high anxious individuals appear to have more negative and fewer positive thoughts about the task and their self. However independent judges and the subjects themselves often did not agree on thought categorization, thereby raising the question of whether anxious individuals can be valid evaluators of their own communication.

Concluding Remarks

These chapters demonstrate that diverse research perspectives can both add to our body of knowledge concerning anxiety and anxiety-related constructs, and introduce viable, new areas for study as well. The reports represent diversity and eclecticism in the specific variables under study and the mechanisms eliciting anxiety, but the central theme is unified. Anxiety is problematic in human endeavors. Whether via nervous arousal or negative cognitions, anxiety has a dysfunctional impact on communication. In no case do we see anxious arousal as an asset to information processing or communication outcomes. Thus it is by studying how anxiety is generated, the processes through which it functions, the responses heightened anxiety elicits, and the role of cognition in this complex process that we can hope to comprehend the influence these interrelationships have on communicative interactions.

I particularly would like to thank my colleagues both in communication and psychology who helped develop this collection: Steve Booth-Butterfield, West Virginia University; Jonathan Cheek, Wellesley College; Rick Crandall, editor of the *Journal of Social Behavior and Personality;* John Daly, University of Texas; John Greene, Purdue University; Michael Motley, University of California, Davis; and Ron Goldsmith, Florida State University. These individuals provided expert and timely assistance with information-gathering, reviewing, and organizing this collection of research on anxiety, cognition, and communication.

REFERENCES

Booth-Butterfield, S., & Booth-Butterfield, M. (1990). The mediating role of cognition in the experience of state anxiety. *Southern Communication Journal.*

Carver, C., & Scheier, M. (1986). Analyzing shyness: A specific application of broader self-regulatory principles. In W. Jones, J. Cheek, & S. Briggs (Eds.) *Shyness: Perspectives on research and treatment* (pp. 173-185). New York: Plenum.

Cheek, J., Melchior, L., & Carpentieri, A. (1986). Shyness and self-concept. In L. Hartman & K. Blankstein (Eds.), *Perception of self in emotional disorder and psychotherapy* (pp. 113-131). New York: Plenum Press.

Norem, J., & Cantor, N. (1986). Defensive pessimism: Harnessing anxiety as motivation. *Journal of Personality and Social Psychology, 51,* 1208-1217.

Anxiety, Cognitive Interference, and Performance

Irwin G. Sarason
Barbara R. Sarason
Gregory R. Pierce
Department of Psychology
University of Washington, Seattle, WA 98195

A cognitive view of anxiety emphasizes the appraisal process that takes place in challenging situations and the debilitating consequences of thoughts laden with negative affect. A crucial aspect of anxiety is the self-preoccupying thoughts which interfere with focusing attention on the task at hand and result in lowered levels of performance. While the cognitive approach to anxiety has been applied mainly to intellectual performance, it also has potential value for the study of social behavior. This article discusses anxiety in terms of the effects of cognitive interference both in performance and interpersonal relationships.

While there is general agreement that anxiety is an important aspect of human life, there is also wide disagreement about its definition. Often it is discussed as being such a complex experience as to make scientific investigation difficult or impossible. If there were such a thing, perhaps the modal definition of anxiety would be in terms of an unpleasant emotional state or condition marked by apprehension. Spielberger (1972) defined anxiety as "an unpleasant emotional state or condition which is characterized by subjective feelings of tension, apprehension, and worry, and by activation or arousal of the autonomic nervous system" (p. 482). Leary (1982) offered this definition of anxiety: "Anxiety refers to a cognitive-affective response characterized by physiological arousal (indicative of sympathetic nervous system activation) and apprehension regarding a potentially negative outcome that the individual perceives as impending" (p. 99). The problem is that many of the terms in these definitions have proven difficult to operationalize. For example, there is little agreement among researchers on how best to conceptualize and measure emotional or affective states.

In addition to the reliability problem, the illustrative definitions of anxiety highlight yet another problem that confronts researchers: the multiple aspects of the concept. What is needed is a component analysis of its ingredients in order to formulate testable hypotheses. For instance, research with a factor analytically derived measure of test anxiety has defined four components: tension, worry, test irrelevant thinking, and bodily reactions (Sarason, 1984). The main focus of this paper is the cognitive components, most particularly, self-related worries and preoccupations. We describe research findings suggesting that these components, which are relatively unambiguous and can be assessed quantitatively and reliably, play a significant role in one important class of situations, those in which people perform and are evaluated.

Those who take a cognitive view of anxiety would agree that what they are studying is a response to perceived danger and perceived inability to handle a challenge in a satisfactory manner. The following cognitive events often occur in anxiety-provoking situations:

1. The situation is seen as difficult, challenging, and threatening.
2. The individual sees himself or herself as ineffective, or inadequate, in handling the task at hand.
3. The individual focuses on undesirable consequences of personal inadequacy.
4. Self-deprecatory preoccupations are strong and interfere or compete with task-relevant cognitive activity.
5. The individual expects and anticipates failure and loss of regard by others.

The cognitive view of anxiety focuses attention on states of heightened self-awareness, perceived helplessness, and expectations of negative consequences which become the content of self-preoccupation. Worried cognitions are aroused when a person perceives his or her ability to cope with a task demand as unsatisfactory, is unable to understand what is going on in a situation, or is uncertain about the consequences of inadequate coping. The self-preoccupations of the anxious person, even in apparently neutral or even pleasant situations, may be due to a history of experiences marked by a relative paucity of signals indicating that a safe haven from danger has been reached.

Anxiety is not the only type of self-preoccupation. Beck has distinguished between the self-preoccupations of anxious and depressed individuals (Beck & Emery, 1985). While the anxious individual sees some prospects for the future, the depressed individual sees the future as bleak; while the anxious person does not regard her/his defects or mistakes as irrevocable, the depressed person is strongly self-condemning. The anxious person *anticipates* possible damage to her/his relations with others and goals and coping ability, while the depressed person *ruminates* about her/his damaged relationships and is preoccupied with past failures.

Reasons why people perceive danger in situations are various, and include the stimulus properties of the situations and unrealistic interpretations of them. Every teacher knows students who, although quite able and bright, are virtually terror stricken at exam time. In these cases, a student often expresses concern about the consequences of not performing at a satisfactory level and embarrassment at what is regarded as probable "failure" despite the fact that these concerns do not seem to be reality based. If stress is viewed as a call for action determined by the properties of situations and personal dispositions, the anxious person might be characterized as feeling unable to respond to that call.

Anxiety is a characteristic that most individuals experience at some times, and its effect may not always be negative. For example, early work in evaluation anxiety showed that a moderate level of anxiety may provide heightened motivation and result in improved performance (Sarason, 1980). The anxiety spectrum ranges from this enhancing effect through mild discomfort and occasional impaired performance to significant degrees of immobilization as seen in those who meet the criteria for one of the anxiety disorders. These disorders, the most common type of psychiatric diagnosis given today, contain subgroups in which cognitive symptoms are most notable, such as in obsessive disorders. The work of Rachman provides a multitude of examples of how cognitions can immobilize an individual (Rachman & Hodgson, 1980).

ANXIETY, SELF-PREOCCUPATION, AND ATTENTION

The cognitive view of anxiety grows out of the conceptualization that personality can be interpreted from an information-processing perspective. This perspective analyzes the ways in which a person searches the environment for cues, selects cues that are relevant to thought and action, integrates new information with old, and makes decisions that result in observable behavior. Self-preoccupying cognitive events are as much behavior as a muscle twitch or signing one's name on a piece of paper. However, cognitive events are not directly observable and inferential support for their existence must come from behavior that can be observed.

While there is general agreement about the need to incorporate cognitive processes in any comprehensive anxiety construct, there are differences concerning the particular processes emphasized. Nevertheless, there is increasing evidence of the important role self-preoccupation plays in behavioral and physiological outcomes. According to this view, how well people perform, how anxious they feel in particular situations, and their levels of physiological activation are powerfully influenced by self-related thoughts. Self-related thoughts are significant influences over behavior because they direct attention in idiosyncratic, and often maladaptive, ways.

Self-preoccupation has a far different significance than preoccupation in general. A preoccupied individual is engrossed in thought. Illustrative preoccupations range from generalized concerns such as worry over the future of humanity, to specific fears such as thoughts about snakes or failing in school, to complete absorption in the solution of some complex intellectual problem. The range of self-preoccupations is narrower because these cognitions are limited to thoughts about oneself. However, as we noted earlier, self-preoccupation is not restricted to the domain of worry or anxiety. While there is overlap in the cognitions of anxious and depressed individuals, the differences are easily observed. There are many clinical examples of the diversity of cognitions with which persons become self-preoccupied, the degree to which self-preoccupation influences attentiveness to external cues, and the ways in which information from the environment is stored, retrieved, and acted upon. Despite the difference in the content of these preoccupations, they all have the effect of lessening the individual's effective behavior by diverting attention from relevant cues and causing misinterpretations of those cues that are perceived.

Anxious self-preoccupation consists of heightened concern over one's inadequacies and shortcomings. The anxious person is concerned about present or potential dangers, threats, and the inability to cope with them. This does not mean that danger and threat necessarily cause anxious self-preoccupation. Self-preoccupation of any type is a function not only of objective life events but also of the interpretation placed on those events by the individual. Whether self-preoccupation occurs depends on the skills a person has learned in coping with dangers and threats. The anxious person often believes him/herself to be deficient in these skills.

Self-preoccupation has attentional properties because it leads people to focus on situational cues which seem to them to have self-reference. The amount and type of self-preoccupation influences the degree to which the person is receptive to the available stimulus information and the amount of physiological arousal. Students who are worried about failure will be especially attentive to stimuli suggestive of possible evaluations of their work. Paranoid persons will be especially attentive to cues that relate to their distinctive systems of ideation. To the extent that the self-preoccupied person attends to environmental cues, the cues are dealt with in terms of the person's idiosyncratic information-processing system.

A task confronting anxiety researchers is identification of the operations and transformations individuals perform on information that result in high levels of worry and anticipations of unpleasant outcomes. Accomplishing this task will require empirical inquiry into the assumptions, strategies, and expectancies of people falling at different points along the continuum of anxious self-preoccupation, as well as into the rules by which they label and make judgments about whether an environmental event represents a personal threat (Deffenbacher, Zwemer, Whisman, Hill, & Sloan, 1986; Sarason, 1980).

ANXIETY AND PERFORMANCE

An important question concerning human performance is: What are the individual difference variables that influence how well people solve problems and perform on intellectual and motor tasks? Cognitive processes influence how people interpret situations and can be thought of as intervening between being presented with a task and performing on it.

Test Anxiety

Test anxiety is widely studied because evaluative situations are very common and measures of the tendency to experience test anxiety are available (Sarason, 1980). There is now considerable evidence that highly test-anxious subjects in situations that pose test-like challenges perform at relatively low levels and experience relatively high levels of task-irrelevant thoughts (such as self-deprecating attributions). For instance, the results of Ganzer's (1968) experiment showed that, while performing on an intellectual task, high test anxious subjects made many more irrelevant comments than did low test-anxiety scorers. A high percentage of these comments were self-deprecatory. Various researchers have found that high test-anxious people are more likely than low test-anxious people to be preoccupied with and blame themselves for their performance level, feel less confident in making perceptual judgments, and set lower levels of aspiration for themselves (Sarason, 1980).

People evaluate various situations in terms of their personal assumptions, concerns, and expectations about themselves and the world. Performance anxiety, which includes fear of evaluation, catastrophizing, and unrealistic assumptions about performance, is an important factor in intellectual performance. A useful starting point in analyzing anxiety begins with the objective properties of situations. However, regardless of the objective situation, it is the cognitive appraisal or personal interpretation of the situation that leads to behavior. A person who has failed a test, but believes he/she has done well will not become upset.

The available evidence suggests that there usually is more to a proclivity to test anxiety than simply a history of failure experiences. In fact, many highly test-anxious persons are quite competent and rarely experience objective failure. Test-anxious people process their objective successes and failures in distinctive ways and their anxiety is related to how they, and significant others in their lives, view test-taking experiences. The evidence also indicates that for the most part individuals at different test-anxiety levels show either smaller or no differences in performance and cognitive interference in nontest situations. This type of evidence is consistent with an attentional interpretation of test anxiety, according to which people at high and low levels of test anxiety differ in the types of thoughts to which their attention is directed only or predominantly in the face of evaluative stressors.

Social Anxiety

Interpersonal relationships and social communication can be thought of as involving special types of human performance. Why are some people so much more socially competent than others? Anxiety from the standpoint of self-preoccupation, together with situational factors, may play as important roles in the social realm as they seem to in the domains of intellectual performance and problem-solving. People who feel they have handled themselves well in a social situation will be relaxed and anticipate recognition for their social presence. An individual who believes he/she has committed a social faux pas, even if this perception is inaccurate, will become distressed and vigilant for signals communicating rejection.

Most of the work on the correlates and effects of cognitive interference has focused on intellectual tasks and experimentally manipulated evaluative stress. There is a need to determine the extent to which the concept of cognitive interference applies to contexts that are not traditionally defined as performance situations. For example, informal social interactions and social communication are topics that might be elucidated by a focus on cognitive processes. It would not be surprising if test anxiety and social anxiety had similar cognitive roots because both intellectual and social situations involve a strong evaluative component for most people.

Like test anxiety, social anxiety might be associated with any or all of the following: anticipating a situation, experiencing it, and "recovering" from it. Both the quantity of anxiety and the mix of situations in which it is experienced vary from person to person. The situations can be vague or well-defined, but the characteristic they share is that the individual feels unable to respond adequately to them. Some situations, e.g., parties, telephone conversations, meeting a new person, talking with a superior, are likely to provoke disruptive thinking for many people. However, for particular people, social anxiety might also be linked to classes of situations defined in idiosyncratic ways, for example, with regard to certain interpersonal relationships or situations. The disabling role of such preoccupying thoughts as negative self-evaluations has been shown to be as important or more important than social skills in influencing a person's behavior in social situations (Clark & Arkowitz, 1975; Leary, 1983). Despite the variety of situations that evoke social anxiety, social anxiety's debilitating effect on performance seems the same in all of them.

COGNITIVE INTERFERENCE

In both test and social anxiety, self-preoccupying thoughts contribute to performance degradation because they interfere with task-relevant thoughts. Support for this contention has been most clear in research on test anxiety. Thoughts that relate to worry about performance and social comparisons related to performance seem to be responsible for much of the performance decrement reported by high test-anxious people. Highly anxious people become preoccupied with possible threat, their ruminations tend to persist and are most potent when situational threats are actually present. Test anxiety is related to the occurrence of frequent negative thoughts about personal abilities as well as the perceived difficulty of questions and mood during exams (Hunsley, 1987).

In an analysis of the components of anxiety, Ingram and Kendall (1987) identified several critical cognitive features. One of these consists of schemata which relate to possible danger or harm to the individual. With regard to test anxiety this often means the perceived possibility of negative evaluation. The word "possibility" is important in relation to both general and specific anxieties, such as test anxiety. When not in an evaluative situation, or anticipating one, the highly test-anxious individual may not worry about possibilities of failure, embarrassment, and social rejection. But in evaluative situations these possibilities become active and salient. When this happens, the test-anxious individual becomes self-absorbed instead of becoming task-absorbed. Schwartz and Garamoni (1986) have estimated that, in general, cognitive functioning consists of roughly twice the amount of positive as compared to negative thoughts. The occurrence of evaluative stressors heavily tips this two-to-one ratio in the opposite direction for test anxiety-prone individuals.

Thoughts about off-task matters and a general wandering of attention from the task, as well as worries also contribute to performance deficits. For instance, Reason and Michielska (1982) have investigated the negative effects of absentmindedness and forgetfulness, or the wandering of attention on performance. Broadbent and his coworkers (Broadbent, Cooper, FitzGerald, & Parkes, 1982) have also focused on these aspects of attention to determine whether they are important predictors of performance in work situations. Their findings suggest that although absentmindedness may be a stable personality characteristic, the effects on performance, like those of cognitive interference, are not seen except in stressful situations.

In general, highly test-anxious individuals experience high levels of intrusive thinking. These interfering thoughts tend to center around worry and self-preoccupation. Although all people think about their personal capabilities in relation to the task at hand, anxious individuals seem to become overly preoccupied with these self-evaluative thoughts. Thoughts such as "I don't know what to do now" can be self-defeating if the person in fact has the wherewithal to handle the situation. Self-evaluative thoughts are also relevant in social anxiety. One type of cognition that may be particularly debilitating in social situations consists of perceptions and thoughts about one's physical attributes. Many socially anxious people worry, often quite unrealistically, about what they see as unappealing or even revolting features of their appearance. These worries, like those of test-anxious individuals, are usually not based on reality. Other common types of interfering cognitions include fear of appearing foolish, fear of not being perceived as interesting or worth knowing, and so on. What these cognitions have in common is the theme of inadequacy in meeting the demands of the situation and the expectations of others. Such self-preoccupying thoughts may arouse strong emotions that interfere with the perception and appraisal of events and of the reactions of others. The anxious person may at the same time notice too much and too little and be prone to overemphasize, distort, misinterpret, or overlook available cues. This is likely to produce errors and uncertainties in performance, discomfort in social situations, and degraded interpersonal behavior.

Assessing Cognitive Interference

Because of growing evidence concerning the cognitive elements of anxiety and their effect on performance, measurement of the tendency to have interfering cognitions, both in general and in specific situations, becomes important. *In vivo* thought sampling methods, often using beepers to identify time points requiring self-reports of cognitions, think aloud procedures, retrospective accounts of thoughts in particular situations, post-task questionnaires, and other techniques are being used in research on cognitive assessment. These procedures produce different pictures of cognitive activity and the content of cognitions (Blackwell, Galassi, Galassi, & Watson, 1985; Clark, 1988). One important challenge in the use of many of these approaches to ongoing thought is the need to employ cognitive categories that are both meaningful and convenient to record. As a broad generalization, the things that people think about in specific situations are as varied and idiosyncratic as the situations that evoke anxiety. How to categorize thoughts in stressful situations represents an important problem for cognitive researchers.

In our laboratory we have developed and used several instruments to assess different aspects of anxiety with a special focus on cognitive interference both as a stable personal characteristic and from an interactive viewpoint. Four instruments designed to meet these needs are the Reactions to Tests (RTT), the Thought Occurrence Questionnaire (TOQ), the Cognitive Interference Questionnaire (CIQ) and the Reaction to Social Situations (RSS).

Assessing Test Anxiety and Cognitive Interference

The Reactions to Tests instrument was created in order to assess separately several components of reactions to test situations (Sarason, 1984). The instrument yields a total score and four factor analytically derived scales: Tension, Worry, Test-Irrelevant Thought, and Bodily Reactions. Table 1 presents some of the items of the four scales. Two of the scales (Worry and Test-Irrelevant Thought) are specifically concerned with interfering cognitions. While the scales are positively intercorrelated, the correlations seem low enough to justify comparisons among them concerning their explanatory and predictive value. In one study, the total score of the RTT was related to performance on a difficult digit-symbol task under evaluative conditions (Sarason, 1984). The Worry scale was more consistently related to performance and postperformance reports of cognitive interference than were the other scales. Further research is needed to determine the effects of specific classes of self-preoccupying cognitions on performance.

The tendency to experience cognitive interference can be approached as a general individual difference variable. The Thought Occurrence Questionnaire is an empirically developed instrument that contains 28 items referring to the general tendency to experience interfering thoughts. It asks subjects to estimate how often each of 28 thoughts typically occur to them in their daily lives (Sarason, Sarason, Keefe, Hayes, and Shearin, 1986). Table 2 illustrates TOQ items. The TOQ may prove useful in assessing the habitual thought content characteristic of individuals as they monitor their own behavior. There is evidence that cognitive interference assessed with the TOQ is related to performance

TABLE 1   Illustrative Items From Four Factor Analytically Derived Reaction to Tests (RTT) Scales

Tension
1. I feel distressed and uneasy before tests.
2. I feel jittery before tests.
3. I find myself becoming anxious the day of a test.

Worry
1. Before taking a test, I worry about failure.
2. During tests, I think about how poorly I am doing.
3. Before tests, I feel troubled about what is going to happen.

Test-Irrelevant Thinking
1. During tests, I think about recent past events.
2. Irrelevant bits of information pop into my head during a test.
3. During tests, I find myself thinking of things unrelated to the material being tested.

Bodily Reactions
1. I get a headache during an important test.
2. My stomach gets upset before tests.
3. My heart beats faster when the test begins.

TABLE 2   Illustrative Thought Occurrence Questionnaire (TOQ) Items

1. I think about what someone will think of me.

2. I think about how I should be more careful.

3. I think about how often I get confused.

4. I think about other activities (for example, assignments, work).

TABLE 3   Illustrative Items from the Cognitive Interference Questionnaire (CIQ)

---

1. I thought about how poorly I was doing.

2 I thought about how I should work more carefully.

3. I thought about how others have done on this task.

4. I thought about how I would feel if I were told how I performed.

---

under stress. Those endorsing a high number of TOQ items perform more poorly under stress than do those who report a weaker tendency to have intrusive thoughts. Interestingly, task-focusing instructions and exercises seem to be helpful in improving the performance of subjects with high TOQ scores (Sarason, Sarason, Keefe, Hayes, & Shearin, 1986).

A third instrument, the Cognitive Interference Questionnaire was developed by Sarason and Stoops (1978) to assess the degree to which people, after working on tasks, report in a post-task assessment the frequency of thoughts of various types, including those that interfered with concentration on the task. Table 3 presents some of the CIQ items. In filling out the CIQ, subjects are asked to estimate retrospectively how often certain thoughts passed through their minds while working on a particular task. In the Sarason and Stoops' study, subjects who differed in test anxiety performed on a series of tasks presented as measures of intelligence. The dependent measures were their performance, estimates of how long they had worked on the tasks, and post-performance reports of task-irrelevant thoughts they may have had during performance. These thoughts were assessed with the CIQ. Sarason & Stoops found that highly test-anxious subjects reported high levels of task-irrelevant thought, judged time spent on the tasks to be longer than did other subjects, and performed at relatively low levels. None of these performance features were observed under neutral, nontestlike conditions.

Assessing Social Anxiety

Like test anxiety, social anxiety refers to a class of situations that can be reliably defined. We are now developing a new instrument, the Reactions to Social Situations, that parallels the RTT. It has been administered to a large group of college students. Factor analysis of its items has yielded essentially the same factors found for the RTT (Sarason and Sarason, 1986a). Table 4 lists some of the items on the Worry scale of the RSS.

TABLE 4 Illustrative Items from the Worry Scale of the Reactions to Social Situations

---

1. Thoughts of doing poorly interfere with my concentration in social situations.

2 I often think about how difficult it is relating to other people.

3. During a social situation, I worry whether I will handle myself effectively.

4. Before entering a social situation, I worry about failure.

We have found that the correlation of the RSS total score with the TOQ is .44 for males and .53 for females. The fact that every item on the TOQ was correlated significantly and positively with the RSS total score reflects the tendency of socially anxious people to experience task-irrelevant thoughts in social situations. It may well be that task-irrelevant thinking plays as detrimental a role in social behavior as it does in test-taking situations. R. Schwarzer and Quast (1985) and C. Schwarzer (1986) have found that when stressful events occur in either social or academic situations, people shift their attention from task to self in the process of assessing their competence and likely outcomes. If competence and likely outcomes are perceived as being insufficient or inadequate, the situation will be appraised as threatening and the individual will experience anxiety. There may also be a degree of resignation, the result of which would be that the individual does not invest enough effort and persistence in the task or in the social interaction, thus increasing the probability of actual failure.

Causes and Mediators of Cognitive Interference

Further research is needed, not only on the effects of cognitive interference in particular types of situations, such as tests and social encounters, but also on the developmental and interpersonal processes that cause or mediate these effects. An example of how this need might be approached is seen in a study by Yee and Pierce (1989) who investigated the developmental and interpersonal correlates of cognitive interference, both as a general disposition and as a response to stressful intellectual tasks. They found that subjects who described themselves as having experienced warm, supportive relationships with their parents in early childhood, and more supportive relationships in adulthood, reported a lower frequency of intrusive thoughts in general, and fewer interfering cognitions while working on experimental tasks. This type of evidence, if extended, might provide information about the link between positive interpersonal experiences and the capacity to remain task focused across a variety of evaluative situations.

This point is further buttressed by findings from I. Sarason and Sarason's (1986b) investigation of the effects on cognitive interference and task performance of experimentally administered social support (i.e., an experimenter's communication of being available to assist subjects if they needed it). Subjects who received the experimenter's communication of interest and who had previously indicated low levels of perceived available social support reported reduced levels of interfering thoughts and successfully solved more anagrams than did low social support subjects in the control condition. In addition, low social support subjects in the treatment condition performed at comparable levels to the high social support subjects in both the control and support conditions. The performance of subjects high in social support did not benefit from the experimenter's communication. The fact that an interpersonal experience (communication of social support) decreased cognitive interference and improved the intellectual performance of subjects low in perceived social support, but not subjects high in perceived social support, is consistent with the idea that the tendency to experience preoccupying thoughts is associated with deficits in interpersonal experiences. This work is also consistent with the idea that the general tendency to experience cognitive interference reflects a stable disposition that is rooted in social experience.

AMELIORATING EVALUATIVE ANXIETY

A generalized tendency toward self-preoccupation seems to be a stable personality characteristic that leaves individuals vulnerable to interfering thoughts in particular kinds of situations. However, other personal characteristics, even in otherwise vulnerable individuals, may serve as protection from cognitive interference under stress. For instance, one such characteristic is perceived social support. Perceived social support may be conceptualized as a schema or working model that leads to perceptions that others are available to help if needed. This relationship is illustrated in a study in which subjects were asked to recall recent negative events they had experienced. Subjects high in perceived social support reported less cognitive interference when it was assessed immediately after the recall task than subjects low in perceived social support (Sarason and Sarason, 1987). It appeared that level of perceived support buffered the reaction to a stressor, the recall of negative events, for subjects high in this personal characteristic.

Consistent with this suggestion of an important influence of social processes on performance and cognitive interference is Sarason's (1981) study which employed a social support manipulation in an experiment with subjects who differed in test anxiety. Social support was provided by a group discussion focused on sharing concerns and solutions regarding students' problems of stress and anxiety in testing situations. Several confederates worked to heighten social association by suggesting a meeting after the experimental session. The group discussion was followed by an anagrams task which was presented as a separate, unrelated experiment run by another experimenter that was combined into the same session for the sake of efficiency.

The results showed that performance and self-preoccupation as measured by the CIQ were affected by this specially created opportunity for social association and acceptance by others. Performance on the anagrams task increased and self-preoccupation decreased as a function of the social support manipulation. However, this change was pronounced only in subjects who were high in test anxiety. The performance of those low in test anxiety was essentially unchanged by the support manipulation.

These findings suggest that knowing that one is cared about and valued by others reduces the effect of the recall of negative experiences on one's cognitions. A social support intervention can also affect cognitive activities. Lindner, Sarason, & Sarason (1988) found that the offer of available help, which was never utilized because of the nature of the task, produced an improved performance in those low in social support and at the same time increased the reported cognitive activity during the task. They interpreted the results to mean that the supportive intervention changed the content of the cognitions from worry to other types of thoughts which did not claim as much of the subject's attention because of their lack of negative valence. Personal characteristics such as perceived social support may be important because they are part of a working model or schema by which a person assesses and interprets the environment and interpersonal relationships. These schemas may provide cognitions that serve as a stress buffer.

Another approach to facilitating the performance of highly test-anxious people is pertinent, easily understood pre-performance instructions that direct subjects' attention to the importance of task-relevant thinking. Sarason and Turk (1983) studied 180 undergraduate students differing on RTT Worry scores who performed on a difficult anagrams task in groups of 15-20. The subjects were told that performance on the anagrams task was a measure of the ability to do college-level work. After this communication, one-third of the subjects were given an attention-directing condition, one-third were given reassurance, and a control group received no additional communication.

The instructions for the anagrams task were contained in the test booklet. The attention-directing and reassuring communications were given by the experimenter after the subjects had read the task instructions which included the achievement-orienting message. Subjects under the Reassurance condition were told not to be overly concerned about their performance on the anagrams. The experimenter made such comments as "Don't worry" and "You will do just fine." Subjects under the Attention-Directing condition were told to absorb themselves as much as possible in the anagrams task and to avoid thinking about other things. The experimenter said, "...concentrate all your attention on the problems...," "think only about the anagrams," and "don't let yourself get distracted from the task." High-Worry subjects under the control condition performed poorly compared to the other control subjects. High-Worry subjects in the Attention-Directing and Reassurance groups performed well. However, consistent with previous evidence, the study showed that reassuring instructions have a detrimental effect on people who are not worriers. Non-worry subjects in the Reassurance group performed poorly, perhaps because non-worriers take the reassuring communication at face value, that is, they take the task lightly and lower their motivational level. The performance levels of all groups that received the Attention-Directing instructions were high. The Attention-Directing approach seems to have all of the advantages of reassurance for high-Worry subjects with none of the disadvantages for low Worry subjects.

After the anagrams task, all the subjects responded to the CIQ, which provided a measure of the number and type of interfering thoughts experienced in that particular situation. Cognitive interference at the end of the anagrams tasks was relatively low under the Attention-Direction condition for high- as well as low-Worry subjects. Similar to previous findings concerning highly test-anxious subjects, the high-Worry groups showed high cognitive interference under the control conditions.

The performance and CIQ scores were reanalyzed in terms of the other RTT scales, but none of these analyses revealed statistically significant results. The findings of this experiment support an attentional interpretation of anxiety and worry. They suggest that simply calling subjects' attention to the need for task-oriented behavior can have a salutary effect on their performance, with a reduction in intrusive thoughts. In another phase of their research, Sarason and Turk found that the coping-enhancing effects of the attention-directing intervention were strengthened significantly when combined with the opportunity for subjects to support each other.

Reducing vulnerability to cognitive interference is an important challenge to researchers. While we have emphasized the potential contributions of social processes and information about coping strategies, a diversity of approaches is needed.

CONCLUSIONS

Anxiety is a widely discussed topic that has aroused controversy. In part, this is because it has been given so many definitions, a large number of which have ambiguous referents. We do not contend that a cognitive approach is a cure-all for all present definitional problems surrounding the anxiety concept. However, we believe increasing evidence suggests that the cognitive component of anxiety plays an important role in intellectual performance and social behavior and that certain aspects of it can be assessed reliably. In addition, a variety of studies now indicate that this aspect of anxiety can be manipulated to reduce decrements in intellectual performance.

While all people experience self-preoccupation, such thoughts become maladaptive when they are excessively preoccupying and when they interfere with task-oriented thinking and attention to situational realities. Further research and theory is needed concerning (1) interactions among cognitive, behavioral, and physiological systems, (2) ways to help people articulate their self-preoccupying thoughts, (3) assessment of profiles of intrusive thoughts, and (4) interventions directed toward modifying the cognitive mediators of maladaptive behavior.

It seems likely that behavior in a wide variety of situations (exams, parties, job interviews) is influenced by self-related cognitions. Available evidence suggests that self-preoccupation often interferes with ongoing activity in situations for which either a task focus (as in performing a task on the job), awareness of subtle cues (as in a social interaction) or spontaneity (as at a party) are desirable. We need ways to measure self-preoccupation and cognitive interference and techniques to evaluate the effects of different types. We ultimately also need interventions to reduce the deleterious effects of self-related cognitions and enhance comfort and problem-solving efforts in clearly evaluative situations and also those situations perceived as evaluative by socially anxious individuals.

Although all people from time to time question their personal capabilities to perform particular types of tasks, anxious individuals tend to become overly preoccupied with such self-derogatory thoughts. Saying such things as "I don't know what to do now" or "I'm dumb" can be self-defeating if the person really has the wherewithal to handle the situation.

High levels of anxious self-preoccupation interfere with the perception and appraisal of events and lead to errors in estimating the possibility of danger, loss (e.g., of love, job, money, reputation), and probability of attaining goals. Research in both naturalistic settings and the laboratory suggests that cognitive interference, often in the form of worry, is a key factor in lowering the performance of highly test-anxious people.

We have emphasized cognitive interference as a mediator between situational conditions, and behavior. There is growing evidence that this mediation plays an important role. A number of questions, some barely touched upon in the literature, now require in-depth study. One concerns assessment: What are the best ways to get information about interfering thoughts? Another has to do with why some people experience high levels of cognitive interference, while others do not: What are the experiential histories of people who differ in cognitive interference? Yet another relates to the role of cognitive interference in the human information-processing system: What are the major facets of this system and how does the system influence the process of self-regulation. All these questions have important implications for human behavior and thus call for direction of effort toward a better understanding of cognitive interference.

REFERENCES

Beck, A.T., & Emery, G. (1985). *Anxiety disorders and phobias.* NY: Basic Books.

Blackwell, R.T., Galassi, J.P., Galassi, M.D., & Watson, T.E. (1985). Are cognitive assessment methods equal? A comparison of think aloud and thought listing. *Cognitive Therapy and Research, 9,* 399-413.

Broadbent, D.E., Cooper, P.E., Fitzgerald, P.T., Parkes, K.R. (1982). The Cognitive Failures Questionnaire (CFQ) and its correlates. *British Journal of Clinical Psychology, 21,* 1-16.

Clark, D.A. (1988). The validity of measures of cognition: A review of the literature. *Cognitive Therapy and Research, 12,* 1-20.

Clark, J.V., & Arkowitz, H. (1975). Social anxiety and self-evaluation of interpersonal performance. *Psychological Reports, 36,* 211-221.

Deffenbacher, J.L., Zwemer, W.A., Whisman, M.A., Hill, R.A., & Sloan, R.D. (1986). Irrational beliefs and anxiety. *Cognitive Therapy and Research, 10,* 281-292.

Ganzer, V.J. (1968) The effects of audience pressure and test anxiety on learning and retention in a serial learning situation. *Journal of Personality and Social Psychology, 8,* 194-199.

Hunsley, J. (1987). Internal dialogue during academic examinations. *Cognitive Therapy and Research, 11,* 653-664.

Ingram, R.E., & Kendall, P.C. (1987). The cognitive side of anxiety. *Cognitive Therapy and Research, 11,* 523-536.

Leary, M.R. (1982). Social anxiety. In L. Wheeler (Ed.), *Review of personality and social psychology* (Vol. 3). Beverly Hills, CA: Sage.

Leary, M.R. (1983). *Understanding social anxiety: Social, personality and clinical perspectives.* Beverly Hills: Sage.

Lindner, K.C., Sarason, I.G., & Sarason, B.R. (1988). Assessed life stress and experimentally provided social support. In C.D. Spielberger, I.G. Sarason, & P.B. Defares (Eds.), *Stress and anxiety* (Vol. 11). Washington, DC: Hemisphere.

Rachman, S.J., & Hodgson, R.J. (1980). *Obsessions and compulsions.* Englewood Cliffs, NJ: Prentice-Hall.

Reason, J.T., & Mychielska, K. (1982). Absentminded: The psychology of mental lapses and everyday errors. Englewood Cliffs, NJ: Prentice Hall.

Sarason, I.G. (Ed.) (1980). *Test anxiety: Theory, research, and applications.* Hillsdale, NJ: Lawrence Erlbaum.

Sarason, I.G. (1981). Test anxiety, stress, and social support. *Journal of Personality, 49,* 101-114.

Sarason, I.G. (1984) Stress, anxiety, and cognitive interference: Reactions to tests. *Journal of Personality and Social Psychology, 46,* 929-938.

Sarason, I.G., & Sarason, B.R. (1986a). Experimentally provided social support. *Journal of Personality and Social Psychology, 50,* 1222-1225.

Sarason, I.G. & Sarason, B.R. (1986b). Anxiety and interfering thoughts: Their effect on social interaction. In W.H. Jones, J.M. Cheek, & S.R. Briggs (Eds.), *Shyness: Perspectives on research and treatment.* NY: Plenum.

Sarason, I.G., & Sarason, B.R. (1987). *Effects of focus on positive and negative life events on cognitive interference and performance of subjects differing in social support.* Unpublished research, University of Washington.

Sarason, I.G., Sarason, B.R., Keefe, D.E., Hayes, B.E., & Shearin, E.N. (1986) Cognitive interference: Situational determinants and traitlike characteristics. *Journal of Perosnality and Social Psychology, 31,* 215-226.

Sarason, I.G. & Stoops, R. (1978). Test anxiety and the passage of time. *Journal of Consulting and Clinical Psychology, 1,* 102-109.

Sarason, I.G., & Turk, S. (1983). *Coping strategies and group interaction: Their function in improving performance of anxious individuals.* Seattle, WA: Unpublished paper.

Schwartz, R.M. & Garamoni, G.I. (1986). A structural model of positive and negative states of mind: Asymmetry and the internal dialogue. In P.C. Kendall (Ed.), *Advances in cognitive-behavioral research and therapy* (Vol. 5). NY: Academic Press.

Schwarzer, C. (Ed.) (1986). *Two studies of anxiety.* West Germany: Unpublished report, University of Dusseldorf.

Schwarzer, R. & Quast, H. (1985). Multidimensionality of the anxiety experience: Evidence for additional components. In H.M. van der Ploeg, R. Schwarzer, & C.D. Spielberger (Eds.), *Advances in test anxiety research* (Vol. 4). Lisse, The Netherlands: Swetz & Zeitlinger.

Spielberger, C.D. (1972). Conceptual and methodological issues in anxiety research. In C.D. Spielberger (Ed.), *Anxiety: Current trends in theory and research* (Vol. 2). NY: Academic Press.

Yee, P.L., & Pierce, G.R. (1989). *Cognitive interference as a personality characteristic.* Paper presented at the annual meeting of the American Psychological Association, New Orleans, LA.

Willingness to Communicate: A Cognitive View

James C. McCroskey
Virginia P. Richmond
Communication Studies, West Virginia University
Morgantown, WV 26506

Willingness to communicate (WTC) is discussed as a personality-based predisposition with a major impact on human communication behavior. The associations of WTC with introversion, self-esteem, communication competence, communication apprehension, and cultural diversity are examined. These predispositional factors are seen as dominating cognitive decision-making processes of communicators.

Talk holds a central place in interpersonal communication. While a very large portion of all the meaning people generate in others' minds through interpersonal communication stems from nonverbal messages, the fact remains that without talk most interpersonal communication would have little reason to exist.

Berger and Calabrese (1975) point to the importance of the amount of talk in the initial stage of an interpersonal relationship. All interpersonal relationships must pass through this stage before reaching more intimate stages, but most never go beyond this stage. At the outset of interaction between strangers, considerable uncertainty exists in the minds of both. Since such uncertainty generally is non-reinforcing to interactants, they would desire to reduce uncertainty. Berger and Calabrese (1975) note that, as both amount of verbal communication and nonverbal affiliative expressiveness increase, the levels of uncertainty of both interactants decreases. Reduced levels of uncertainty lead to higher levels of intimacy and liking. The development of strong interpersonal relationships, then, is heavily dependent on the amount of communication in which interactants are willing to engage. The more a person is willing to talk and to be nonverbally expressive, the more likely that person is to develop positive interpersonal relationships.

In the general North American culture, interpersonal communication is highly valued. People are evaluated in large part on the basis of their communication behavior. While there are exceptions, people who communicate well typically are evaluated more positively than people

© 1990 Select Press

who do not. In fact, in most instances the more a person communicates, up to a very high extreme, the more positively the person is evaluated (Daly, McCroskey, & Richmond, 1977; Daly & Stafford, 1984; Hayes & Meltzer, 1972; McCroskey, 1977; Richmond, 1984).

Although talk is a vital component in interpersonal communication and the development of interpersonal relationships, people differ dramatically from one another in the degree to which they actually do talk. Some people talk very little, they tend to speak only when spoken to—and sometimes not even then. Others tend to verbalize almost constantly. Many people talk more in some contexts than in others. Most people talk more to some receivers than they do to others. This variability in talking behavior is rooted in a personality-based predisposition which we call "Willingness to Communicate" (WTC: McCroskey & Richmond, 1985, 1987; Richmond & McCroskey, 1989).

THE COGNITIVE NATURE OF WILLINGNESS TO COMMUNICATE

To a major extent, verbal communication is a volitional act. People have the ability to choose to communicate or to choose not to communicate. This does not deny the existence of ritualized communication which exists with little or no cognitive awareness—the "Hi, how are you?" greeting followed by the ritual "Fine." Although this type of communication exists and virtually everyone participates in it every day, even this ritualized behavior is subject to volitional control and modification. As an example, consider how ritualized behavior might be changed when two individuals have sustained conflict.

Nonverbal communication is subject to far less volitional control in human interactions. One of the cardinal tenets of contemporary communication theory is that "one cannot not communicate" in the presence of another. This view holds that nonverbal aspects of individuals constantly communicate to others who are present, even if all verbal communication ceases. In fact, the cessation of verbal communication itself is seen as a powerful nonverbally communicative message. Hence, viewed from a nonverbal perspective, individuals cannot truly avoid communication when others are present, they only may choose what messages they will send.

The above facts point to the essentially cognitive nature of human communication. Messages are subject to choice. People do make such choices, although some choices are made so consistently that the communication behaviors become habituated and little cognitive involvement is required in a given instance unless diversion from habit is contemplated. Since cognition is critical to volitional choice, all that is known about human cognition may be brought to bear to improve understanding of how these choices are made. We take the view that cognition itself and, hence, cognition about human communication is heavily influenced by the personality of the individual. Whether a person is willing or not willing to communicate, either in a given instance or more generally, is a volitional choice which is cognitively processed. The personality of the individual may be the determining factor in the manner in which that choice is made and what that choice will be.

WILLINGNESS TO COMMUNICATE AS A PERSONALITY CONSTRUCT

Whether a person is willing to communicate with another person in a given interpersonal encounter certainly is affected by the situational constraints of that encounter. Many situational variables can have an impact: how the person feels that day, what communication the person has had with others recently, who the other person is, what that person looks like, what might be gained or lost through communicating, and other demands on the person's time.

WTC, then, is to a major degree situationally dependent. Nevertheless, individuals exhibit regular WTC tendencies across situations. Consistent behavioral tendencies with regard to frequency and amount of talking have been noted in the research literature for decades (Chapple & Arensberg, 1940; Goldman-Eisler, 1951; Borgatta & Bales, 1953). Such regularity in communication behaviors across interpersonal communication contexts suggests the existence of a predisposition. It is this orientation which explains why one person will communicate and another will not under identical or virtually identical situational constraints.

The present WTC construct has evolved from the earlier work of Burgoon (1976) on unwillingness to communicate, Mortensen, Arntson, and Lustig (1977) on predispositions toward verbal behavior, and Leary (1983) and McCroskey and Richmond (1982) with a behavioral approach toward shyness. All of these writings center on a presumed trait-like predisposition toward communication.

MEASURING THE WILLINGNESS TO COMMUNICATE CONSTRUCT

Abundant evidence exists to support the argument that people exhibit differential behavioral tendencies to communicate more or less across communication situations. A recently developed self-report instrument, known as the Willingness to Communicate (WTC) Scale (see Figure 1), appears to be a valid operationalization of the construct (McCroskey & Richmond, 1987; Richmond & McCroskey, 1985; 1989).

FIGURE 1   Willingness to Communicate Scale

Williness to Communicate Scale

Directions: Below are 20 situations in which a person might choose to communicate or not to communicate. Presume you have *completely free choice*. Indicate the percentage of time you would choose *to communicate* in each type of situation. Indicate in the space at the left what percent of the time you would choose to communicate. 0=never, 100=always.

    1. *Talk with a service station attendant.
    2. *Talk with a physician.
    3. Present a talk to a group of strangers.
    4. Talk with an acquaintance while standing in line.
    5. *Talk with a salesperson in a store.
    6. Talk in a large meeting of friends.
    7. *Talk with a policeman/policewoman.
    8. Talk in a small group of strangers.
    9. Talk with a friend while standing in line.
   10. *Talk with a waiter/waitress in a restaurant.
   11. Talk in a large meeting of acquaintances.
   12. Talk with a stranger while standing in line.
   13. *Talk with a secretary.
   14. Present a talk to a group of friends.
   15. Talk in a small group of acquaintances.
   16. *Talk with a garbage collector.
   17. Talk in a large meeting of strangers.
   18. *Talk with a spouse (or girl/boy friend).
   19. Talk in a small group of friends.
   20. Present a talk to a group of acquaintances.
* Filler item

Scoring: To compute the subscores add the percentages for the items indicated and divide the total by the number indicated below.

Public: 3 + 14 + 20; divide by 3.
Meeting: 6 + 11 + 17; divide by 3.
Group: 8 + 15 + 19; divide by 3.
Dyad: 4 + 9 + 12; divide by 3.
Stranger: 3 + 8 + 12 + 17; divide by 4.
Acquaintance: 4 + 11 + 15 + 20; divide by 4.
Friend: 6 + 9 + 14 + 19; divide by 4.

To compute the total WTC score, add the subscores for Stranger, Acquaintance, and Friend. Then divide that total by 3.

Normative means, standard deviations, and internal reliability estimates for the scores, based on a sample of 428 college students, are as follows:

Score	Mean	Standard Deviation	Reliability
Total WTC	67.3	15.2	.92
Public	56.1	22.2	.76
Meeting	60.0	20.9	.70
Group	73.4	15.8	.65
Dyad	79.5	15.0	.69
Stranger	41.3	22.5	.82
Acquaintance	75.0	17.9	.74
Friend	85.5	13.8	.74

It has strong content validity and there is some support for its construct (McCroskey & McCroskey, 1986 a,b) and predictive validity (Chan, 1988; Chan & McCroskey, 1987; Zakahi & McCroskey, 1986).

Underlying the WTC construct is the general assumption it is a personality- based, trait-like predisposition which is relatively consistent across a variety of communication contexts and types of receivers. For us to argue that the predisposition is trait-like, it is necessary to assume the level of a person's WTC in one communication context (like small group interaction) is correlated with the person's WTC in other communication contexts (such as public speaking, talking in meetings, and talking in dyads). Further, it is necessary to assume that the level of a person's WTC with one type of receiver (like acquaintances) is correlated with the person's WTC with other types of receivers (such as friends and strangers).

These assumptions do not mandate that a person be equally willing to communicate in all contexts or with all receivers, only that the level of willingness in various contexts and with various receivers be correlated. Thus, if Person A is much more willing to communicate in small groups than in a public speaking context, the underlying assumption is not necessarily violated. However, if Person A is more willing to communicate than Person B in one context, it is assumed that Person A will be more willing to communicate than Person B in other contexts as well. If no such regularity exists when data are aggregated for a large number of people, WTC in one context will not be predictive of WTC in another context and WTC with one type of receiver will not be predictive of WTC with another type of receiver. In this event, the data would invalidate the assumption of a trait-like predisposition and necessitate we redirect attention to predispositions that are context-based and/or receiver-based, or forgo the predispositional approach in favor of a purely situational explanation of WTC.

The WTC scale includes items related to four communication contexts—public speaking, talking in meetings, talking in small groups, and talking in dyads—and three types of receivers—strangers, acquaintances, and friends. The scale includes twelve scored items and eight filler items (those marked with an asterisk in Figure 1 are filler items). In addition to an overall WTC score, presumably representing the general personality orientation of WTC, seven subscores may be generated. These represent the four types of communication contexts and three types of receivers.

Available data on the instrument are very promising (McCroskey & Baer, 1985; McCroskey & McCroskey, 1986a,b; McCroskey, Richmond, & McCroskey, 1987). The internal reliability of the total

WTC score is .92. Internal reliabilities for the subscores for communication context range from .65 to .76. Internal reliabilites for the subscores for types of receivers range from .74 to .82. The mean correlation among context subscores is .58. The mean correlation among receiver-type subscores also is .58. After correction for attentuation, the mean correlation among context subscores is .88 and among receiver-type subscores it is .82. Factor analysis indicates that all twelve scored items load most highly on the first unrotated factor, indicating the scale is unidimensional. No interpretable multidimensional structure could be obtained through forced rotations in the McCroskey and Baer (1985) study.

The above correlations and reliabilites suggest that an individual's WTC in one context or with one receiver type is highly related to her/his WTC in other contexts and with other receiver types. This does not mean, however, that individuals are equally willing to communicate in all contexts and with all types of receivers. In fact, major mean differences were observed across the sample of subjects studied on the basis of receiver type. The observed mean percentage of time people would be willing to communicate with friends was 85.5. For acquaintances and strangers the percentages were 75.0 and 41.3, respectively. Contexts produced less dramatic differences in willingness. The percentages for the contexts were as follows: dyad, 79.5; group, 73.4; meeting, 60.0; and public, 56.1. In general, the larger the number of receivers and the more distant the relationship of the individual with the receiver(s) the less willing the individual is to communicate.

The data generated by the WTC scale suggest the validity of our construct of a general predisposition toward being willing or unwilling to communicate. The scale also appears to be valid. The items clearly represent the construct as we have outlined it and the subscore correlations suggest the instrument is measuring a broadly based predisposition rather than a series of independent predispositions. Whether the WTC can be used as a valid predictor of actual communiction behavior is another question. Early results have been extremely encouraging (Chan, 1988; Chan & McCroskey, 1987; Zakahi and McCroskey, 1986). When subjects' communication behavior was observed in these studies under circumstances where they truly had free choice of whether to communicate or not, their scores on the WTC scale were highly predictive of their actual behavior. Students who had higher WTC scores talked more in class than those with lower scores and students with higher scores were more likely than students with lower scores to arrive for scheduled out-of-class appointments for research projects in which some minimal interpersonal interaction could be expected.

ANTECEDENTS OF WILLINGNESS TO COMMUNICATE

That there is regularity in the amount of communication behavior of an individual across situations has been clearly established in many research studies. We have posited a personality-based, cognitively mediated variable as the immediate cause of that regularity—Willingness To Communicate. The question which we will now address is why people vary in this predispositional orientation. We will refer to the variables which we believe lead to differences in WTC as "antecedents." It is likely that many of these "antecedents" develop concurrently with the WTC predisposition. Hence, it cannot be clearly established that the "antecedents" are the causes of variablity in WTC. It is more likely that these variables may be involved in mutual causality and even more likely both the "antecedents" and WTC are produced in common by other causal elements.

The antecedents which we will consider below are variables which have received considerable attention from scholars in communication and/or psychology. Each of them is of interest to scholars for a variety of reasons, only one of which is a possible relationship with WTC. The variables we will consider are introversion, self-esteem, communication competence, communication apprehension, and cultural diversity.

Introversion. The construct of extraversion-introversion has received considerable attention from scholars in psychology for several decades (eg. Eysenck, 1970; 1971). The construct postulates a continuum between extreme extraversion and extreme introversion. The nearer the individual is to the extraversion extreme, the more "people oriented" the person is likely to be. The more introverted the individual, the less need the individual feels for communication and the less value the person places on communicating. Introverts tend to be inner-directed and introspective. They tend to be less sociable and less dependent on others' evaluations than more extraverted people.

Introverts often are characterized as quiet, timid, and shy. Other things being equal, they prefer to withdraw from communication. This may stem in part from anxiety about communication. However, the relationship between introversion and communication apprehension is modest (r = .33, Huntley, 1969). Numerous studies have indicated a relationship between introversion and communication behaviors characteristic of people presumed to have a low WTC. For example, Carment, Miles, and Cervin (1965) found introverts participated in a small group discussion singnificantly less than extroverts and tended to speak only when spoken to rather than initiating interaction. Similarly, Borg and Tupes (1958) found introverts were significantly less likely to engage in the communication behaviors necessary to exercise leadership in small groups than were extraverts. McCroskey & McCroskey (1986 a) found extraversion and WTC to be significantly correlated ($r = .29$).

Self-Esteem. A person's self-esteem is that person's evaluation of her/his own worth. If a person has low self-esteem it might be expected the person would be less willing to communicate because he/she feels he/she has little of value to offer. Similarly, the person with low self-esteem may be less willing to communicate because he/she believes others would respond negatively to what would be said. Although we believe there is good reason to consider self-esteem to be an antecedent of WTC, little research support is available which directly bears on this issue.

The only research reported to this point which provides data directly bearing on the relationship between self-esteem and WTC was provided by McCroskey and McCroskey (1986a,b). They observed a modest correlation between the two, $r = .22$. In an unpublished study we found self-esteem to be significantly related to amount of times people talk in a small group setting—the higher the self-esteem the more times talked. However, we also found that if the variance attributable to communication apprehension were removed first, self-esteem accounted for no significant variance in times talked. Thus, it may be that self-esteem is related to WTC but only as a function of the relationship between self-esteem and anxiety about communication, a relationship which has been found to be quite strong (McCroskey, Daly, Richmond, & Falcione, 1977).

Communication Competence. Work in the area of reticence (Phillips, 1968; 1977; 1984) leads us to believe that a major reason why some people are less willing to communicate than others is because of deficient communication skills. To be reticent is to avoid social interaction; to be reserved, to say little. It is to behave in the way exactly opposite to how one would expect a person who is willing to communicate to behave.

Early work in the area of reticence focused on the behavior as a function of anxiety about communication and was essentially similar to the work to be discussed below related to communication apprehension. The original definition of a reticent individual advanced by Phillips (1968, p. 40) was "a person for whom anxiety about participation in oral communication outweighs his projection of gain from the situation."

More recent work in this area has moved away from anxiety and chosen to focus on communication skills. Although Phillips and others working with the reticence construct do not deny that many people engage in reduced communication because they are apprehensive about communicating, they choose to focus their attention on people who may or may not be anxious but who definately are deficient in their communication skills.

Examples drawn from Phillips' (1968; 1977) work on communication skills training with reticent individuals indicate that when skills are increased WTC in contexts related to the training also increases. This reinforces our belief that for some people WTC in some contexts and/or with some receivers is reduced as a function of not knowing how to communicate. The relationship between communication skills and a general predisposition to be willing to communicate is unknown at this time. Most likely, small skill deficits would have little relationship. However, the perception of one's own skill level may be more important than the actual skill level. Hence, people with low self-esteem may see their skills as deficient and be reticent , even if their skills in reality are quite satisfactory.

Of primary concern here, then, is the way an individual perceives her/his own communication competence. As most people learn from experience, there are many incompetent communicators in the world who think they are competent and proceed to communicate much more willingly than those around them would prefer! Although probably less obvious to most people, there are also those who have quite adequate communication skills who see themselves as incompetent. Hence, they tend to be quite unwilling to communicate. Self-perceptions of competence, then, may have a strong influence on individuals' WTC.

Research to date has shown a substantial association between self-perceived communication competence and WTC. The McCroskey and McCroskey (1986 a,b) research with U.S. college students has observed a correlation between the two of .59. In their report of these results they advanced the argument that self-perceived communication competence may be more associated with both WTC and volitional communication behavior than is actual communication skill. Since the choice of whether to communicate is a cognitive one, it is likely to be more influenced by one's perceptions of competence (of which one usually is aware) than one's actual competence (of which one may be totally unaware).

Communication Apprehension. Communication apprehension (CA) is "an individual's level of fear or anxiety associated with either real or anticipated communication with another person or persons" (McCroskey,1970; 1977; 1984). An individual's level of CA probably is the single best predictor of the person's WTC. The higher the CA level, the lower the level of WTC. To understand the relationship between CA and WTC, and the important distinctions between them, we need to distinguish between the internal and the external effects of CA.

Internal Effects of CA. The effects of traitlike CA have been the focus of extensive research. Much of that work has been summarized elsewhere (Daly & Stafford, 1984; McCroskey, 1977). Unfortunately, much of the research has centered on the impact of CA on communication behaviors. This research is not completely compatible with the conceptualization of CA as a cognitively based variable. Although CA indeed may be linked with communication behavior, it can be so only through its impact on the mediating variable of WTC.

As has been noted elsewhere (McCroskey, 1984), *the only effect of CA that is predicted to be universal across both individuals and types of CA is an internally experienced feeling of discomfort.* As CA is heightened, feelings of discomfort increase and WTC is predicted to decline.

The importance of this conceptualization of CA must be emphasized. Since CA is experienced internally, the only potentially valid indicant of CA is the individual's report of that experience. Thus self-reports of individuals, whether obtained by paper-and-pencil measures or careful interviews, obtained under circumstances where the individual has nothing to gain or avoid losing by lying, provide the only potentially valid measures of CA.

CA is *not* a behavioral construct. It is a cognitive one. "Fear" and "anxiety" are labels for physiological activiation applied by some people while others apply labels such as "excitement" and "anticipation" to essentially similar activation. Once the label is applied it has been found that cognitive disruption can occur in an individual without engaging in a single bit of communication behavior. Simply being alerted to future communication with another person can institute the cognitive disruption (Booth-Butterfield, 1988a,b). CA can be reduced by methods which either reduce the physiological activation (eg. systematic desensitization, McCroskey, 1972) or change the labeling (eg. cognitive restructuring, Fremouw, 1984).

CA is experienced cognitively, and the experience may or may not be manifested by changes in physiological activiation or externally observable symptoms. Hence, measures of physiological activation and observations of communication behavior can provide, at best, only indirect evidence of trait-like CA and thus are inherently inferior approaches to measuring CA. Physiological and behavioral instruments intended to measure CA must be validated with self-report measures, not the other way around. To the extent that such measures are not related to self-report measures, they must be judged invalid. Currently available data indicate that such physiological measures and behavioral observation procedures generally have low validity as measures of trait-like CA but may be somewhat more valid for measuring state CA (Clevenger, 1959; Behnke & Beatty, 1981).

External Effects of CA

As noted above, there is no single behavior that is predicted to be a universal product of varying levels of traitlike CA. Any impact of CA on behavior must be mediated by WTC in interaction with situational constraints. Nevertheless, there are some externally observable behaviors that are more likely to occur or less likely to occur as a function of varying levels of CA. Behavioral prediction from traitlike CA should only be assumed to be correct when considering aggregate behavioral indicants of the individual across time, contexts, and receivers.

Three patterns of behavioral response to high traitlike CA may be predicted to be generally applicable: communication avoidance, communication withdrawal, and communication disruption. A fourth pattern is atypical but sometimes does occur—excessive communication. Let us consider each.

When people are confronted with a circumstance they anticipate will make them uncomfortable, and they have a choice of whether or not to confront it, they may decide either to confront it and make the best of it or avoid it and thus avoid the discomfort. Some refer to this as the choice between "fight" and "flight." Research in the area of CA indicates that the latter choice should be expected in most cases. In order to avoid having to experience high CA, people may become less willing to communicate and therefore select occupations that involve low communication responsibilities, may pick housing units that reduce incidental contact with other people, may choose seats in classrooms or in meetings that are less conspicuous, and may avoid social settings. Avoidance, then, is a common behavioral response to high CA.

Avoidance of communication is not always possible no matter how high a person's level of traitlike CA or low a person's level of WTC. A person can find her/himself in a situation that demands communication with no advance warning. Under such circumstances, withdrawal from communication is the behavioral pattern to be expected. This withdrawal may be complete (absolute silence) or partial (talking only as much as absolutely required). In a public speaking setting, this response may be represented by the very short speech. In a meeting, class, or small group discussion, it may be represented by talking only when called upon. In a dyadic interaction, it may be represented by only briefly answering questions or supplying agreeing responses with no initiation of discussion.

Generally, then, verbal communication is substantially reduced when a person wishes to withdraw from communication. Nonverbal communication, on the other hand, may not be reduced but the nonverbal messages which are sent may be primarily of one type. That type is referred to as "nonimmediate." Nonimmediate messages include such things as frowns, standing or sitting away from other people, avoiding eye contact, and standing with arms folded. These messages signal others that a person is not interested in communicating and tend to reduce communication initiation attempts from others.

Communication disruption is the third typical behavioral pattern associated with high CA. The person may have disfluencies in verbal presentation or unnatural nonverbal behaviors. Equally as likely are poor choices of communicative strategies. It is important to note, however, that such behaviors may also be produced by introversion, low self-esteem, inadequate communication skills, low self-perceived communication competence and/or cultural divergence. Thus inferring the existence of high CA from observations of such behavior often is inappropriate.

Overcommunication as a response to high traitlike CA is uncommon but does exist as a pattern exhibited by a small minority. This behavior may involve overcompensation for a person's high level of apprehension and low level of WTC. It also might represent a circumstance where a person has a high need and WTC but also has high apprehension. Willingness and apprehension are presumed to be substantially, but not perfectly, negatively correlated. Thus, this may represent the "fight" response, an attempt to communicate in spite of the presence of high apprehension. The person who elects to take a public speaking course in spite of her/his extreme stage fright is a classic example. Less easily recognizable is the individual with high CA who attempts to dominate social situations. Most of the time people who employ this behavioral option are seen as poor communicators but are not recognized as having high CA. In fact, they may be seen as people with very low CA.

Although most of the research related to CA has been done under the CA label (McCroskey, 1970; 1977; Daly & McCroskey, 1984), very similar work has been done under other labels. Some of these include "stage fright" (Clevenger, 1959), the early work on "reticence" (Phillips, 1968), "unwillingness to communicate" (Burgoon, 1976), "social anxiety" (Leary, 1983), "audience anxiety" (Buss, 1980), and "shyness" (Buss, 1980; Zimbardo, 1977).

Although there are very meaningful differences in the conceptualizations advanced under these various labels, the main differences involve the operational measures employed under each. Both subjective examination of the measures and correlational analyses (Daly, 1978), however, indicate that the measures are highly related and probably are all tapping into the same global construct.

Regardless of the operationalization of the construct, research overwhelmingly indicates people who experience high levels of fear or anxiety about communication tend to avoid and withdraw from communication. Although not measured directly, these research results strongly suggest CA directly impacts an individual's WTC. The reported research which directly bears on this question supports the hypothesis that CA and WTC are substantially related. In the McCroskey and McCroskey (1986 a,b) research with college students the observed correlation was -.50. Similar correlations have been found for college students in Australia (r = -.49; Barraclough, Christophel, & McCroskey, 1988) and Sweden (r = -.44; Daun, Burroughs, & McCroskey, 1988).

Cultural Diversity. Although communication exists in all human cultures and subcultures, communication norms are highly variable as a function of culture. Thus, one's communication norms and competencies are culture-bound. Recent studies have indicated United States college students are significantly more willing to communicate than are similar students in Australia (Barraclough, Christophel, & McCroskey, 1988) and Sweden (Daun, Burroughs, & McCroskey, 1988). Such norms are reflected in what often is called the "personality" of a culture. Some cultures are seen as quiet while others are characteristically loquacious. Although mean willingness may differ substantially from culture to culture, we would still anticipate major variations among people in any given culture, no matter how homogeneous that culture might be.

In a few countries, like Japan, a single culture is almost universally dominant. In other countries, like the United States, there is a majority culture and many subcultures. These subcultures exist both as a function of geographic region and ethnicity. People from Texas and people from Maine have differing communication norms. So too do Mexican Americans, African Americans, Japanese Americans, Native Americans, Irish Americans, and so forth.

Whenever a person finds her/himself in an environment in which her/his own subculture is in a minority position compared to other people with whom he/she must communicate, that person may be described as culturally divergent. It is incumbent on the individual to adapt to the larger group's communication norms to be effective in communication in that environment. As anyone who has traveled extensively can testify, such adaptation can be very difficult or impossible to achieve.

Culturally divergent people are very similar to people who have deficient communication skills. They do not know how to communicate effectively so they tend to be much less willing to communicate at all to avoid failure and possible negative consequences. The difference between the culturally divergent and the skill deficient is that the culturally divergent individual may have excellent communication skills for one culture but not for the other. Cultural divergence, then, is seen as being highly related to WTC if a person regularly resides in a culture different from her/his own. On the other hand, if the person communicates primarily in her/his own culture and only occasionally must do so in another culture, the impact would only be transitory and situational. Culture, of course, may have an impact on WTC beyond its direct impact and the impact resulting from an individual going from one culture to another. The relationship between WTC and its various antecedants may be substantially different in one culture than in another. This was evidenced in the previously noted studies comparing students in the U.S. with those in Australia and Sweden. The association between WTC and self-perceived communication competence was found to be .59 (R^2 = .35) in the U.S. and .57 (R^2 = .32) in Australia, but only .44 (R^2 = .19) in Sweden (Barraclaugh, Christophel, & McCroskey, 1988; Daun, et al. 1988).

EFFECTS OF WILLINGNESS TO COMMUNICATE IN COMMUNICATION

Research relating to the impact of WTC in communication has been conducted under a variety of constructs—CA, shyness, unwillingness to communicate, predisposition toward verbal behavior, talkativeness, reticence, quietness, and social anxiety, to name a few. Such research has been reported in the literature of psychology and communication for over four decades. The three basic research models that have been employed have been 1) direct observation of amount of communication with assessment of outcomes, 2) measurement of a predisposition (such as CA) which is presumed to be related to WTC, allowing communication to occur, and assessing outcomes, and 3) simulation of talkativeness variation with assessment of outcomes.

Regardless of the research model employed, the results of this research have been remarkably consistent. The general conclusion that can be drawn from this immense body of research is that reduced WTC results in an individual being less effective in communication and generating negative perceptions of him or her self in the minds of others involved in the communication.

Since this research has been thoroughly summarized (Daly & Stafford, 1984) and interpreted (Richmond, 1984) previously, we will not take the space here to repeat those efforts. Instead, we will simply draw from that work some of the conclusions that appear most obvious from the research results.

Interpersonal communication occurs primarily within three general environments—school environments, organizational environments, and social environments. While these three environments are neither mutually exclusive nor exhaustive of all environments in which interpersonal communication can occur, they will suffice for our illustrative purposes here.

In the school environment students with high WTC characteristically have all the advantages, even though they may be reprimanded occasionally for communicating when they are not supposed to. Teachers have positive expectations for students who are highly willing to communicate and negative ones for those less willing. Student achievement, as measured by teacher made tests, teacher assigned grades, and standardized tests, is consistent with these expectations— in spite of the fact that intellectual ability has not been found to be associated with communication orientations.

Students who are less willing to communicate are also seen in negative ways by their peers. Such negative perceptions have been observed all the way from the lower elementary level through graduate school. Students who are willing to communicate have more friends and report being more satisfied with their school experience. With both academic achievement and social support on the side of the student who is willing to communicate, it should not be surprising that such students are more likely to remain in school and graduate than those who are less willing.

The impact of WTC in the organizational environment is no less than that in the school. People who are highly willing to communicate receive preference in the hiring process and are more likely to be promoted to positions of importance in the organization. People who are less willing to communicate tend to self-select themselves into occupational roles that insure themselves lower social status and lower economic standing. People who report higher WTC also report being more satisfied with their employment and are much more likely to remain with an organization. People with lower WTC tend to generate negative perceptions in the minds of their co-workers. They are seen as neither task attractive nor credible and are rejected for leadership positions.

On the social level, the picture is very similar. People with high WTC have more friends and are less likely to be lonely. They are likely to have more dates and to date more people than people less willing to communicate. The latter are more likely to engage in exclusive dating and to marry immediately after completing their schooling. People who are highly willing to communicate are seen as more socially and physically attractive by others, which may explain some of the other effects noted above.

CONCLUSION AND IMPLICATIONS

The general conclusion we draw from the research and theory summarized above is that a global, personality-type orientation (WTC) exists which has a major impact on cognitive choices regarding interpersonal communication in a wide variety of environments. While WTC in a given situation can be impacted by situational constraints, trait-like WTC has potential impact in all communication settings. High willingness is associated with increased frequency and amount of communication which are associated with a wide variety of positive communication outcomes. Low willingness is associated with decreased frequency and amount of communication which are associated with a wide variety of negative outcomes.

The above conclusion appears to be true for individuals in the general American culture and highly similar cultures. It very likely is *not* true in many other cultures. Cultures vary in the degree to which they value oral communication. Authors of works on both intercultural communication (eg. Samovar & Porter, 1982; Klopf & Park, 1982; Klopf & Ishii, 1984) and nonverbal communication (eg. Burgoon & Saine, 1978; Hinde, 1972; Knapp, 1978; Richmond, McCroskey, & Payne, 1987) have tended to focus their attention on the nonverbal aspects of communication in intercultural contexts. For the most part differences in verbal communication between cultures have been left to the concern of linguists. Differences in the *amount* of verbal communication have received comparatively little attention from either group.

The view taken here is that the most basic difference in communication patterns between cultures may indeed be the amount of verbal communication which is preferred and the circumstances calling for talk as opposed to those which call for silence. A primary direction for future research in the WTC area is in the intercultural arena. With the global expansion of business, government, and other intercultural contacts, the need for people able to communicate effectively in multicultural settings has far outstriped academia's output of knowledge needed in this area, to say nothing of its output of people with command of that knowledge. The impact of willingness to communicate within the general American culture is now fairly well understood, although additional research in this area certainly is needed. Comparable knowledge concerning other cultures, for the most part, is virtually nonexistent. Filling this void should be the primary concern for scholars interested in conducting research in this area.

REFERENCES

Barraclaugh, R. A., Christophel, D. M. & McCroskey, J. C. (1988). Willingness to communicate: A cross-cultural investigation. *Communication Research Reports, 5,* 187-192.

Behnke, R. R., & Beatty, M. J. (1981). A cognitive-physiological model of speech anxiety. *Communication Monographs, 48,* 158-163.

Berger, C. R., & Calabrese, R. J. (1975). Some explorations in initial interaction and beyond: Toward a developmental theory of interpersonal communication. *Human Communication Research, 1,* 99-112.

Booth-Butterfield, S. (1988a). The effect of communication apprehension and anticipated interaction on student recall of information. Doctoral dissertation, West Virginia University.

Booth-Butterfield, S. (1988b). Inhibition and student recall of instructional messages. *Communication Education, 37,* 312-324.

Borg, W. R., & Tupes, E. C. (1958). Personality characteristics related to leadership behavior in two types of small group situational problems. *Journal of Applied Psychology, 42,* 252-256.

Borgatta, E. F., & Bales, R. F. (1953). Interaction of individuals in reconstituted groups. *Sociometry, 16,* 302-320.

Burgoon, J. K. (1976). The Unwillingness-to-Communicate Scale: Development and validation. *Communication Monographs, 43,* 60-69.

Burgoon, J. K. & Saine, T. (1978). *The unspoken dialogue: An introduction to nonverbal communication.* Boston: Houghton Mifflin.

Buss, A. H. (1980). *Self-consciousness and social anxiety.* San Francisco, CA: W. H. Freeman.

Carment, D. W., Miles, C. G., & Cervin, V. B. (1965). Persuasiveness and persuasibility as related to intelligence and extraversion. *British Journal of Social and Clinical Psychology, 4,* 1-7.

Chan, B. M. (1988). The effects of willingness to communicate on student learning. Doctoral dissertation, West Virginia University.

Chan, B. M., & McCroskey, J. C. (1987). The WTC scale as a predictor of classroom participation. *Communication Research Reports, 4,* 47-50.

Chapple, E. D., & Arensberg, C. M. (1940). Measuring human relations: An introduction to the study of the interaction of individuals. Genetic *Psychology Monographs, 22,* 3-147.

Clevenger, T., Jr. (1959). A synthesis of experimental research in stage fright. *Quarterly Journal of Speech, 45,* 134-145.

Daly, J. A. (1978). The assessment of social-communicative anxiety via self-reports: A comparison of measures. *Communication Monographs, 45,* 204-218.

Daly, J. A., & McCroskey, J. C. (1984). *Avoiding communication: Shyness, reticence, and communication apprehension.* Beverly Hills, CA: SAGE.

Daly, J. A., & Stafford, L. (1984). Corrrelates and consequences of social-communicative anxiety. In J. A. Daly and J. C. McCroskey (Eds.), *Avoiding communication: Shyness, reticence, and communication apprehension.* Beverly Hills, CA: SAGE.

Daly, J. A., McCroskey, J. C., & Richmond, V. P. (1977). The relationships between vocal activity and perception of communicators in small group interaction. *Western Speech Communication Journal, 41,* 175-187.

Daun, A., Burroughs, N. F., & McCroskey, J. C. (May, 1988). Correlates of quietness: Swedish and American perspectives. Paper present at the annual convention of the International Communication Association, New Orleans.

Eysenck, H. J. (1970). *Readings in extraversion-introversion: Volume I.* New York: Wiley-Interscience.

Eysenck, H. J. (1971). *Readings in extraversion-introversion: Volume II.* New York: Wiley-Interscience.

Fremouw, W. J. (1984). Cognitive-behavioral therapies for modification of communication apprehension. In J. A. Daly and J. C. McCroskey, Eds. *Avoiding communication: Shyness, reticence, and communication apprehension.* Beverly Hills, CA: Sage.

Goldman-Eisler, F. (1951). The measurement of time sequences in conversational behavior. *British Journal of Psychology, 42*, 355-362.

Hayes, D., & Meltzer, L. (1972). Interpersonal judgements based on talkativeness: I. Face or artifact? *Sociometry, 35*, 538-561.

Hinde, R. A. (Ed.) (1972). *Non-verbal communication.* London: Cambridge University Press.

Huntley, J. R. (1969). An investigation of the relationships between personality and types of instructor criticism in the beginning speech-communication course. Unpublished doctoral dissertation, Michigan State University.

Klopf, D. W. & Ishii, S. (1984). *Communicating effectively across cultures.* Tokyo: NAN"UN-DO.

Klopf, D. W. & Park, Myung-Seok. (1982). *Cross-cultural communication: An introduction to the fundamentals.* Seoul, Korea: Han Shin Publishers.

Knapp, M. L. (1978). *Nonverbal communication in human interaction.* (2nd. ed.) New York: Holt, Rinehart & Winston.

Leary, M. R. (1983). Understanding social anxiety: Social, personality, and clinical perspectives. Beverly Hills, CA: Sage.

McCroskey, J. C. (1970). Measures of communication-bound anxiety. *Speech Monographs, 37*, 269-277.

McCroskey, J. C. (1972). The implementation of a large-scale program of systematic desensitization for communication apprehension. *Speech Teacher, 21*, 255-264.

McCroskey, J. C. (1977). Oral communication apprehension: A summary of recent theory and research. *Human Communication Research, 4*, 78-96.

McCroskey, J. C. (1984). The communication apprehension perspective. In J. A. Daly and J. C. McCroskey (Eds.). Avoiding communication: Shyness, reticence, and communication apprehension. Beverly Hills, CA: SAGE.

McCroskey, J. C., & Baer, J. E. (November, 1985). Willingness to communicate: The construct and its measurement. Paper presented at the annual convention of the Speech Communication Association, Denver.

McCroskey, J. C., & McCroskey, L. L. (February, 1986a). Correlates of willingness to communicate. Paper presented at the annual convention of the Western Speech Communication Association, Tucson, AZ.

McCroskey, J. C., & McCroskey, L. L. (May, 1986b). Predictors of willingness to communicate: Implications for screening and remediation. Paper presented at the annual convention of the International Communication Association, Chicago, IL.

McCroskey, J. C., & Richmond, V. P. (1982). Communication apprehension and shyness: Conceptual and operational distinctions. *Central States Speech Journal, 33*, 458-468.

McCroskey, J. C., & Richmond, V. P. (March, 1985). Willingness to communicate and interpersonal communication. Paper presented at the Symposium on Personality and Interpersonal Communication, West Virginia University, Morgantown, WV.

McCroskey, J. C., & Richmond, V. P. (1987). Willingness to communicate. In J.C. McCroskey and J.A. Daly, Eds. *Personality and Interpersonal Communication*. Newbury Park, CA: Sage, 129-156.

McCroskey, J. C., Richmond, V. P., & McCroskey, L. L. (1987). Correlates of self-perceived communication competence. Paper presented at the annual convention of the International Communication Association, Montreal, Canada.

McCroskey, J. C., Daly, J. A., Richmond, V. P., & Falcione, R. L. (1977). Studies of the relationship between communication apprehension and self-esteem. *Human Communication Research, 3*, 264-277.

Mortensen, D. C., Arnston, P. H., & Lustig, M. (1977). The measurement of verbal predispositions: Scale development and application. *Human Communication Research, 3*, 146-158.

Phillips, G. M. (1968). Reticence: Pathology of the normal speaker. *Speech Monographs, 35*, 39-49.

Phillips, G. M. (1977). Rhetoritherapy versus the medical model: Dealing with reticence. *Communication Education, 26*, 34-43.

Phillips, G. M. (1984). Reticence: A perspective on social withdrawal. in J. A. Daly and J. C. McCroskey (Eds.). *Avoiding communication: Shyness, reticence, and communication apprehension*. Beverly Hills, CA: SAGE.

Richmond, V. P. (1984). Implications of quietness: Some facts and speculations. In J. A. Daly and J. C. McCroskey (Eds.). *Avoiding communication: Shyness, reticence, and communication apprehension*. Beverly Hills, CA: SAGE, 145-156.

Richmond, V. P. & McCroskey, J. C. (1985). *Communication: Apprehension, avoidance, and effectiveness*. Scottsdale, AZ: Gorsuch Scarisbrick Publishers.

Richmond, V. P., & McCroskey, J. C. (1989). Willingness to communicate and dysfunctional communication processes. In C.V. Roberts and K.W. Watson, Eds. *Intrapersonal communication processes: Original essays*. Scottsdale, AZ: Gorsuch Scarisbrick Publishers.

Richmond, V. P., McCroskey, J. C., & Payne, S. K. (1987). *Nonverbal behavior in interpersonal relations*. Englewood Cliffs, NJ: Prentice-Hall, Inc.

Samovar, L. A. & Porter, R. E. (1982). *Intercultural communication: A reader*. (3rd. Ed.). Belmont, CA: Wadsworth.

Zakahi, W. R., & McCroskey, J. C. (November, 1986). *Willingness to communicate: A confounding variable in communication research*. Paper presented at the annual convention of the Speech Communication Association, Chicago, IL.

Zimbardo, P. G. (1977). *Shyness: What it is and what to do about it*. Reading, MA: Addison-Wesley.

Anxiety, Cognition, and Behavior:
In Search of a Broader Perspective

Mark R. Leary

Department of Psychology, Wake Forest University
Winston-Salem, NC 27109

This article draws connections among various lines of research that have examined the affective, cognitive, and behavioral aspects of social anxiety. The two lead articles in this volume are discussed within a broad perspective that proposes three primary paths among cognition, anxiety, and behavior.

The study of anxiety was once the purview of experimental psychologists (who were interested in its effects on learning) and clinical psychologists (who were interested in the treatment of neurotic disorders). Recently, however, researchers from many areas of behavioral science have converged to study the worries of everyday life. This growth of interest in socially-relevant anxieties has been pronounced during the past 10-15 years.

Most writers have regarded the anxious state as a multifaceted response, characterized not only by the subjective distress we typically call "anxiety," but also by certain patterns of thought and behavior. When anxious, people are troubled by fearful and self-deprecating thoughts, their behavior tends to become hesitant, inhibited, and, occasionally, disrupted. One of the more complex and problematic issues in the anxiety literature involves the relationships among the affective, cognitive, and behavioral components of the anxious response.

The articles by Sarason, Sarason, and Pierce (1990) and by McCroskey and Richmond (1990), as well as other articles in this volume, address aspects of these relationships. My objective in this commentary is to examine the two lead papers with an eye toward providing a broader perspective for understanding the links among anxiety, cognition, and behavior.

The article by Sarason and his colleagues dealt primarily with the effects of anxious self-preoccupation on behavioral performance. When anxious, people tend to ruminate about impending disasters and personal deficiencies. Evidence shows that such thoughts interfere with their

© 1990 Select Press

performance in both testing and interpersonal settings by distracting the individual from the task at hand. McCroskey and Richmond (1990) were interested not in behavioral disruption resulting from cognitive interference but in the degree to which people are willing to communicate with others. Importantly, one of the best predictors of the willingness to communicate is communication apprehension—anxiety experienced in communication settings—highlighting, again, a link between anxiety and behavior.

Although these papers share a general interest in cognition, anxiety, and behavior, their specific foci may appear, at least initially, to be unrelated. The phenomenon examined by Sarason and his colleagues is largely nonvolitional and beyond the individual's control—a dysfunctional by-product of certain cognitive processes. McCroskey and Richmond, on the other hand, discussed communicative behaviors that are largely a matter of personal choice. The divergence in their topics is perhaps best reflected in the fact that their reference lists have very few citations in common.

Despite their differences, it seems to me that the phenomena discussed in these two articles are, in fact, more closely related than they may first appear. Specifically, two points of connection may be drawn: (1) both papers involve phenomena associated with anxious thoughts and behaviors and (2) both deal with behavioral effects of anxious cognition, albeit cognitions that occur at different points in the sequence of anxious responses. I'll discuss each of these points in turn.

Conceptual Similarities

Like many areas of behavioral research, the literature that deals with social anxieties and their concomitants is quite fragmented. Although some cross-fertilization between researchers in communication and psychology has occurred (as exemplified by this volume), these two fields have tended to remain relatively insulated. Furthermore, even researchers from various subfields of psychology (social, developmental, personality, clinical, and counseling psychology, for example) have sometimes paid scant attention to one another's work.

Specialists in each field have adopted different terms for the phenomena they study and, as a result, the area has witnessed a proliferation of constructs that deal with anxiety and behavior in social and evaluation settings: social anxiety, communication apprehension, test anxiety, audience anxiety, shyness, willingness-to-communicate, separation anxiety, and so on. As I have discussed elsewhere (Leary, 1983b, 1986), these constructs can be clustered into two primary groups—those that deal with the affective experience of anxiety and those that focus on behavioral concomitants, such as inhibition and reticence. With the Sarasons' recent work on cognitive components of test and social anxiety, we may add a third group of constructs—those that involve cognitive aspects of anxiety.

We should not let these various terms blind us to the fact that all of these constructs—whether they are affective, behavioral, or cognitive—are related to people's reactions in social/evaluative situations. Even test anxiety, which has developed a literature quite distinct from social anxiety, can be regarded as a "social anxiety" at heart, a reaction to the belief that one will be perceived and evaluated negatively by others (Leary, 1983a).[1] Clearly, conceptual differences exist among these constructs, but they are none-the-less closely related. In light of this, it behooves researchers who are interested in one particular construct to pay attention to work that deals with the others.

Paths Among Cognition, Anxiety, and Behavior

Given their interrelationships, we must begin to address more explicitly how the affective, cognitive, and behavioral aspects of anxiety are related. Both Sarason/Sarason/Pierce and McCroskey/Richmond address aspects of these relationships, but each serves us only a slice of the pie. Although many potential paths exist among anxiety, cognition, and behavior, I will highlight three of the primary ones.

Path 1: Behavior as a result of cognitive assessment. People regulate their behavior by assessing the likelihood that they will achieve certain goals or meet certain standards (Carver, 1979). In social settings, people weigh the potential rewards and costs involved with certain behavioral options and estimate the likelihood that these outcomes will occur. Potential costs of interaction include not only social failure and rejection, but their subjective consequences such as anxiety.

In some settings, the individual will conclude that the likelihood of failure and its accompanying costs is unacceptably high, relative to potential rewards, and the person will opt against performing the behavior in question. Thus, in some social situations, one possible outcome of this analysis is that the individual will simply not interact—they will be unwilling to communicate.

As McCroskey and Richmond observe, persons who perceive themselves to be deficient in communication skills are less willing to commu-

---

[1] *More precisely, some sources of test anxiety are social, whereas other sources are not. When people worry about their test performance because they are concerned about how others will evaluate them ("My parents will be mad and my friends will think I'm stupid if I fail this test"), their test anxiety reflects a form of social anxiety. However, when the person is worried about nonsocial outcomes that may result form poor performance ("If I won't do well on this test, I won't get the job, and the bank will foreclose on my house"), their test anxiety is not primarily social.*

nicate. In my view, this is because they perceive fewer rewards and greater risks associated with interacting. Similarly, those who are high in communication apprehension may decline to communicate to avoid the aversiveness of social anxiety. Thus, willingness to communicate may reflect a volitional and relatively reasoned choice given one's analysis of the rewards and costs that are likely to occur. Viewed another way, withdrawal and reticence may reflect an interpersonal strategy that minimizes one's social risks. Whether we are dealing with one's willingness-to-communicate in a particular situation or with the trait measured by the Willingness-to-Communicate (WTC) Scale, antecedents of willingness-to-communicate have their effects by tipping the person's reward/cost analysis in the direction of withdrawal rather than interaction.[2]

Path 2: Behavioral disruption as a consequence of cognitive interference. In some instances, individuals find it difficult to avoid or disengage themselves from an anxiety-producing situation. Occasionally, students leave examinations before completion and speakers flee from the podium in mid-speech, but such instances of premature exit are rare once the individual is engaged in the situation.

In his cybernetic model of self-attention, Carver (1979) suggested that individuals who perceive that their likelihood of achieving success is low, but who cannot withdraw from the situation, are "frozen in the self-assessment phase of the sequence, where they repeatedly confront the evidence of their own inadequacy" (p. 1266). As Sarason et al. correctly note, this task-irrelevant thinking distracts the individual from devoting sufficient attention to the immediate situation, whether it be a test, a social interaction, or whatever. As a result, behavior is disrupted.

In the literatures on both test and social anxiety, writers have tended to view these disruptions as entirely dysfunctional. Granted, anxious inhibition typically creates problems for the test anxious or socially anxious person, but it may in fact have a function. Specifically, anxiety may serve as an "interrupt mechanism" that breaks an ongoing behavioral performance to reassess its direction or success (Baumeister & Tice, in press; Simon, 1967). Indeed, this reassessment function may be part of the cognitive disruption discussed by Sarason et al.

---

[2] *In their article, McCroskey and Richmond discuss trait WTC as an "immediate cause" of communication behaviors. In my view, a dispositional variable such as WTC is best regarded as a description of behavioral styles that are consistent across situations rather than as the cause of those behaviors. After all, WTC is measured by asking respondents the percentage of time they communicate in various settings. Thus, WTC is a self-reported summary of the frequency with which they communicate. This in no way diminishes the conceptual or empirical usefulness of WTC, but questions its status as a causal construct.*

In the case of performing a physically dangerous action (preparing to leap across a precipice, for example), such an interruption and reassessment has distinct advantages. In th case of symbolic and social threats, such as those that underlie test and social anxiety, this interrupt mechanism is less useful. Occasionally, anxious disruption of a socially misguided action (insulting the boss' spouse, for example) may be helpful, but more often, it is simply debilitating.

Path 3: Behavior as an antecedent of anxious cognition and affect. A third path, which has received little attention, involves the fact that behavioral inhibition and disruption may precede anxious cognitions and subjective anxiety. For example, an individual who realizes that his or her performance (on a test or in an interaction) is below par will become concerned about the consequences of a poor performance and experience social anxiety. In such instances, the problematic behaviors precede anxious cognition and affect.

In addition, some individuals—introverts and persons who are low in willingness-to-communicate, for example—interact less frequently and fully than other people. They are not necessarily nervous about interacting; they simply prefer solitary over gregarious activities. Even so, they may recognize that their quiet demeanor results in negative evaluations from others, and this realization may result in social anxiety.

In brief, I see three primary paths between anxiety, cognition, and behavior. In the first, one's cognitive assessment of likely outcomes affects one's willingness to participate in a particular situation. In the second, an individual is distracted from a behavioral performance by worrisome and self-relevant thoughts. And, in the third, one's analysis of one's behavior results in anxiety and worry.

Summary

This brief analysis suggests that researchers must be careful to distinguish between cognitions and behaviors that are antecedents versus consequences of subjective anxiety. Anxiety is perhaps best regarded as a recursive process. Cognitive appraisal precipitates subjective anxiety, which disposes people to ruminate further and may interfere with ongoing behavior. As behavioral performance is degraded, intrusive thinking escalates, which results in increased anxiety and additional interference. Of course, the entire cycle is avoided when an individual simply declines to communicate or interact.

Previous researchers have entered this anxiety-cognition-behavior cycle at different places without discussing that they were, in fact, studying different aspects of a single, complex process. Sarason et al., for example, enter where the already-anxious individual finds his or her behavior disrupted by cognitive interference. McCroskey and Richmond jump in where the individual declines to enter a potentially threatening encounter. My own work on the self-presentational theory of social anxiety starts where the individual assesses how he or she is being perceived and evaluated by others (Leary, 1983a; Schlenker & Leary, 1982). As they continue to study the connections among cognition, anxiety, and behavior, researchers should remain aware of the fact that they are, in fact, studying different facets of the same process.

REFERENCES

Baumeister, R.F., & Tice, D. (in press). Anxiety and social exclusion. *Journal of Social and Clinical Psychology*.

Carver, C.A. (1979). A cybernetic model of self-attention processes. *Journal of Personality and Social Psychology, 37*, 1251-1281.

Leary, M.R. (1983a). *Understanding social anxiety*. Beverly Hills: Sage.

Leary, M.R. (1983b). The conceptual distinctions are important: Another look at communication apprehension and related constructs. *Human Communication Research, 10*, 305-312.

Leary, M.R. (1986). Affective and behavioral components of shyness: Implications for theory, measurement, and research. In W.H. Jones, S.R. Brigs, & J.M. Cheek (Eds.), *Shyness: Perspectives on research and treatment* (pp. 27-38). New York: Plenum.

McCroskey, J.C., & Richmond, V.P. (1990). Willingness to communicate: A cognitive view. In M. Booth-Butterfield, Communication, cognition, and anxiety [Special Issue]. *Journal of Social Behavior and Personality, 5* (2), 19-38.

Sarason, I.G., Sarason, B.R., & Pierce, G.R. (1990). Anxiety, cognitive interference, and performance. In M. Booth-Butterfield, Communication, cognition, and anxiety [Special Issue]. *Journal of Social Behavior and Personality, 5* (2), 1-18.

Schlenker, B.R., & Leary, M.R. (1982). Social anxiety and self-presentation: A conceptualization and model. *Psychological Bulletin, 92*, 641-669.

Simon, H.A. (1967). Motivational and emotional controls of cognition. *Psychological Review, 74*, 29-39.

Toward a Hemispheric Processing Approach To Communication Competence

Daniel E. Sellers
Department of Speech Pathology and Audiology,
University of South Alabama, Mobile, AL 36688

Don W. Stacks
Department of Speech Communication,
University of Alabama, Tuscaloosa, AL 35487-0240

The way in which people process communication is viewed as one avenue for understanding why some people are competent communicators at times, yet incompetent at other times. The essay presented here argues that this processing involves the access of brain modules in a "normal" functional manner. The underlying premise is that communication occurs at the intrapersonal level through the interaction of a variety of brain modules which produce "normal" and "abnormal" responses to the communication situation. Abnormal communication—fear or apprehension toward communication—may be perceived as either state- or trait-oriented, depending upon the pathology of the particular brain module influencing the processing system.

INTRODUCTION

It has often been said that most of what we believe and act upon exists in the *"mind* of the actor." The mind, however, is not a simple subject of study and for years philosophers and scientists have tried to come to grips with that which "makes us human." What is the mind? How does it impact at both the cognitive and lower (precognitive) levels of daily communication? What role does the mind play in an individual's ability to communicate with "competence"—or to communicate "normally" in day-to-day interaction? What role does the mind play in the formation of communication avoidance or apprehension? How does the mind operate in the functioning of pre-communication, or int*ra*personal

---

Authors Note: We wish to thank the University of South Alabama, Dept. of Speech Pathology & Audiology and College of Allied Health, for its generosity in underwriting the project.

© 1990 Select Press

communication? What effect does this functioning have on communication behavior at the conscious level? These questions and others are the focus of this essay.

For some time now research and theory have placed the mind somewhere within the brain, in particular within the functioning of the two major hemispheres of the cerebral cortex. This body of thought and research has evolved over the years from a rather simple model whereby one brain hemisphere controlled our conscious actions and communications. This model saw one (left) hemisphere "dominate" the other (right) hemisphere as the repository for language and logic; the right hemisphere's function was to interpret the nonverbal elements of communication. Biologically, damage to this dominant hemisphere *did* change the impact and function of the individual's communication, especially his or her verbal behavior. Additionally, research established that the right hemisphere controlled the *motor functioning* of the left side of the body; the left hemisphere controlled the right side of the body.

This very parsimonious right-left brain theory fell into disrepute in the late 1970s when it was recognized that the brain, rather than being two differing cerebral units was actually an organized whole. This "holistic" theory of brain functioning placed greater emphasis on the type of analysis and function each brain hemisphere accomplished than on the dominance each had for communication. The focus, then, changed from an analysis of *structure* to an analysis of *process and interpretation*. An extension of this line of thought presents the brain as composed of a variety of stages, centers, or *modules* which interact with each other to process stimuli according to a particular style or specialization. Within this perspective, the brain *communicates with itself* as a precursor to actual (conscious) communication. This form of "modular communication" takes place at the intrapersonal level of communication (Stacks and Andersen, 1989).

It is assumed that communication at the intrapersonal level affects communication at other levels: interpersonal, small group, large group, etc. Further, as discussed later, it is assumed that intrapersonal communication exists below the cognitive level of analysis, that it is part and parcel a part of the mind as composed of brain modules.

Communication competence is the individual's ability to properly process information in such a way that communicative behaviors occur in some orderly, rule-governed way. That is, the competent communicator is able to relate some message, either verbally or nonverbally, in a manner appropriate for the situation. The initial stimuli for such communication may be either external or internal to the communicator. Lack of communication competence is perceived as an inability to produce messages appropriate to the situation, or to even attempt a communication. In this regard we suggest that inability to communicate is associated with both conscious and unconscious forces within the individual. These forces may manifest themselves in terms of inappropriate cognitive associations with a particular communication situation, producing a state of communication apprehension, or may exist as a trait found within the individual. McCroskey (1983; McCroskey & Beatty, 1984) has adequately addressed this issue. The treatment which follows suggests that anxiety in the form of communication avoidance or apprehension may be explained by the way in which the mind perceives the situation both specifically (state-like) and across contexts (trait-like).

This essay first examines the modular mind as a precursor to discussion about hemispheric processing of information by that mind. It then examines how this functioning may be interrupted, interfered with, or corrupted in such as way as to induce anxiety and reduce communication competence. We turn first to a discussion of the modular mind.

THE MODULAR MIND

The concept of modularity in general is not new (cf., Fodor, 1983) and it is not the purpose of this essay to review it great detail. Instead a general review of the modular mind sets the stage for the hemispheric processing of information as analyzed by the various modules engaged in "normal" communication. Gazzaniga, as early as 1978 (Gazzaniga & LeDoux, 1978; Gazzaniga, 1985), suggested that the human brain operates on a modular basis—like a federation of governments, each module consisting of a state which has the independent abilities of cognition, feeling, memory, and action:

> A cognitive system of mental modules, each one of which could act independently from the other but all together forming a mental federation, would be most likely to assign to one cognitive system the chore of establishing and maintaining a theory about the federation's actions. Part and parcel of the process would be the necessary concept that the organism was acting freely, that in fact the organism was governable (Gazzaniga, 1985, p. 146).

As with any federation, one state or module can influence the actions of the other modules or the entire federation. The analogy to the brain is consistent with neurophysiological research, as pointed out by Stacks and Andersen (1989):

> Witelson (1987) suggested that a number of distinct memory systems exist in each individual's mind. These systems are functionally organized and each is independently capable of learning. Damage to one system may have little or no effect on memory (p. 276).

In a similar theoretical perspective Stacks (1983) posited a parallel model which described how preverbal brain "centers" prepared the individual for communication. Both Gazzaniga and Stacks theorize that their components are (1) capable of independent action and cognitive activity; (2) that each is able to receive and process external, as well as internal, information; and (3) that each is capable of providing us with unified cognitions and behavior. Hence, it follows that modular functioning may be directly related to feelings of anxiety as differing modules interpret internal and external stimuli; functioning that may produce both normal and abnormal behaviors.

The modular mind, however, is not simply a psychological concept, it exists within the various parts of the brain (Ojemann, 1986). The brain's modules have specific duties and functions, are specialized from birth for those functions (Andersen, Garrison, & Andersen, 1979; Witelson, 1987), and are arranged functionally in hierarchical groupings (Stacks, 1983). As Gazzaniga (1985) concluded, it is "clear that modularity has a real anatomical base" (p. 128).

The mind's modularity as it relates to the intrapersonal processes of communication becomes important as it influences the cognitive manifestations of communication. As Stacks (1983; Stacks & Sellers, 1989) posits, the preverbal stage, the preinterpersonal stage of communication, serves as a "loading" mechanism for an individual's verbal and nonverbal communication. "This stage is generally unconscious, intrapersonal, and serves as a screening mechanism for subsequent behavior. This stage serves to establish the intrapersonal system, operating as a storage center for such concepts as attitudes, values, scripts, goals, plans and beliefs; concepts which make us human" (Stacks & Andersen, 1989, p. 279). As has been established by a number of researchers, the intrapersonal impact on subsequent communication is both predictable and important (cf., Barker, 1986; Borden & Stone, 1976; Cunningham, 1989; Goss, 1982).

Of importance to our study of communication, then, is the way in which the various brain modules receive, process, and communicate the stimuli (information) they work with. The next section examines the processing mechanisms and modular networks which interact to produce hemispheric modular cooperation and dissonance, the precursors to anxiety and resultant degrees of communication competence as affected by that anxiety.

MODULAR PROCESSING

Perhaps the largest of the brain's modules are the two cerebral hemispheres themselves. Each brain hemisphere can be conceived as an alliance of federations with a particular aim or function in mind. This metaphorical analysis clearly is close to the earlier held notion that each brain hemisphere was dominant for a particular function of communication (i.e., verbal or nonverbal functioning). However, it is clear that the modules located in the left hemisphere have a particular *style* of operation that may be characterized as more logical and verbal, while the right hemisphere's style is more affective and nonverbal (Stacks & Sellers, 1986; 1989). In reviewing the previous literature, it is clear that the right hemisphere's input is stylistically and functionally different than its left counterpart. These stylistic differences, then, underlie the nature of the processing itself.

Hemispheric Communication

At one level we can operationalize hemispheric communication as the communication of the "cerebral hemispheres...[as] central superprocessing modules" (Zaidel, 1985a, p. 135). Such communication is limited, however, by the anatomical boundaries of the brain and lack of interconnections, other than the corpus callosum, between them. As Zaidel (1985b) noted, the brain hemispheres "have sharp anatomic boundaries and some apparently sharp functional demarcation as well. The interaction between hemispheres thus becomes a paradigm case for information transfer within the cognitive-cerebral network" (pp. 54-55). The implication is clear: the modules located within each hemisphere work together in some loose federation under the guiding control of the "superprocessing" mechanism of that hemisphere. Further, it is conceivable that "backup" modules may exist within the other hemisphere which approximate the function of the other. As Zajonc (1984a; 1984b) has pointed out, affect (right superprocessing module) and cognition (left superprocessing module) are independent, separate and parallel systems which often function together. Support for this cognitive-affective dichotomy is offered by Swann et al. (1987) who proposed that the cognitive system is designed for classification and assessment while the affective system is designed to provide rapid responses for the individual's safety. Additionally, studies of language acquisition and the "neuromaturational" process indicate a left hemisphere predisposition for language processing. As a child matures, however, the right hemisphere becomes more involved in language activities. Between ages five to 13 years of age such predisposition for language (cognition) begins to equalize (Keith, 1981; Williford, 1978).

The type of communication employed by the brain's major modules has been studied for a number of years as interhemispheric communication, communication between brain hemispheres, cross-callosal interaction, and as cross-talk between left and right hemispheres (Andersen, Garrison, & Andersen, 1979; Bogen, 1985; Gazzaniga & LeDoux, 1978;

TenHouten, 1985; Sperry, 1985). The transfer of information between the hemispheres, then, is an important function in the creation of the mind. Essentially one brain becomes a sender of a message which is transmitted through the corpus callosum (channel) to the other hemisphere (the receiver).

In the approach proposed herein, it is this transmission of messages between hemispheres—and within hemispheres—that constitutes the intrapersonal processing of communication. Such communication is *not* "thinking," since modules and hemispheres can "think" and operate on information independently. The modular approach clearly implies that complete messages—"thoughts"—are communicated within and between modules. Each impacts on the processing of the other and the final interpretation of the communication situation and the ultimate communicative behavior exhibited by the individual.

How do these modules operate in the process of "normal" communication? As of now we know that hemispheric communication occurs, but as Gardner (1983) argued, "communication between modules occurs, only subsequently in ways that remain obscure" (p. 132). Stacks and Andersen (1989) suggest that "In a metaphorical sense brain modules and hemispheres behave much like individual interpersonal interactions in everyday communication; they inhibit, struggle for control, compete, cooperate, facilitate, create paradoxes, coexist, and promote harmoniousness" (p. 281). *As such, we can conceptualize "normal" communication as the healthy interpersonal relationships of modules within first the superprocessing module in which they exist and, second, between the two major modules themselves.* This form of communication may be termed "modular cooperation" and "modular dissonance."

Before discussing the cooperative and dissonance functions of hemispheric processing we must digress shortly and explore "normal" modular functioning. This functioning, as Stacks (1983) posits, serves two functions. First, it serves to prepare the individual from birth for future communication. That is, while some modules are only partially prepared for use, others are hardware-oriented—preprogrammed ROM so to speak. This establishes the human elements of communication; including perhaps centers for such things as drives, fears, phobias, recognition, and deep structure (as in language). These modules, Stacks would argue, establish the traits associated with the particular individual and will influence his or her communication as it develops. Hence, if the modules are normal, normal functioning should begin at birth with the acquisition of "normal" language and an understanding of cultural norms. Additionally, those behaviors necessary for survival should begin to develop. In some instances the traits associated with communication competence may be short-circuited, may be genetically or in some other way damaged, thus producing less than normal communications. These, as Stacks points out, are often seen in children with Downs' syndrome or other brain malfunctions. However, they may also be a product of low birth weight, drug abuse of the mother, etc.

In some instances this preparation may yield traits producing distorted information processing later in life. As such, anxiety in general may become a trait-like state within the individual. The individual's communication may be the product of inappropriate modular communication, resulting in less than normal, or a limited capacity for, information processing.

Second, modular functioning serves to interpret the information received by the brain and create the mind's view of "reality." While some brain modules are fully preprogrammed for processing, other brain modules are only partially prepared for use. Their use may occur only after some time passes or they are called up or created by other modules in some time sequence. These modules may be state-oriented and serve as processing agents for more transitory information used in daily activity. Such modules may deal with the more complex and variable cognitions associated with attitudes, beliefs, and values. As they "develop" and come on-line they in turn influence and are influenced by the trait-like modules. As such, these modules affect each other and may at times alter the individual's communicative behavior in less than predictable or normal ways.

Modular Cooperation

In the modular approach, normal communication is a function of cooperation between the hemispheres. In the interpersonal analogy previously offered, this cooperation can be both harmonious and disharmonious. To what extent is each hemisphere's cooperation necessary for the processing of normal communication? This will differ according to a number of factors, including the complexity of the task, processing of certain types of information, creativity, and dialectical thinking (Stacks & Andersen, 1989).

How the brain receives and processes information has been detailed elsewhere (cf., Shedletsky, 1981, 1983; Segalowitz, 1985; Stacks & Sellers, 1989). A brief review of the processing mechanisms in relation to modular cooperation should help flesh out the role of information and task in hemispheric cooperation. Recent research has demonstrated that while the left hemisphere is primarily responsible for verbal communication, both brain hemispheres have the capacity for language and contribute to the final analysis of intent. How that analysis is carried out and with what effect, however, is a result of the particular hemisphere's function and style.

In most daily communication, the left hemisphere's ability to logically interpret events and information makes it truly "dominant" for most processing tasks. In this manner the modules contained in the left hemisphere federation exert more influence and ultimately control the situation. This occurs, however, only when the interpretation of the situation fits with the logical processes associated with *current* cultural mores, rules, and laws. The function of the right hemisphere federation is more affective in nature and serves to guide the left in situations where the "norm" has been deviated from (Hickson & Stacks, 1989; Zaidel, 1985b) and in situations where anxiety may be present.

A large body of *clinical* research demonstrates the integrative function of hemispheric cooperation. Research on split-brain patients, for example, suggests that when the left hemisphere must interpret messages without right hemispheric input due to a severing of the corpus callosum, that message is interpreted literally. As such, sarcasm, emotion, and humor are lost to the processor of the message. Moscovitch (1983) has suggested that high imagery or highly affective tasks require processing through the right hemisphere, which then functions as a "priming mechanism" for the left's logical interpretation of the affective mood or intent of the message. This priming is a major function of normal intrapersonal communication. Safer and Leventhal (1977) support this interpretation in "normal" people. They found that use of both hemispheres produced more accurate ratings of message content *and* the tone of voice used to present messages. However, subjects who processed messages via the left ear (right hemisphere processing) primarily used tone of voice to rate messages, whereas right ear (left hemispheric processing) subjects primarily used message content to rate messages.

Behavioral research has demonstrated that, in normal situations, the left hemisphere can and does operate basically alone. Stacks and Sellers (1986) presented messages of varying intensity to *either* one hemisphere or the other and noticed no apparent behavioral changes for messages characterized by low to moderate language intensity. However, when exposed to highly intense messages, the left hemisphere only subjects perceived the message as *more* positive and persuasive and the source *more* credible than their right hemisphere counterparts. They explained these findings in part due to a lack of the right hemisphere's "priming" function. That is, without the priming function in operation *during message processing* the left hemisphere had to make interpretations based on the *literal* meaning of the message, interpretations were then sent to the right. Hence, they suggest that when communication situations are outside the accepted norms associated (such as inappropriately high language intensity) with a communication (and these may change as the individual becomes assimilated to a particular environment), increased right hemisphere processing is necessary, especially "priming" the left for non-normative information. This right hemispheric function is carried out through transfer of information through the corpus callosum (cf., Shedletsky, 1981; 1983).

Other research has demonstrated that hemispheric cooperation is necessary for tasks requiring creativity or dialectic types of thinking. TenHouton (1985) found that split brain patients showed a lack of creativity, that is, they failed to verbally express fantasies, symbols, insights or feelings. As with creativity, TenHouton (1985) maintained:

> the dialects of hemispheric interaction also imply a complementarity between the two hemispheres. This does not mean that more proficiency is developed in both modes, so that a person can carry out tasks with one and tasks with the other. Dialectical thinking, as complementarity, means that both appositional and propositional thought are brought to bear on one problem (pp. 344-345).

Obviously, the processing of both hemispheres is superior to that of one. Many times, however, it is more parsimonious for the "dominant" hemisphere to process and interpret information leading to communication. This is possible during "normal" communicative situations—where societal rules are followed. However, there are times when for a variety of reasons "normal" communication is not possible. The next section details both "normal" disharmony and pathological disharmony and their effects on communication.

Modular Dissonance

At times the harmonious interchange of information between modules and hemispheres becomes disrupted. This, Stacks and Andersen (1989) suggest, develops along the line of Festinger's (1957) theory of cognitive dissonance, one of the more developed models of consistency and change. When modules "collide" regarding a belief, attitude, or processing nuance two things may happen. First, change occurs. The reasons for such conflict are worked through, stored in the effected modules memory and the mind moves to another state. Second, however, would be chaotic, unorganized, and fragmented behavior. Stacks and Andersen believe that the experience of dissonance and its reduction are beneficial to the mind. They point out that if "there was no means for resolution or dissonance reduction, mental confusion and disarray would predominate. The human brain may be constructed for this process to prevail" (p. 285-286). Gazzaniga (1985) further proposes that dissonance allows for the constant testing and retesting of beliefs, yielding an array of modules harmoniously testing new situations, retesting old situations, and possibly pretesting situations into the future.

Modular dissonance, then, can be perceived as a function of normal hemispheric processing. It occurs when either internal or external stimuli produce changes in processing such that memories or predisposed processing mechanisms come into conflict. Such conflict—and its resolution—is good, promotes growth in the individual through a constant reevaluation of beliefs and attitudes, and serves to test the "normalcy" of the current situation. There are times, however, when this modular dissonance gets out of control. That is, one module temporarily interferes with normal processing and inhibits the other module. At the hemispheric level this modular inhibition may produce confusion and anxious behavior. These minor inhibitions may explain how logical-affective discrepancies are resolved through intrapersonal communication. Along this same line, Swain et al. (1987) posited that people are often caught in a "cognitive-affective crossfire" whereby the cognitive system infringes on the affective system over time. This interference yields a change in the affective "coloring" of the situation, making it more normal than it had previously been (cf., Sarason & Sarason, 1986). Stacks and Andersen (1989) suggest that this may be part of the basis of cognitive therapy "which encourages patients to reinterpret negative events" (p. 286). As with many affective interpretations, the conscious (left) module may actively suppress the information to the less conscious right hemisphere, thus ensuring that any distress, grief, or agony do not overcome the conscious awareness of the situation.

There are times, however, when such inhibition fails within the processing of information. Such forms of pathological inhibition have been detailed relating to schizophrenia (Beaumont & Dimond, 1973; Diamond, Scammell, Bryce, Huws, & Gray, 1979) and other psychopathologies (Beaton, 1985). The modular processing either from within a hemisphere or between hemispheres has been disrupted in such a manner as to allow control of processing to a single hemisphere. Langs (1986) suggests that such processing defects yield internal messages sent to inappropriate modules for processing, resulting in psychosis, hallucination, and extreme anxiety.

At their extreme such pathologies are fairly easily diagnosed. However, in non-psychotic individuals, the results of poor rather than defective modular communication may produce the communication patterns associated with communication apprehension. Such apprehension may be the result of two parallel processing problems. First, the affected modules within a particular hemisphere may communicate extreme messages relating to fear of the situation or interpretation of the individual's past experiences in the particular situation that invoke conscious defensive communications similar to pathological repression, denial, or avoidance. This form of apprehension might yield moderate avoidance/apprehension behavior, behavior that still would be under the conscious control of the individual.

Second, one hemisphere may "short-circuit" the other through a massive neural charge (Galin, 1974; 1976), similar to that found in epilepsy. In such situations the left hemisphere's normal control over cognition may yield to right hemisphere control, producing more affective responses to the situation. In such instances nonpropositional messages (messages verbalized but not consciously produced) may result (cf., Buck, 1982). If the left hemisphere perseveres, the right hemisphere's input is repressed and the resulting anxiety or stress may be manifested in nightmares or anxiety and even in later breakdown. As noted earlier, such repressed messages may later become "normal" within the processing of the situation by the modules involved and the perceptions may become "real."

From this perspective, then, an individual whose communication is described as apprehensive may be experiencing extreme modular dissonance—or even pathological modular dissonance. From this approach, the interpretation of the situation is strong enough to create anxiety and possibly even pathological reactions to, or perceptions of, the situation. If the processing creates modular interpretations as sufficiently negative, it may yield interference or inhibition of the "normal" exchange of information between hemispheres. In some instances it may yield enough of a processing problem to effectively block input across the corpus callosum by one hemisphere or the other. It may be that in such cases the individual is unaware of his or her actions, implying clearly right hemispheric or modular control of the situation.

Anxiety, as a form of intrapersonal communication may be perceived as a multidimensional function of modular processing related to trait-like and state-like processing of information from the individual communicator, the environment, the situation, or the interaction between the three. In a 1986 cognitive interpretation of anxiety and shyness as a function of interfering thoughts, Sarason and Sarason argue along a similar line when they note that "How information is acted on is the result of the interaction between the individual's personal characteristics [intrapersonal—modular—communication] and the environmental events ... The joint contributions of personal resources [modular processing] and personal interpretations [intermodular communication] and the situational requirements determine overt behavior" (p. 254). Hence, anxiety may be the product of either inappropriate modular dissonance regarding the situation (perceptions of helplessness, for instance) or a trait-like tendency toward social interaction (extreme modular dissonance or pathological modular processing).

SUMMARY

Healthy communication, like healthy interpersonal relationships requires the cooperation of all parties involved. This essay has examined one approach to an understanding of communication at the intrapersonal level. It suggests that communication is influenced, perhaps predetermined, by a mind that is composed of a variety of brain modules.

How well the individual communicates is seen as a function of modular communication at a less than conscious level. This form of intrapersonal communication yields cognitions specific to internal or external stimuli which ultimately influence behavior. Modular communication, at the intrapersonal level, serves as a processing mechanism for initial analysis. At the interhemispheric level, modular communication establishes the conscious, cognitive, and affective responses found in daily communication.

There are times, however, when modular communication becomes disrupted through inappropriate or faulty perception of the situation or through modular interference, yielding anxiety or apprehensive avoidance behavior. Anxiety behavior may be present even among "normal" communicators. In such instances, normal modular processing of the dissonant information is interfered with in such a way as to create inappropriate modular communication or the blockage of normal information processing between the two major modules, the hemispheres. If the individual is predisposed toward apprehension through some modular trait or defective processing system, pathological behaviors will be experienced. (This is similar to the recently reported trait-processing pathology associated with certain stutterers [Freeman et al., 1988].) Most often, however, the disruption is less serious, resulting in a modular dissonance that is potentially treatable through such treatment paradigms as systematic desensitization or cognitive therapy (Sellers & Stacks, 1985).

Hemispheric modularity as an explanatory principle provides a potential area of research and theory for both communication and neurophysiological researchers. Future research and theory needs to begin identifying these modules and their processing rules and ranges. Of particular interest is their impact on more conscious intrapersonal variables and as the self-system and self-concept (eg., Greene, 1984; Greene & Geddes, 1988), imagined interactions (Honeycutt, Zagacki, & Edwards, 1989), voicing (Hamilton, Anderson, & Pineo, 1988), and emotion (Vinson, 1989; Vinson & Biggers, 1988) as well as related work in language.

REFERENCES

Andersen, P.A., Garrison, J.P., & Andersen, J.F. (1979). Implications of a neurophysiological approach for the study of nonverbal communication. *Human Communication Research, 6,* 74-89.

Barker, L.L. (1986, November). *Intrapersonal communication in communication.* Paper presented at the annual convention of the Speech Communication Association, Chicago.

Beaumont, G., & Dimond, S. (1973). Brain disconnection and schizophrenia. *British Journal of Psychiatry, 123,* 661-662.

Beaton, A. (1985). *Left side, right side: A review of laterality research.* London: Batsford.

Bogen, J.E. (1985). The dual brain: Some historical and methodological aspects. In D.F. Benson & E. Zaidel (Eds.) *The dual brain: Hemispheric specialization in humans* (pp. 27-43). New York: Guilford Press.

Borden, G.A., & Stone, J.D. (1976). *Human communication: The process of relating.* Reading, MA: Cummings.

Buck, R. (1982). Spontaneous and symbolic nonverbal behavior and the ontogeny of communication. In R.S. Feldman, (Ed.) *Development of nonverbal behavior in children* (pp. 29-62). New York: Springer-Verlag.

Cummings, J. (1985). Hemispheric specialization: A history of current concepts. In M. Burns, A. Halper, & S. Mogil, (1985). *Clinical Management of Right Hemisphere Dysfunction* (p. 4). Rockville, MD: Aspen Systems Corp.

Cunningham, S.B. (1989). Defining intrapersonal communication. In C.V. Roberts & K.W. Watson (Eds.) *Intrapersonal communication processes: Original essays* (pp. 82-94). Auburn, AL: Spectra Publishers.

Dimond, S.J., Scammell, R.E., Bryce, I.G., Huws, D., & Gray, C. (1979). Callosal transfer and left-hand anomia in schizophrenia. *Biological Psychiatry, 14,* 735-739.

Festinger, L. (1957). *A theory of cognitive dissonance.* Stanford: Stanford University Press.

Fodor, J.A. (1983). *The modularity of mind.* Cambridge, MA: MIT Press.

Freeman, F.J., Watson, B.C., Dembowski, J.S., Finitzo, T., Pool, K.D., Chapman, S.B., Devous, M.D., Schaefer, S., Kondraske, G., Donnell, A., & Mendelschon, D. (1988, November). *LRT profiles of adult stutterers.* Paper presented to the American Speech-Language-Hearing Association, Boston.

Galin, D. (1974). Implication for psychiatry of left and right specialization: A neurophysiological context for unconscious processes. *Archives of General Psychiatry, 31,* 572.

Galin, D. (1976). Hemispheric specialization: Implications for psychiatry. In R.G. Grenell & S. Gabay (Eds.), *Biological foundations of psychiatry.* New York: Raven Press. Cited in R. Restak, *The brain: The last frontier* (pp. 33-54). New York: Doubleday.

Gardner, H. (1983). *Frames of mind: The theory of multiple intelligences.* New York: Basic Books.

Gardner, H. (1985). *The mind's new science: A history of the cognitive revolution.* New York: Basic Books.

Gazzaniga, M.S. (1985). *The social brain: Discovering the networks of the mind.* New York: Basic Books.

Gazzaniga, M.S., & LeDoux, J.E. (1978). *The integrated mind.* New York: Plenum Press.

Goss, B. (1982). *Processing Communication.* Belmont, CA: Wadsworth.

Greene, J.O. (1984). A cognitive approach to communication: An action assembly theory. *Communication Monographs, 51,* 289-306.

Greene, J.O, & Geddes, D. (1988). Representation and processing in the self-system: An action-oriented approach to self and self-relevant phenomena. *Communication Monographs, 55,* 287-314.

Hamilton, M.A., Anderson, K., & Pineo, S. (1988, November). *Type of conscious thought and the effectiveness of rational- versus rule-oriented appeals.* Paper presented to the Speech Communication Association, New Orleans, LA.

Hickson, M.L., & Stacks, D.W. (1989). *NVC: Nonverbal communication studies and applications,* (2nd ed.). Dubuque, IA: Wm. C. Brown.

Honeycutt, J.M., Zagacki, K.S., & Edwards, R. (1989). Intrapersonal communication, social cognition, and imagined interactions. In C.V. Roberts and K.W. Watson, (Eds.) *Intrapersonal communication processes: Original essays* (pp. 166-184). Auburn, AL: Spectra Publishers.

Keith, R.W. (1981). *Central auditory and language disorders in children.* Houston: College-Hill.

Langs, R. (1986). Clinical issues arising from a new model of the mind. *Contemporary Psychoanalysis, 22,* 418-244.

McCroskey, J.C. (1983). The communication apprehension perspective. *Communication, 12,* 1-25.

McCroskey, J.C., & Beatty, M.J. (1984). Communication apprehension and accumulated communication state anxiety experiences: A research note. *Communication Monographs, 51,* 79-84.

Moscovitch, M. (1983). The linguistic and emotional functions of the normal right hemisphere. In E. Perecman (Ed.) *Cognitive processing in the right hemisphere* (pp. 57-82). New York: Academic Press.

Ojemann, G. (1986). Brain mechanisms for consciousness and conscious experience. *Canadian Psychology, 27,* 158-168.

Safer, M.A., & Leventhal, H. (1977). Ear differences in evaluating emotional tones of voice and verbal content. *Journal of Experimental Psychology: Human Perception and Performance, 3,* 75-82.

Sarason, I.G., & Sarason, B.R. (1986). Anxiety and interfering thoughts: Their effect on social interaction. In W.H. Jones, J.M. Cheek, & S.R. Biggs (Eds.) *Shyness: Perspectives on Research and Treatment* (pp. 253-264). New York: Plenum Press.

Segalowitz, S.J. (1983). *Two sides of the brain: Brain lateralization explored.* Englewood Cliffs, NJ: Prentice-Hall.

Sellers, D.E., & Stacks, D.W. (1985). Brain processing and therapy. *Journal of Communication Therapy, 3,* 30-50.

Shedletsky, L.J. (1981). Cerebral asymmetry for aspects of sentence processing. *Communication Quarterly, 29,* 3-11.

Shedletsky, L.J. (1983). Cerebral asymmetry for aspects of sentence processing: A replication and extension. *Communication Quarterly, 31,* 78-84.

Sperry, R.W. (1985). Consciousness, personal identity, and the divided brain. In

D.F. Benson & E. Zaidel (Eds.) *The dual brain: Hemispheric specialization in humans* (pp. 27-43). New York: Guilford Press.

Stacks, Don W. (1983). Toward the establishment of a preverbal stage of communication. *Journal of Communication Therapy 3*, 39-60.

Stacks, D.W., & Andersen, P.A. (1989). The modular mind: Implications for intrapersonal communication. *Southern Communication Journal, 54*, 273-293.

Stacks, D.W., & Sellers, D.E. (1986). Toward a holistic approach to communication: The effect of "pure" hemispheric reception on message acceptance. *Communication Quarterly, 34*, 266-285.

Stacks, D.W., & Sellers, D.E. (1989). Understanding intrapersonal communication: neurological processing implications. In C.V. Roberts and K.W. Watson, (Eds.) *Intrapersonal communication processes: Original essays* (pp. 243-267). Auburn, AL: Spectra Publishers.

Swann, W.B. Jr., Griffin, J.J., Predmore, S.C., & Gaines, B. (1987). The cognitive-affective crossfire: When self-consistency confronts self-enhancement. *Journal of Personality and Social Psychology, 52*, 881-889.

TenHouten, W.D. (1985). Cerebral-lateralization theory and the sociology of knowledge. In D.F. Benson & E. Zaidel (Eds.) *The dual brain: Hemispheric specialization in humans* (pp. 341-358). New York: Guilford Press.

Vinson, L.R. (1989). The relative importance of three sources of emotion-eliciting stimuli: Toward an integrative model of naturally occurring emotion. In C.V. Roberts and K.W. Watson, (Eds.) *Intrapersonal communication processes: Original essays* (pp.337-349). Auburn, AL: Spectra Publishers.

Vinson, L.R., & Biggers, T. (1988, November). *An emotion based model of compliance-gaining message selection: Refining, testing, and extending Hunter's and Boster's theory*. Paper presented to the Speech Communication Association, New Orleans, LA.

Williford, J. (1978). Sentence test of central auditory dysfunction. In J. Katz, (Ed.) *Handbook of clinical audiology* (2nd ed.) (pp. 252-261). Baltimore: William & Wilkins.

Witelson, S.F. (1987). Neurobiological aspects of language in children. *Child Development, 58*, 653-688.

Zaidel, E. (1985a). Academic implications of dual-brain theory. In D.F. Benson & E. Zaidel (Eds.) *The dual brain: Hemispheric specialization in humans* (pp. 393-397). New York: Guilford Press.

Zaidel, E. (1985b). Biological and physiological studies of hemispheric specialization. In D.F. Benson & E. Zaidel (Eds.) *The dual brain: Hemispheric specialization in humans* (pp. 47-63). Guilford Press.

Zajonc, R.B. (1984a). The interaction of affect and cognition. In K.R. Scherer & P. Ekman (eds.) *Approaches to emotion* (pp. 239-246). Hillsdale, NJ: Lawrence Erlbaum.

Zajonc, R.B. (1984b). On primacy of affect. In K.R. Scherer & P. Ekman (eds.) *Approaches to emotion* (pp. 259-270). Hillsdale, NJ: Lawrence Erlbaum.

Chronic Issue-Specific Fear Inhibits Systematic Processing Of Persuasive Communications

Christopher Jepson
Fox Chase Cancer Center, 510 Township Line Road Cheltenham, PA 19012

Shelly Chaiken
Department of Psychology, New York University 6 Washington Place (7th floor), New York, NY 10003

Two studies investigated the hypothesis that fear about a health topic reduces the tendency to process a persuasive message systematically. Subjects' naturally-occurring levels of fear about cancer were measured. They then read a message about cancer checkups that contained logical errors, simultaneously listing their thoughts. In both experiments, high-fear subjects found fewer errors and wrote fewer message-related thoughts than low-fear subjects. In Experiment 1, high-fear subjects were also more persuaded by the message. These effects are not accounted for by trait anxiety, perceived susceptibility to cancer, or cognitive or behavioral style variables.

Between the mid-1950s and the mid-1970s, much theoretical and empirical work was devoted to the study of fear-arousing persuasive messages, and in particular, to the question of how effective such messages are in inducing people to change their beliefs, intentions, and behavior. More recently, some persuasion theorists have focused on how people process information in persuasive messages (Chaiken, 1980, 1987; Chaiken, Liberman, & Eagly, 1989; Chaiken & Stangor, 1987; Eagly & Chaiken, 1984; Petty & Cacioppo, 1981). For these authors, the emphasis has shifted from the outcomes of processing—belief, intention, or behavior change—to processing itself.

Authors Note: This research was supported by NIMH Training Grant #MH16734-04, awarded to the first author; and NSF Grant #BNS-8309159 and NIMH Grant #R01 MH43299-01, held by the second author. The authors wish to thank Charles Brown, Linda Collins, and John Graham for advice on statistical analyses; Tracy Allen for acting as Experimenter in Experiment 2 and assisting with coding; and Chang Ming Duan for collecting pilot study data.

© 1990 Select Press

One issue central to most process theories of persuasion is the extent to which people expend cognitive effort in attending to, understanding, and elaborating upon persuasive message content. This type of careful attention and evaluation has been referred to by Chaiken (1980, 1987; Chaiken et al., 1989) as "systematic" processing, and by Petty and Cacioppo (1981, 1986a) as reflecting the "central" route to persuasion.

This raises new questions about the effects of fear appeals. Does fear increase or decrease systematic processing? When people accept the recommendations of a fear-arousing message, is it because they have paid close attention to its content and carefully evaluated its worth; or is it a "blind" acceptance, accompanied by a low level of comprehension and cognitive elaboration?

Early theorists of fear appeals (Hovland, Janis, & Kelley, 1953; Janis, 1967) assumed that fear acted as a drive and that responses to fear messages were essentially attempts to reduce this drive. Although these theories were not primarily concerned with the question of fear's effect on the recipient's processing of the information in a fear appeal, they did contain conjectures as to the possible nature of such effects. In particular, these theories postulated that fear would lead to avoidance under certain conditions—especially when the level of fear was high and the message failed to reduce it—and suggested that avoidance might be accomplished through an inhibition of processing. For example, Hovland et al. (1953) proposed "inattentiveness to the communication" as one of the main types of avoidance behavior.

These early theorists predicted that avoidance would result in reduced persuasion (e.g. Janis & Feshbach, 1953). Thus, messages arousing high levels of fear should be less effective than messages arousing moderate fear. In general, however, subsequent research has failed to document such a phenomenon. Instead, higher levels of fear typically produce greater persuasion than lower levels (Leventhal, 1970; Sutton, 1982). This fact was widely taken to mean that high fear does not produce avoidance. Thus, according to the reasoning outlined above, the idea that fear inhibits processing seemed to be refuted.

The recent process theories of persuasion, however, have challenged the traditional and implicit assumption that a reduction in systematic processing always leads to reduced persuasion. In some cases, people may be persuaded by a communication without thoroughly evaluating the quality of its arguments (Axsom, Yates, & Chaiken, 1987; Chaiken, 1980, 1987), and systematic processing can sometimes lead to decreased persuasion (Langer, Blank, & Chanowitz, 1978; Petty, Cacioppo, & Goldman, 1981). Thus, the question of the effect of fear on processing is still open. It may well be that fear produces avoidance in the form of reduced systematic processing: People might accept the recommendations of a fear appeal, while reducing their unpleasant affect by spending as little time and effort as possible in processing its arguments. This type of response should be especially likely when well-learned habits of defensive avoidance are present (that is, when the person has had numerous experiences with fear-arousing messages and has learned to respond by a reduction in processing) and the present message is sufficiently similar to past messages to trigger the habitual response.

The other possibility, that fear facilitates systematic processing, is consistent with more recent theories of fear appeals such as those of Rogers (1975, 1983) and Sutton (1982). These are based on the assertion that, although messages of the kind traditionally referred to as "fear appeals" do produce fear, this fear is not in fact causally involved in persuasion. Rather, fear appeals are effective because they alter recipients' perceived susceptibility to, and perceived severity of, the threat in question. Thus, in these theories, fear is merely an epiphenomenon that happens to covary with the increases in perceived susceptibility and severity which actually influence persuasion. As Sutton (1982) stated, "Fear is not one of the components of the model. ... fear is assumed to have no causal role in mediating the effects of fear-arousing communications" (p. 329).

These theories, like the earlier drive theories, are not primarily concerned with predicting the effect of fear appeals on processing itself. We can derive such a prediction, however, by looking at a related theoretical construct. Perceived susceptibility can be construed as an operationalization of the construct issue involvement or personal relevance (Apsler & Sears, 1968; Petty & Cacioppo, 1979, 1986b). This has been defined as the extent to which the recipient of a message believes that the issue in question is likely to have important personal consequences. Process theories of persuasion suggest that issue involvement should facilitate systematic processing by increasing recipients' motivation to attend carefully to the information presented (Chaiken, 1980, 1987; Petty & Cacioppo, 1981, 1986a). Thus, if fear appeals increase perceived susceptibility (and therefore, presumably, issue involvement), they should result in increased systematic processing.[1]

This reasoning assumes that fear itself, as an emotional state, has no independent effect on processing. The evidence we have reviewed, however, suggests that fear and issue involvement may produce competing response tendencies. Thus, when fear and issue involvement are both

---

[1] *The analogy between fear arousal and involvement is restricted to issue involvement as defined herein. Involvement has been defined in different ways by different authors and may be multidimensional (see Chaiken & Stangor, 1987; Johnson & Eagly, 1989).*

high, we might expect the result to vary according to other aspects of the situation. For example, if strong, well-learned habits of defensive avoidance are triggered by the message, the tendency to suppress systematic processing may override the competing response tendency that would normally be produced by issue involvement alone. In such a case, both fear and issue involvement could actually show an inverse relationship with systematic processing.

Thus, while the literature on persuasion certainly suggests that fear should influence processing, it is far from unequivocal on the direction of that influence. Studies of the impact of affect on cognitive processes yield a similar conclusion. With regard to basic processes such as recall, Isen (1984) has noted that negative feeling states tend to give rise to a process of "mood repair"—that is, the selection of responses aimed at reducing the negative affect and reinstating positive affect (see also Worth & Mackie, 1987). This in itself does not suggest what type of processing might be most efficacious for mood repair. However, as Hoffman (1986) points out, the research on perceptual defense and motivated unconscious processing indicates that at least one useful strategy for avoiding unpleasant affect is to "shut off the processing of certain stimuli" (p. 270).

Our discussion so far has focused on the issue of motivation: how fear might increase or decrease motivation to process a fear-arousing message systematically. It is also possible, however, that fear might affect capacity to engage in systematic processing (see Chaiken et al., 1989). Ever since the formulation of the Yerkes-Dodson law (Yerkes & Dodson, 1908) it has been known that high levels of arousal can impair performance. There is evidence that this is true for cognitive performance as well as other kinds. The fact that high arousal levels cause a narrowing of attention was established three decades ago (Easterbrook, 1959). Recently, Nemeth (1986) has suggested that arousal fosters convergent thought and inhibits creative thought. In addition, the literature on social facilitation (Zajonc, 1965) indicates that the kinds of behaviors most impeded by arousal are those that are complex and effortful, whereas those that are simple and automatic are more likely to be facilitated. Thus, to the extent that fear represents a relatively high degree of arousal, it might be expected to interfere with the capacity to process messages systematically.

In the two studies reported here we measured subjects' naturally occurring levels of fear about a topic, and investigated the relationship between fear and amount of systematic processing. The topic we chose was cancer, because we felt it was one about which many people have an appreciable degree of fear. We expected chronic fear of cancer to be inversely related to systematic processing, because we felt that high-fear subjects would have developed habits of defensive avoidance that would lead to an inhibition of systematic processing.

To measure systematic processing, we planted several logical errors, designed to be potentially noticeable by laypeople, in a short written message advocating regular cancer-related checkups for young adults. While reading the message, subjects wrote down their thoughts. We predicted that subjects with high chronic fear of cancer would mention fewer errors in their thought lists, as well as listing fewer message-related thoughts in general, than subjects with lower levels of fear. In Experiment 1 (but not Experiment 2), we also made the prediction that high-fear subjects would exhibit greater persuasion than would low-fear subjects. This follows from the hypothesis that high-fear subjects would notice fewer errors than low-fear subjects. If so, they should find the message more persuasive. In addition, we included measures assessing subjects' perceived susceptibility to cancer and their perceptions of cancer's severity. These measures were intended to serve as indicators of the degree of subjects' involvement with the cancer issue. We predicted that chronic fear, perceived susceptibility, and perceived severity would exhibit moderate positive intercorrelations, and that the correlations of susceptibility and severity with processing would be similar in direction to the correlations of chronic fear with processing.

In choosing to focus on naturally occurring levels of fear we were departing from standard practice in the study of fear appeals. In this literature, fear has generally been dealt with as a message variable rather than a person variable. The focus has typically been on acute fear, induced by the message itself. Effects of subjects' pre-existing, chronic levels of fear regarding the topic in question have usually been ignored. In our view the use of chronic fear rather than acute fear as a predictor of processing style is essential, because chronic fear, and not acute fear, should be an indicator of the presence of habits of defensive avoidance. This is illustrated by the following thought experiment. Imagine that a group of individuals is presented with a fear-arousing message concerning some threat they have heretofore been unaware of—for example, a newly discovered disease. Thus, they have low levels of chronic fear concerning the topic, but high levels of acute fear. These people might be expected to attend carefully to the information presented. In the absence of habits of defensive avoidance regarding messages on this topic, they respond with a high level of systematic processing, because the message has raised their level of involvement by informing them that the threat is likely to have important consequences. Now suppose that these individuals are presented with a message on some topic they are familiar with, and about which they have a high level of chronic fear—for example, cancer. Such individuals have had the opportunity to develop habits of defensive avoidance regarding information on this topic. They are more likely to skim the message once they become aware of its subject matter. Moreover, to the extent that suppression of systematic processing is successful in reducing acute fear, we should not expect such people to exhibit much higher levels of acute fear than people with lower levels of chronic fear about cancer.

To examine the relative effects of chronic and acute fear, we included a self-report measure of fear induced by the message. We expected a moderate positive correlation between chronic fear and message-induced fear. We also predicted that the correlations between message-induced fear and processing would be similar in direction to, but smaller in magnitude than, the correlations between chronic fear and processing.

Our prediction of an inverse relationship between fear and systematic processing was based on the idea that high fear should be associated with a high likelihood that habits of defensive avoidance will be triggered. This likelihood may also be influenced by other individual difference variables in addition to fear—for example, cognitive and behavioral styles such as monitoring and blunting (Miller, 1980, 1987). Monitoring refers to the tendency to seek out and attend to information concerning disturbing or stressful topics. Blunting, by contrast, is the tendency to react to stressful situations by distracting oneself (i.e., focusing on nondisturbing stimuli). If monitoring and blunting styles play an important role in subjects' responses, several results should be seen in Experiment 1. First, because the message concerns a health threat and is therefore potentially disturbing, high monitors should exhibit greater systematic processing than low monitors. Likewise, low blunters should exhibit greater systematic processing than high blunters. Second, and more important, we might expect an interaction between monitoring and chronic cancer fear. Among high monitors (information seekers), fear should increase processing; among low monitors (information avoiders), fear should decrease processing. An analogous interaction effect between blunting and chronic fear might also be found.

EXPERIMENT 1
Method
Subjects

Eighty-six male and female Vanderbilt University introductory psychology students participated in small group sessions in exchange for extra course credit.

Procedure

At the laboratory, the Experimenter (the first author) described the experiment as a pilot study designed to test materials for future research, and explained that the session would involve filling out a questionnaire, followed by reading a message while listing thoughts, and then filling out a second questionnaire. The Experimenter described the message as a persuasive message about cancer, written by "a doctor at the Med Center." Subjects then filled out the first questionnaire (see Premeasures, below), after which the Experimenter elaborated on the instructions for the next task. He told subjects to write down whatever crossed their minds as they read the message, but stressed that they should note any "strengths or weaknesses" of the message. The purpose of this was to increase the likelihood that subjects would notice the planted errors, which were necessarily relatively subtle in order to maintain the message's credibility. Subjects then read the message (described below) and listed their thoughts. There was no time limit. As each subject finished this task, they began the second questionnaire (see Postmeasures, below). Afterwards, subjects were debriefed, given credit slips, and excused.

Materials

Premeasures

The first premeasure consisted of the "monitor" and "blunter" subscales of the Miller Behavioral Style Scale (Miller, 1980, 1987). Miller (1987) reports test-retest reliability coefficients of .72 and .75 for these subscales. Next came five items tapping subjects' beliefs and feelings about cancer, accompanied by 10-point response scales. Two of these items were designed to measure chronic fear of cancer ("How scared are you of getting cancer?", "How upsetting do you find it when you read or hear something about cancer?"). Two other items were related to perceived severity of cancer ("To what extent do you feel that getting cancer would be devastating to your life?", "If you were to develop cancer, how likely do you think you would be to die from it?"). The fifth item assessed perceived susceptibility to cancer ("How likely do you think it is that you personally will develop cancer at some point in your life?"). Factor analysis revealed that the four items designed to assess fear and perceived severity formed a single factor. Thus, an index of chronic cancer fear was created by averaging subjects' responses to these four items. The reliability of the index was high (Cronbach's alpha = .76).

Message

The message, written by the first author with the aid of literature from the American Cancer Society (ACS), was approximately 600 words long and contained nine general arguments in favor of regular cancer checkups for young adults. The first five arguments concerned cancer in general (e.g. cancer is widespread and serious; the crucial factor in curing cancer is early detection; the best means of early detection is regular checkups); the rest concerned cancer in relation to young adults (e.g. the danger of cancer to the young is increasing; cancer in young adults is more curable, if treated early, than in older adults; young adults should have regular checkups rather than wait for warning signals). In most cases, an argument was followed by one to three supporting statistics. The statistics supporting the first three arguments were accurate, and were taken from the ACS literature. The statistics supporting the other arguments were invented for the purposes of the experiment, and were designed to include logical errors or weaknesses. For example, the argument that the danger of cancer to the young is increasing was followed by the statistic that the number of new cancer cases among young adults increased from the 1920s to the 1970s; total population increase was not taken into account. As another example, the argument that cancer in young adults is more curable, if treated early, than in older adults was followed by the statistic that a patient aged 18 to 29 who is treated early has a better chance of surviving ten years than a patient over 60; the fact that people over 60 are less likely to live another ten years anyway was not taken into account. In all, five errors were planted in the message.[2]

Postmeasures

The postmeasures came from the thought lists subjects generated while reading the message, and from the posttest questionnaire.

Thought lists. Two measures of processing were developed from subjects' thought lists: the number of planted errors mentioned by the subject and the total number of message-related thoughts listed. To get credit for mentioning an error, subjects had to refer to the specific passage containing the error and indicate that they felt that there was something wrong with it. Coding was performed by the first author. To assess reliability, an independent rater coded twenty thought lists. For this subset, the two coders displayed exact agreement in every case. Coding of thought lists for total number of message-related thoughts was performed similarly. Exact agreement occurred in 85% of the cases.

Emotional reactions. In the posttest questionnaire, subjects rated, on 10-point scales, the extent to which they had experienced the following

---

[2] *Neither the message nor its supporting statistics were reviewed or approved by the National Cancer Institute.*

feelings while reading the message: fearful, nervous, uncomfortable, and relaxed (the scores for the "relaxed" item were reversed for purposes of analysis). An index of message-induced fear was formed by averaging subjects' responses to the items (alpha = .86).

Behavioral intention. The posttest questionnaire also included an item designed to measure change in behavioral intention: "Did the message you read today make you feel more or less likely to have regular cancer-related checkups?" As with the other items, it was accompanied by a 10-point scale. This measure was designed to assess the extent to which subjects were persuaded by the message.

RESULTS

Effects of Chronic Cancer Fear

Effects of chronic cancer fear were assessed by means of Pearson correlations. Where specific predictions were made, one-tailed significance levels are reported; where predictions were not made, or results were opposite from predictions, two-tailed levels are given. Unless otherwise specified, p-values appearing below are one-tailed.

Our predictions regarding the effects of chronic cancer fear were supported, as shown in the left-hand column of Table 1. Chronic fear was negatively correlated with number of planted errors mentioned in the thought list and number of message-related thoughts listed.[3] Also as predicted, chronic cancer fear was associated with greater persuasion, evidenced by the significant positive correlation between fear and change in behavioral intention.[4]

We tested for curvilinear relationships between chronic fear and processing by means of quadratic regressions. Errors mentioned and message-related thoughts were each regressed on two predictors—a linear term (chronic fear, transformed into Z-scores) and a quadratic term (the square of the linear term). The quadratic term displayed a marginally significant effect on errors mentioned (t = 1.83, two-tailed p < .10), but did not approach significance for message-related thoughts. In neither case was the effect of the quadratic term as strong as the linear effect.

---

[3] *Because the measure of errors mentioned was entirely contained within the measure of message-related thoughts, the effect of chronic fear on the latter is confounded with its effect on the former. To remove this confounding, we repeated the correlation between chronic fear and message-related thoughts, with errors partialed out. The correlation was reduced from -.23 (p < .001) to -.16 (p < .10). In Experiment 2, however, partialing out errors left the correlation between fear and message-related thoughts unchanged.*

[4] *In this experiment, the observed correlations between chronic cancer fear and the various postmeasures tended to be stronger among men than among women; however, none of these differences were statistically significant. For each postmeasure, the correlations with chronic fear were in the same direction among men and women. A similar pattern of results was found in Experiment 2.*

TABLE 1 Simple and Partial Correlations, Experiment 1

Postmeasure	Simple correlation of postmeasure with:			Partial correlation of postmeasure with chronic cancer fear, controlling for:	
	Chronic cancer fear	Message induced fear	Perceived susceptibility	Message induced fear	Perceived susceptibility
Errors found					
r	-.30	-.22	-.13	-.24	-.29
p value	.002	.02	ns	.02	.005
Message-related thoughts					
r	-.23	-.06	-.20	-.22	-.21
p value	.02	ns	.05	.02	.05
Change in behavioral intention					
r	.54	.31	-.08	.48	.55
p value	.001	.002	ns	.001	.001

To assess the exact form of the relationship between chronic fear and errors, we divided subjects into three groups according to their level of chronic fear, and determined the mean number of errors mentioned for each group. The figures, for low-, medium-, and high-fear subjects respectively, were 0.62, 0.32, and 0.17. Thus, the overall negative relationship between fear and errors mentioned was not reversed at any level of fear. There was simply a decline in the strength of that relationship at higher fear levels.

Effects of Message-Induced Fear

Our prediction of a moderate positive correlation between chronic fear and message-induced fear was supported: The correlation between the two measures was .36 ($p < .001$).

Pearson correlations between message-induced fear and the other postmeasures are presented in Table 1. As predicted, these correlations were in the same direction as the correlations between chronic fear and the same measures, but weaker.

The low correlations between message-induced fear and the postmeasures suggest that the effects of chronic fear are not mediated by message-induced fear. As a specific test of this, correlations between chronic fear and the postmeasures were performed with message-induced fear partialed out. These correlations are presented in Table 1. The correlations, although reduced somewhat, remained significant. By contrast, when correlations between message-induced fear and the other postmeasures were performed with chronic fear partialed out, none were significant (rs = -.13 to .15).

Effects of Perceived Susceptibility to Cancer

In contrast to our prediction, perceived susceptibility did not correlate with chronic cancer fear ($r = .11$, $p = .16$), although it did correlate with message-induced fear ($r = .27$, $p < .01$).

Pearson correlations between susceptibility and the postmeasures are presented in Table 1. Our prediction that these correlations would be similar in direction to the correlations of chronic fear with the postmeasures received partial support. Susceptibility correlated negatively with all postmeasures, although the only correlation to reach significance was that with message-related thoughts.

To assess the extent to which susceptibility accounted for the effect of chronic fear, correlations between chronic fear and the postmeasures were performed with susceptibility partialed out. These correlations are presented in the right-hand column of Table 1. In all cases, the correlations remained essentially unchanged. By contrast, when correlations between susceptibility and the postmeasures were performed with chronic fear partialed out, none were significant (rs = -.11 to -.16).

Effects of Monitoring and Blunting

For both the monitor and blunter scales there were trends toward positive correlations with chronic cancer fear (r = .19, two-tailed p < .10, and r = .15, two-tailed p = .17, respectively). Neither scale correlated with perceived susceptibility, message-induced fear, or any other postmeasure (rs = -.14 to .14, two-tailed ps > .20).

Multiple regression was used to test for interactions between monitoring and chronic cancer fear. Each postmeasure was regressed on three predictors: chronic fear, the monitor scale, and an interaction term consisting of the product of the first two predictors.[5] The effect of the interaction term did not approach significance for any postmeasure. This procedure was repeated using the blunter scale; again, no significant interaction effects were found.

EXPERIMENT 2

Experiment 2 was designed to replicate and to redress certain limitations of Experiment 1.

The possibility exists that the scale used to measure chronic cancer fear in Experiment 1 was in fact measuring generalized anxiety. In that case, the correlations observed in Experiment 1 might simply be due to an inhibitory effect of general anxiety on processing of messages—regardless of their topic. To rule out this explanation, we introduced two revisions. First, we included a measure of trait anxiety (Spielberger, 1972). We predicted that the effects of chronic cancer fear on processing would remain even after controlling statistically for trait anxiety. Second, we added a message on a neutral topic (i.e., not related to cancer). Subjects read this message before reading any cancer-related message and listed their thoughts as they read. We predicted that chronic cancer fear would not influence the processing of this message.

A third revision concerned the measures of cognitive and behavioral style used in Experiment 1—the monitoring and blunting scales—which failed to show either main effects or interactions with chronic fear. We thought it possible that effects of cognitive and behavioral style did exist but were not captured by these measures. Therefore, in Experiment 2, we replaced them with a repression-sensitization scale (Epstein & Fenz, 1967), which is conceptually similar: It seeks to differentiate people who habitually block out disturbing stimuli (repressers) from those who habitually seek out or are especially sensitive to such stimuli (sensitizers).

---

[5] *To prevent multicollinearity, we transformed the first two predictors into Z-scores and computed the interaction term from them.*

Thus, we might expect a main effect of repression-sensitization, such that sensitizers would exhibit more systematic processing than repressers, and an interaction with chronic fear, such that fear would increase processing among sensitizers and decrease processing among repressers.

In Experiment 1, the measures of subjects' initial opinions on the topic of the message indicated that subjects with high levels of chronic cancer fear tended to be more in initial agreement with the message's position than low-fear subjects. The possibility therefore exists that the results of Experiment 1 can be explained by a tendency of people to spend less effort processing messages they already agree with—perhaps because there is no need to generate counterarguments. This phenomenon has been documented by Lord, Ross, and Lepper (1979). To rule out this possibility, we introduced a fourth revision. Subjects in Experiment 2 read two messages regarding cancer checkups for young adults, one in favor ("Pro") and one opposed ("Con"). Because of this design, however, no clear prediction could be made concerning the relationship between chronic fear and persuasion. Therefore, no measure of persuasion was included in Experiment 2.

Method

Subjects

Eighty-six male and female Vanderbilt University undergraduate psychology students participated in small group sessions in exchange for extra course credit.

Procedure

Each subject attended two experimental sessions. As in Experiment 1, the experiment was described as a pilot study testing materials for future research. In Session 1, subjects filled out a questionnaire containing the premeasures (see Premeasures, below); they were then scheduled for Session 2 and dismissed. In Session 2, held approximately 1 to 2 weeks later, subjects began by reading a message on a neutral (i.e., non-cancer-related) topic, simultaneously listing their thoughts (see Messages, below). They then read the Pro and Con messages (described below) about cancer checkups. The order of these two messages was counterbalanced across subjects. Once again, subjects listed their thoughts as they read. After finishing this task, subjects filled out a questionnaire consisting of the various postmeasures (see Postmeasures, below). Afterwards, subjects were debriefed, given credit slips, and excused.

Materials

Premeasures

Three premeasures were included in the questionnaire given in Session 1. The first was the set of five items used in Experiment 1 to measure chronic fear of and perceived susceptibility to cancer. A four-item index of chronic fear of cancer, identical to that used in Experiment 1, was formed. Coefficient alpha for this scale was .66 (as compared to .76 in Experiment 1).

The second premeasure was the repression-sensitization scale. Low scores on this scale represent repression; high scores represent sensitization. The scale used in this experiment was devised by Epstein and Fenz (1967) as a shortened version of the repression-sensitization scale developed by Byrne (1961), who reported a split-half reliability coefficient of .88 for the scale. The third premeasure was Spielberger's (1972) trait anxiety scale (alpha = .88).

Messages

Neutral message. The neutral message consisted of the text of an editorial from the March 8, 1985 edition of one of Nashville's major newspapers, *The Tennessean*, and was identified as such. It was approximately 375 words long, and advocated farm debt relief.

Cancer messages. As mentioned earlier, subjects received both a Pro and a Con message about cancer checkups for young adults. Each message was about 500 words long. The Pro message was a revised version of the message used in Experiment 1; the general arguments and supporting statistics were roughly similar in both cases. The Con message contained two general arguments: very few young adults would be saved by checkups; and cancer-preventive behaviors would be more effective. The Pro message included four of the logical errors used in Experiment 1; no errors were inserted into the Con message.[6]

Postmeasures

As in Experiment 1, the postmeasures came from the thought lists

---

[6] *A secondary purpose of Experiment 2 was to examine the effects of argument strength and author expertise on processing. To do this, we created strong and weak versions of each cancer-related message. This was accomplished by varying the strength of the figures given in the statistics supporting the arguments. Also, the logical errors in the Pro message were corrected in the strong version. Prior to Session 2, subjects were dichotomized according to level of chronic cancer fear. Half the subjects within each fear level read the strong version of the Pro message and the weak version of the Con; the rest read the other versions. Author expertise was manipulated by attributing the strong version of each message to a nonexpert author and the weak version to an expert. These manipulations proved to be ineffective. Thus, no analyses involving them are presented, and the data are collapsed across conditions. Because equal numbers of low- and high-fear subjects were in each condition, overall relationships between fear and processing should not have been affected.*

generated by the subjects and from the posttest questionnaire.

Thought lists. The total number of message-related thoughts listed by each subject was tabulated for each message (Pro, Con, and neutral). As in Experiment 1, the first author coded all thought lists. An independent rater then coded a set of twenty lists for each message. For the Pro message, exact agreement between the coders occurred in 85% of the cases; for the Con message, in 80% of the cases; and for the neutral message, in 100% of the cases. For each subject, message-related thoughts for the Pro and Con messages were totaled to form a combined score of message-related thoughts. (The correlation between Pro and Con message-related thoughts was .54.) For the Pro message only (see description of messages above), the number of planted errors mentioned by each subject was also tabulated. All 86 thought lists were coded by the first author and an independent rater. Exact agreement occurred in 91% of the cases.

Emotional reactions. In the posttest questionnaire, subjects indicated the extent to which they had experienced the following feelings while reading the messages: fearful, nervous, uncomfortable, and relaxed (reverse-scored for purposes of analysis). For each feeling, subjects gave two ratings, one for the Pro message and one for the Con message, yielding eight items in all. An index of message-induced fear was created by averaging subjects' responses to the eight items (alpha = .89).

Results

Effects of Chronic Cancer Fear

As shown in the left-hand column of Table 2, the findings of Experiment 1 with regard to the effects of chronic cancer fear were replicated, although the significance levels were slightly lower. Chronic fear was negatively correlated with number of planted errors mentioned in the thought lists, and also with number of message-related thoughts, although the latter correlation was of marginal significance.

As in Experiment 1, we tested for possible curvilinear relationships between chronic fear and processing by means of quadratic regressions. The effect of the quadratic term did not approach significance for either of the postmeasures.

Effects of Message-Induced Fear

As in Experiment 1, a moderate positive correlation was found between chronic fear and message-induced fear ($r = .42$, $p < .001$).

Pearson correlations between message-induced fear and the other postmeasures are presented in Table 2. For errors found, the correlation with message-induced fear was in the same direction as the correlation

TABLE 2 Simple and Partial Correlations, Experiment 2

Postmeasure	Simple correlation of postmeasure with:				Partial correlation of postmeasure with chronic cancer fear, controlling for:		
	Chronic cancer fear	Message-induced fear	Perceived susceptibility	Trait anxiety	Message-induced fear	Perceived susceptibility	Trait
Errors found							
r	-.21	-.17	-.17	-.10	-.18	-.21	-.23
p value	.05	.10	.10	ns	.10	.05	.02
Message related thoughts							
r	-.15	.13	-.11	-.22	-.24	-.14	-.15
p value	.10	ns	ns	.05	.02	.10	.10

with chronic fear but weaker, repeating the pattern found in Experiment 1. For message-related thoughts the correlation was positive and nonsignificant.

Correlations between chronic fear and the postmeasures with message-induced fear partialed out are presented in Table 2. The correlation with errors found decreased slightly, reducing its significance to a marginal level. The correlation with message-related thoughts, by contrast, increased substantially. Correlations were also performed between message-induced fear and the other postmeasures with chronic fear partialed out. The only resulting correlation that was of even marginal significance was the positive correlation with message-related thoughts, which increased from .13 to .20 (two-tailed $p < .10$). Thus, as in Experiment 1, the effects of chronic fear did not appear to be mediated to any large degree by message-induced fear.

Effects of Perceived Susceptibility to Cancer

In Experiment 1, perceived susceptibility to cancer correlated with message-induced fear but, contrary to predictions, not with chronic fear. In Experiment 2 the opposite occurred: Susceptibility correlated with chronic fear ($r = .31$, $p = .002$) but not with message-induced fear ($r = .05$).

Pearson correlations between susceptibility and the postmeasures are presented in Table 2. The pattern of results was similar to that found in Experiment 1. The correlations of susceptibility with errors found and message-related thoughts were in the same direction as the correlations between chronic fear and those measures, but lower.

Correlations between chronic fear and the postmeasures with susceptibility partialed out are presented in Table 2. The correlations remained essentially unchanged. When correlations between susceptibility and the postmeasures were performed with fear partialed out, neither was significant (rs = -.05 and -.08 for errors and message-related thoughts respectively).

Effects of Trait Anxiety

Trait anxiety did not correlate with either chronic cancer fear ($r = .09$), message-induced fear ($r = .11$), or perceived susceptibility ($r = .13$). Trait anxiety was, however, highly correlated with repression-sensitization ($r = .61$, two-tailed $p < .001$), with sensitizers scoring high on trait anxiety.

Pearson correlations between trait anxiety and the postmeasures are presented in Table 2. The correlations were in the same direction as the correlations between chronic cancer fear and these measures, although the correlation with errors found was not significant.

Correlations between chronic cancer fear and the postmeasures with trait anxiety partialed out are presented in Table 2. All correlations remained essentially unchanged. Similarly, when correlations between trait anxiety and the postmeasures were performed with chronic fear partialed out, the correlations were not greatly affected.

Because of the strong association between trait anxiety and repression-sensitization, we also performed correlations between trait anxiety and the postmeasures with repression-sensitization partialed out. The correlation with errors remained unchanged; the correlation with message-related thoughts was reduced to -.15 ($p < .10$).

Effects of Repression-Sensitization

Repression-sensitization exhibited moderate positive correlations with chronic cancer fear and message-induced fear (rs = .18 and .21 respectively; two-tailed ps = .10 and .05). Repression-sensitization was uncorrelated with perceived susceptibility to cancer ($r = .00$). Repression-sensitization was uncorrelated with errors found ($r = -.03$), but exhibited a correlation of -.16 with message-related thoughts. This correlation was not in the expected direction: Sensitizers listed fewer thoughts than repressers, not more. Using a two-tailed test of significance, this correlation was not significant (two-tailed $p = .15$). Because of the strong association between repression-sensitization and trait anxiety (mentioned earlier), this correlation was repeated with trait anxiety partialed out; the correlation was reduced to -.04.

As in Experiment 1, we used multiple regression to test for an interaction between repression-sensitization and chronic fear of cancer. The interaction effect did not approach significance for either errors found or message-related thoughts.

Processing of the Neutral Message

As we anticipated, number of message-related thoughts listed in response to the neutral message was uncorrelated with chronic cancer fear, perceived susceptibility, trait anxiety, and repression-sensitization (rs = -.02 to -.13). When correlations between chronic fear and the postmeasures were performed with neutral-message thoughts partialed out, the correlations remained essentially unchanged.

GENERAL DISCUSSION

Theoretical Implications

In two studies using several measures of systematic processing, we have found that chronic fear about a threatening topic (cancer) has a detrimental effect on processing of messages about the topic. This finding is consistent with the concept of fear as an aversive drive, and of defensive avoidance as a fear-reducing response.

Early studies that failed to document defensive avoidance tended to follow the widespread assumption that avoidance would manifest itself in reduced persuasion (e.g. Janis & Feshbach, 1953). Our findings indicate that this may have been one reason for their failure. In Experiment 1, subjects high in chronic cancer fear processed the message less carefully, but were also more persuaded by it, than low-fear subjects. This supports the contention, made by proponents of process theories of persuasion, that the relationship between systematic processing and persuasion is not invariant.

Previous research on fear appeals has tended to focus on acute or message-induced fear rather than chronic, pre-existing fear about the message topic. We argued that chronic fear was the proper predictor of processing style because chronic fear, and not acute fear, should indicate the presence of habits of defensive avoidance. Our results supported this contention. Although the correlations between message-induced fear and the measures of processing were almost all in the same direction as the correlations of chronic fear with processing, in no case was message-induced fear as good a predictor of processing as chronic fear. The correlations between chronic fear and processing changed little when message-induced fear was partialed out. By contrast, nearly all correlations between message-induced fear and processing were nonsignificant with chronic fear partialed out. This suggests that the relationship between chronic fear and processing is not mediated by acute fear. Rather, any relationships between acute fear and processing are largely accounted for by chronic fear, which presumably directly affects both.

The above results provide a tentative answer to an issue raised in the Introduction. Because evidence exists to suggest that fear might reduce both motivation and capacity for systematic processing, there is a question as to whether our findings represent an effect of fear on motivation or on capacity (see Chaiken et al., 1989; Mackie & Worth, in press). In the Introduction we stated that the basis for expecting fear to influence capacity is that fear is a type of arousal, which has been shown to impede capacity to perform complex tasks. We would expect arousal to be reflected in our measure of fear induced by the message. Thus, any effect of chronic fear on capacity to process should be mediated by message-induced fear. The fact that the relationships of chronic fear with processing were not so mediated indicates that chronic fear may have influenced motivation rather than capacity. This indication is far from conclusive, however; much stronger evidence is needed to settle this issue decisively.

Process theories of persuasion have proposed that issue involvement facilitates systematic processing. This suggests that, in our experiments, high-involvement subjects should have processed messages more carefully than low-involvement subjects. We predicted the opposite result, however. We expected that subjects high in issue involvement would also be high in chronic fear, and that fear-reducing responses (i.e., avoidance) would occupy a dominant position in these subjects' response hierarchies. This would cause both chronic fear and issue involvement to be negatively related to processing.

The balance of our results favored this prediction. We used perceived susceptibility to cancer as a measure of issue involvement. Susceptibility correlated positively with chronic cancer fear in both experiments, although the correlation reached significance only in Experiment 2. Subjects reporting greater susceptibility to cancer tended to score lower on our measures of systematic processing. Also, correlations between chronic fear and processing changed little when susceptibility was partialed out. By contrast, no correlations between susceptibility and processing were significant with chronic fear partialed out. These results indicate that the positive relationship between issue involvement and processing typically found in past research (see Chaiken, 1987; Petty & Cacioppo, 1986a) does not necessarily hold when fear and issue involvement co-occur. It may be that issue involvement does not exert a unidirectional effect on processing, but only amplifies whatever response tendency is present.

Alternative Interpretations of Findings

Two possible alternative explanations of the results of Experiment 1 were addressed by Experiment 2. The first of these was that the supposed effects of chronic cancer fear on processing of a cancer-related message were in fact due to an inhibitory effect of generalized anxiety on message processing regardless of topic. Two pieces of evidence from Experiment 2 refute this. First, chronic cancer fear did not influence the processing of a message unrelated to cancer. Second, the relationships between chronic fear and processing of cancer-related messages were not greatly affected when trait anxiety was partialed out. Unlike message-induced fear, trait anxiety was not correlated with chronic fear, and the relationships between trait anxiety and processing were not greatly affected when chronic fear was partialed out, suggesting that the effects of trait anxiety and chronic fear on processing are largely independent of one another.

The second of the two possible alternative explanations was that the supposed effects of chronic cancer fear on processing were in fact due to a tendency for people to spend less effort processing a message they already agree with. This explanation is refuted by the fact that, in Experiment 2, in which subjects read both a Pro and a Con message regarding cancer checkups for young adults, the same negative relationships between chronic fear and processing were found.

A clearer test of this second explanation is obtained by examining the relationship between chronic cancer fear and processing for each message separately in Experiment 2. If subjects' processing of a message is primarily influenced by their initial agreement with the message's position, then chronic fear should be negatively related to processing of the Pro message and positively related to processing of the Con message. If, on the other hand, subjects' processing is primarily influenced by chronic cancer fear, then chronic fear should be negatively related to processing of both messages. One measure of processing was available in Experiment 2 to test this: message-related thoughts listed for each message separately, rather than for both messages combined. The correlations of chronic cancer fear with Pro and Con message-related thoughts were -.11 ($p = .15$) and -.16 ($p < .10$) respectively. Thus, far from being positive, the relationship between fear and processing seems, if anything, to be even more negative for the Con message than for the Pro message.

LIMITATIONS

The primary limitations of this research are the small sample sizes in both experiments, resulting in low power, and the fact that some of the measures used were not highly reliable, tending to bias the results towards the null value. Examples of the latter are the measures of perceived susceptibility to cancer (in both experiments) and of change in behavioral intention (in Experiment 1), both of which were single-item measures, and the measure of chronic fear in Experiment 2, which had an alpha coefficient of only .66. Both of the abovementioned limitations increase the likelihood that these experiments failed to detect some true effects, the first by reducing significance levels and the second by reducing effect sizes. Thus it is not appropriate to place a high degree of confidence in any null results observed in this research. This is particularly true for interaction effects.

Effects of Cognitive and Behavioral Style

In this research, we were primarily concerned with issue-specific influences on processing. That is, we expected that the processing of messages about a given topic would be affected by chronic fear about that topic. Another possibility, however, was that subjects' processing would be influenced by more generalized processing styles that are not specific to any one topic. This idea is supported by work on cognitive and behavioral style concepts such as monitoring, blunting, and repression-sensitization (cf. Zanna & Olson, 1982; Miller, 1987). These concepts suggest not only a main effect of overall style on processing, but also a possible interaction with chronic fear. That is, the relationship between fear and processing may differ for people with different processing styles, and may even reverse its direction: Fear should decrease processing among low monitors, high blunters, and repressers, and should increase processing among high monitors, low blunters, and sensitizers. We included the monitoring, blunting, and repression-sensitization scales and tested both for main effects and for interactions with chronic fear. Little or no main effect on processing was found for these variables. With respect to interactions, no evidence was found of any reversal of the overall negative relationship between fear and processing as a function of any cognitive and behavioral style variable. The relationship remained negative across all levels of these variables. Overall, these results provide little evidence that generalized cognitive or behavioral style had an important effect on how subjects processed the messages. However, as discussed above, the low power of these studies prevents us from concluding with confidence that such effects do not exist.

Directions for Future Research

The present data are confined to the responses of subjects to written persuasive messages on a single topic—cancer. Fear may have different effects on processing for other topics. Factors such as the perceived preventability or controllability of the threat in question, for example, may affect the relationship between fear and processing. Thus, further research to test the generality of the present findings would be useful.

Our measure of chronic cancer fear included items that were originally intended to measure perceived severity of cancer. In retrospect, and in light of previous research on fear appeals (e.g. Rippetoe & Rogers, 1987), it is not surprising that fear and perceived severity should be closely related. This raises the question, however, of whether the results we have observed should be interpreted as effects of fear or of perceived severity. The theoretical justification for our hypotheses suggests the former. Some empirical support for this position was obtained by splitting the four-item chronic fear measure into two subscales, one composed of the two items originally intended to measure fear and the other composed of the two items originally intended to measure perceived severity, and by correlating each with the main postmeasures (errors found and message-related thoughts listed). In Experiment 1, the correlations between the two-item "fear" subscale and these postmeasures were -.31 ($p < .002$) and -.21 ($p < .05$)—similar to the correlations of the original four-item scale with these measures (-.30, $p < .002$, and -.23, $p < .02$, respectively). When the two-item "severity" subscale was partialed out, these correlations were somewhat reduced (-.25, $p < .02$, and -.13, $p = .12$, respectively). By contrast, however, the correlations between the "severity" subscale and the postmeasures were -.20 (p < .05) and -.19 (p < .05), and partialing out the "fear" subscale reduced them to -.06 (p = ns) and -.10 (p = ns). Similar results were found in Experiment 2. While these correlational analyses suggest that fear rather than perceived severity was the predominant factor in the processing effects we observed, this issue should be addressed experimentally in subsequent research.

Finally, as noted previously, although our data tentatively endorse a motivational rather than a capacity interpretation for the effects of fear on processing, future research that systematically explores the relative merits of these explanations is warranted.

REFERENCES

Apsler, R., & Sears, D. O. (1968). Warning, personal involvement, and attitude change. *Journal of Personality and Social Psychology, 9*, 162-166.

Axsom, D., Yates, S., & Chaiken, S. (1987). Audience response as a heuristic cue in persuasion. *Journal of Personality and Social Psychology, 53*, 30-40.

Byrne, D. (1961). The repression-sensitization scale: Rationale, reliability, and validity. *Journal of Personality, 29*, 334-349.

Chaiken, S. (1980). Heuristic versus systematic information processing and the use of source versus message cues in persuasion. *Journal of Personality and Social Psychology, 39*, 752-756.

Chaiken, S. (1987). The heuristic model of persuasion. In M. P. Zanna, J. M. Olson, & C. P. Herman (Eds.), *Social influence: The Ontario Symposium* (Vol. 5, pp. 3-39). Hillsdale, NJ: Erlbaum.

Chaiken, S., Liberman, A., & Eagly, A. H. (1989). Heuristic and systematic information processing within and beyond the persuasion context. In J. S. Uleman and J. A. Bargh (Eds.), *Unintended thought*. (pp. 242-252). New York: Guilford Press.

Chaiken, S., & Stangor, C. (1987). Attitudes and attitude change. *Annual Review of Psychology, 38*, 575-630.

Eagly, A. H., & Chaiken, S. (1984). *Cognitive theories of persuasion*. In L. Berkowitz (Ed.), *Advances in experimental social psychology* (Vol. 17, pp. 267-359). New York: Academic Press.

Easterbrook, J. A. (1959). The effect of emotion on the utilization and the organization of behavior. *Psychological Review, 66*, 183-201.

Epstein, S., & Fenz, W. D. (1967). The detection of emotional stress through variations in perceptual threshold and physiological arousal. *Journal of Experimental Research in Personality, 2*, 191-199.

Hoffman, M. L. (1986). Affect, cognition, and motivation. In R. Sorrentino & E. T. Higgins (Eds.), *Handbook of motivation and cognition* (pp. 244-279). New York: Guilford Press.

Hovland, C. I., Janis, I. L., & Kelley, H. H. (1953). *Communication and persuasion*. New Haven: Yale University Press.

Isen, A. M. (1984). Toward understanding the role of affect in cognition. In R. S. Wyer & T. K. Srull (Eds.), *Handbook of social cognition* (pp. 179-236). Hillsdale, NJ: Lawrence Erlbaum.

Janis, I. L. (1967). Effects of fear arousal on attitude: Recent developments in theory and research. In L. Berkowitz (Ed.), *Advances in experimental social psychology* (Vol. 3, pp. 166-224). New York: Academic Press.

Janis, I. L., & Feshbach, S. (1953). Effects of fear-arousing communications. *Journal of Abnormal and Social Psychology, 48*, 78-92.

Johnson, B., & Eagly, A. H. (1989). The effects of involvement on persuasion: A meta-analysis. *Psychological Bulletin, 105*, 635-642.

Langer, E. J., Blank, A., & Chanowitz, B. (1978). The mindlessness of ostensibly mindful action: The role of "placebic" information in interpersonal interaction. *Journal of Personality and Social Psychology, 36*, 635-642.

Leventhal, H. (1970). Findings and theory in the study of fear communications. In L. Berkowitz (Ed.), *Advances in experimental social psychology* (Vol. 5, pp. 119-186). New York: Academic Press.

Lord, C. G., Ross, L., & Lepper, M. R. (1979). Biased assimilation and attitude polarization: The effects of prior theories on subsequently considered evidence. *Journal of Personality and Social Psychology, 37*, 2098-2109.

Mackie, D. M., & Worth, L. T. (in press). Cognitive deficits and the mediation of positive affect in persuasion. *Journal of Personality and Social Psychology*.

Miller, S. M. (1980). When is a little information a dangerous thing? Coping with stressful events by monitoring vs. blunting. In S. Levine & H. Ursin (Eds.), *Coping and health* (pp. 145-169). New York: Plenum Press.

Miller, S. M. (1987). Monitoring and blunting: Validation of a questionnaire to assess styles of information seeking under threat. *Journal of Personality and Social Psychology, 52*, 345-353.

Nemeth, C. J. (1986). Differential contributions of majority and minority influence. *Psychological Review, 93*, 23-32.

Petty, R. E., & Cacioppo, J. T. (1979). Issue involvement can increase or decrease persuasion by enhancing message-relevant cognitive responses. *Journal of Personality and Social Psychology, 37*, 1915-1926.

Petty, R. E., & Cacioppo, J. T. (1981). *Attitudes and persuasion: Classic and contemporary approaches*. Dubuque, Iowa: Wm. C. Brown.

Petty, R. E., & Cacioppo, J. T. (1986a). *Communication and persuasion: Central and peripheral routes to attitude change*. New York: Springer-Verlag.

Petty, R. E., & Cacioppo, J. T. (1986b). The elaboration likelihood model of persuasion. In L. Berkowitz (Ed.), *Advances in experimental social psychology* (Vol. 19, pp. 123-205). Orlando, FL: Academic Press.

Petty, R. E., Cacioppo, J. T., & Goldman, R. (1981). Personal involvement as a determinant of argument-based persuasion. *Journal of Personality and Social Psychology, 41*, 847-855.

Rippetoe, P. A., & Rogers, R. W. (1987). Effects of components of protection-motivation theory on adaptive and maladaptive coping with a health threat. *Journal of Personality and Social Psychology, 52*, 596-604.

Rogers, R. W. (1975). A protection motivation theory of fear appeals and attitude change. *Journal of Psychology, 91*, 93-114.

Rogers, R. W. (1983). Cognitive and physiological processes in fear appeals and attitude change: A revised theory of protection motivation. In J. T. Cacioppo & R. E. Petty (Eds.), *Social psychophysiology* (pp. 153-176). New York: Guilford Press.

Spielberger, C. D. (1972). Anxiety as an emotional state. In C. D. Spielberger (Ed.), *Anxiety: Current trends in theory and research* (Vol. 1, pp. 23-49). New York: Academic Press.

Sutton, S. R. (1982). Fear-arousing communications: A critical examination of theory and research. In J. R. Eiser (Ed.), *Social psychology and behavioral medicine* (pp. 303-337). New York: John Wiley & Sons.

Worth, L. T., & Mackie, D. M. (1987). The cognitive mediation of positive affect in persuasion. *Social Cognition, 5*, 76-94.

Yerkes, R. M., & Dodson, J. D. (1908). The relation of strength of stimulus to rapidity of habit formation. *Journal of Comparative Neurology of Psychology, 18*, 459-482.

Zajonc, R. B. (1965). Social facilitation. *Science, 149*, 269-274.

Zanna, M. P., & Olson, J. M. (1982). Individual differences in attitudinal relations. In M. P. Zanna, E. T. Higgins, & C. P. Herman (Eds.), *Consistency in social behavior: The Ontario Symposium* (Vol. 1, pp. 75-103). Hillsdale, NJ: Erlbaum.

Public Speaking Anxiety Qua Performance Anxiety: A Revised Model and an Alternative Therapy

Michael T. Motley
Department of Rhetoric and Communication
University of California, Davis, CA 95616

Based upon counseling sessions with subjects experiencing high public-speaking anxiety (PSA), informal data are presented as evidence for the viability of a new PSA therapy technique, and for revision of existing models of PSA. Subjects' cognitive orientation to public speaking as either a "performance" event (with priority on audience assessment of the speaker's oratorical skills), or as a "communication" event (with priority on the audience's understanding of the message), seems to be a key determinant of PSA levels—lower levels being associated with, or resulting from, the "communication" orientation. A therapy technique for replacing a "performance" orientation with a "communication" orientation is described, and implications for the role of cognitive orientation in models of PSA are discussed.

Given the considerable research during the last two decades on correlates, treatments, manifestations, and measurements of communication apprehension (e.g., see reviews by Daly & McCroskey, 1984; McCroskey, 1977), it is not surprising that attention to a theory of underlying causal mechanisms is often called for (e.g., Daly, 1978; Richmond & McCroskey, 1985; Clevenger, 1984). One of the more valuable responses to that call has been the Behnke & Beatty (1981) adaptation of Schacter & Singer's (1962) model of general emotional response as a model of public-speaking anxiety in particular, and perhaps of communication apprehension more generally.

While the Schacterian model seems to answer several questions about the covert components of communication apprehension, it seems

© 1990 Select Press

incomplete in certain respects. This is not an indictment of Schacter and Singer (1962), since they were not addressing communication anxiety, nor of Behnke & Beatty (1981), since they were addressing the relevance to public-speaking anxiety of the Schacterian model in its pure form. That the model seems incomplete does, however, provide part of the rationale for the present discussion. More specifically, this discussion is to suggest an additional component for a Schacterian model of public-speaking anxiety, and to suggest resulting implications for the treatment of that anxiety.

The Schacterian model is a two-variable system. As adapted by Behnke & Beatty (1981), one component is the physiological arousal familiar to anxious public speakers before, during, and sometimes after their speeches. The other component is a cognitive interpretation of the physiological-arousal symptoms as representing public-speaking anxiety. Both components are presumably required for the anxiety experience. For example, a high level of physiological arousal interpreted positively as something other than speech anxiety (e.g., as "emotional readiness") would not constitute public-speaking anxiety. Nor would the cognitive recognition of a potential speech-anxiety situation in the absence of physiological arousal.

The physiological-arousal variable in the model would include a variety of heightened autonomic-nervous-system (ANS) responses. This is consistent with the wide range of physiological manifestations reported by anxious speakers. Descriptions of the cognitive component are less clear, however. Behnke and Beatty (1981) discuss the cognitive-interpretation variable as the simple cognitive recognition or labeling of the experience as public-speaking anxiety. They operationalize the variable as responses to McCroskey's (1978) Personal Report of Communication Apprehension, a self-report of behavioral preferences and relative comfort in a variety of communication situations.

The implication is that the cognitive labeling depends in part upon recognition of a personal predisposition toward the behaviors characterized by the label. A variation of the cognitive-interpretation variable (e.g., Motley, 1988) posits a more elaborate process in which the heightened ANS activity is interpreted as the fear emotion, which in turn requires cognitive justification. The emotion is presumably rationalized by recognizing (or inventing) fear objects, these often taking the form of the imagined failures, consequences, embarrassments, and other such negative predictions familiar in discussions of the cognitive targets of rational emotive therapy for public-speaking anxiety (e.g., Fremouw, 1984; Richmond & McCroskey, 1985). In other words, the ANS arousal is interpreted as fear which in turn is justified via cognitions along the lines of "What am I afraid of? *I must be afraid of the speech.* Why? *There must be potential negative consequences.* Like what? *Like making a fool out of myself if ....*"

In combination, these views suggest the cognitive component of the Schacterian model to be a labeling function, probably influenced by self-image or personal expectations, and probably combined with rationalizations for the labeled emotion. It has been hypothesized also (e.g., Motley, 1988), that the ANS and cognitive components may interactively accelerate in a cyclical "snowballing" fashion. That is to say, the rationalization of a tangible fear object (real or imagined) may provide fuel to increase the original ANS arousal, which in turn necessitates more catastrophic cognitions, which in turn again increases ANS arousal, etc. Thus, public-speaking anxiety reaches, for some individuals in some cases, a sort of worst-case-scenario level, both physiologically and cognitively.

In either its most simple or its more elaborate versions, the Schacterian view of public-speaking anxiety remains essentially a two-variable model in which heightened ANS anxiety and anxiety-oriented interpretations interact. As for the underlying mechanisms responsible for instigating the cycle in the first place, however, there has been very little conjecture. That question is the focus of the present discussion.

The Schacterian model practically begs the question: *Why do some individuals experience much higher degrees of the relevant arousal/ interpretation interaction than do others?* Efforts to answer this question generally have been casual and inadequate. That some speakers assign positive interpretations to their ANS arousal (Behnke & Beatty, 1981), for example, still leaves the question of why anxious speakers assign negative interpretations. The related question of why some speakers experience both much lower ANS arousal and much less negative interpretation (e.g., Behnke & Beatty, 1981) remains, as well. The explanation that the classic arousal/interpretation interaction results from the individual's association with earlier similar experiences of the same emotion (e.g., Schacter & Singer, 1962), begs the questions of what accounts for the ANS arousal in the initial instance, and, moreover, from whence comes the interpretive label in one's initial experience of the emotion. The answer that emotional labels are, in effect, taught us at an early age (e.g., Buck, 1988) is a partial answer at best, since children sometimes report stage-fright experiences (by various names) without apparent prompting by peers, parents, or teachers. The possibility that anxious speakers remember having had an earlier traumatic experience in a public-speaking situation is simply not borne out by examination, nor is it the case that these individuals have witnessed failures or traumatic experiences by other speakers as salient.[1]

I wish to propose that an additional cognitive variable instigates and interacts with the two classic Schacterian variables, at least in many (if not most), cases of public-speaking anxiety. I will argue primarily from my experience of several years as a private speech-anxiety counselor (of more that 80 adult subjects treated specifically for public-speaking anxiety) and as an instructor of public-speaking courses (including more than 500 identified high-anxiety subjects). While some empirical data will be provided, they are meant to represent only preliminary and tentative support of certain claims. This report should be taken more as a case-study summary by an individual therapist than as a formal test of a priori hypotheses.

Public-Speaking Orientations: Performing versus Communicating

As is clear from an examination of the innumerable text books on the subject, there are different opinions on the objectives and criteria for public speaking. One somewhat oversimplified but nevertheless viable classification of these approaches is represented by a simple continuum. At one end, public speaking is viewed as a situation demanding special delivery techniques to make a positive aesthetic impression on an audience. At the other end, public speaking is viewed as a situation demanding one's ordinary everyday communication style during an effort to cause, in the audience, cognitive changes regarding the speech topic. To exemplify these extremes, speech instructors favoring the first approach—which I will call a "performance orientation"—are likely to grade speeches on the basis of a check-list of criteria including gestures, eye-contact, vocal range, vocabulary, and other supposed indicators of eloquence, in an effort to evaluate audience reactions to the speaker. Those favoring the other approach—which I will call a "communication orientation"—might grade on the basis of audience responses to relevant information-gain or attitude-change questionnaires, in an effort to gauge reaction to the speech content. In one case, what matters most is the audience's evaluation of the speaker's oratorical behaviors. In the other

---

[1] *This is based on interviews with scores of adult subjects the author has treated privately for public-speaking anxiety. Only two of these subjects reported having had a particularly bad experience in a public-speaking situation. Both of these acknowledged, however, that their anxiety preceded these experiences. (The possibility that all of these subjects have repressed or otherwise denied some past causal public-speaking trauma seems to me to be remote.) Most subjects, moreover, have difficulty identifying instances of having witnessed serious negative consequences experienced by other speakers, and all acknowledge that their personal experience, both as a speaker and as an audience member, indicates the probability of a relevant traumatic experience to be extremely small.*

case, what matters most is the audience's response to the message.

This difference in orientation to the public-speaking situation is found in speakers as well, with or without formal training. I am becoming increasingly convinced that this difference in orientation accounts, in large measure, for differences in public-speaking anxiety (PSA). Stated in the strongest terms (although I will temper the implied hypothesis somewhat as the discussion proceeds), I have never encountered a high PSA subject who did not have a strong performance orientation to public speaking, and I have encountered only one subject for whom a significant shift toward a communication orientation was not accompanied by a dramatic decease of (self-reported) PSA. My basic claim is that one's cognitive orientation to the public-speaking task is critical interactive variable in an otherwise Schacterian account of PSA.

The performance orientation is characterized by a set of attitudes and beliefs that make public speaking analogous to the performances of Olympic figure skaters and concert pianists. The speaker's overriding impression is that the audience is hypercritically focused on his/her every move, and that success is measured by how flawlessly his/her oratorical skills are demonstrated. Thus, for example, minor mistakes are assumed to be unforgivable. Performance-oriented speakers are often unable to articulate what the critical behaviors are, but they invariably assume them to be more "formal," "polished," and "practiced" than the skills in their ordinary communication repertoire. Of equal importance, the performance orientation to public speaking assumes that the audience is involved primarily in *evaluation*, and that the evaluation is based on an aesthetic impression of the speaker *qua* speaker.

That elements of this orientation are anxiety-arousing is not original here, of course. It is generally accepted, for example, that PSA is associated with impending evaluation and supposed audience scrutiny (e.g., Daly & Buss, 1984). Indeed PSA is often included within the larger category of "performance anxieties." Most of the earlier discussions along these lines, however, implicitly concede that many elements of performance anxiety are inherent conditions of public speaking. To put it another way, the common implication is that it is not surprising that public speaking evokes anxiety since several elements of the public speaking situation—evaluation, scrutiny, novelty, formality, etc.—are known to induce anxiety in a variety of other contexts.

Generally missing from these earlier discussions, however, is the notion that the anxiety-arousing performance demands of public speaking are more the result of misconceptions about public speaking than of inherent situational demands, at least according to one readily available alternative perspective. Specifically, the communication orientation removes most elements of novelty, evaluation, and audience scrutiny from the public speaking situation. This perspective is characterized by a set of attitudes that make public speaking analogous to everyday conversation (thus reducing the novelty dimension, for example). Here, the assumption is that the audience is focused with curiosity upon the speaker's message, and that success is measured by the extent to which the audience understands the message and its point of view. Thus, minor "mistakes" are as tolerable as in everyday communication, and appropriate delivery techniques—being generally those of everyday communication—are well within the range of the speaker's existing repertoire.[2] Most importantly, this orientation assumes that the audience is more focused on understanding the message than on evaluating the speaker. By this account, the novelty, audience scrutiny, formality, and evaluative objectives of the performance orientation are considerably exaggerated.

As suggested above, the performance orientation seems by far the more common perspective of high PSA individuals. It is beyond the author's expertise to make claims about the origins of the performance orientation among those who share it. My therapy interviews with high PSA subjects suggest, however, that part of the answer lies in certain early classroom experiences for which oral presentations are, by nature of the assignment, without apparent pragmatic communicative consequence. Recitations of poems, historic documents, and other nonoriginal material (often already known to classmates), as well as oral reports on topics of relatively little interest to speaker or classmates, may promote a speaking-for-the-sake-of-speaking (rather than for the sake of communicating) attitude. This can occur in combination with teacher and classmate feedback directed more toward analyzing the delivery than understanding the content.

At any rate, one may view public speaking as more an aesthetic performance task or as more a pragmatic communication task. That the former orientation is generally more anxiety-ridden than the latter assumes that the demands of performance are generally anxiety producing, and that the demands of communication generally are not. Of course, while most people are more comfortable in ordinary communication than in performance, certainly there are exceptions. For example, certain professional actors have expressed that they are more comfortable in a role than in ordinary conversation. And, of course, there are countless others who, whether comfortable in performance or not, are unusually apprehensive in ordinary communication situations. This discussion is not meant to imply that a shift toward a pragmatic communication orien-

---

[2] *This is different than the assumptions of rhetoritherapy and other "skills" approaches to PSA, by the way.*

tation to public speaking will have a significant effect on PSA among subjects who are very high in general communication apprehension. Rather, it addresses the more typical high PSA subject who is generally functional in most ordinary communication situations.

PSA Reduction via Pragmatic Communication Orientation

As has been acknowledged elsewhere (e.g., Daly & McCroskey, 1984), certain existing therapeutic techniques for PSA may be thought of as targeting the variables within the classic Schacterian model. Thus, systematic desensitization methods may be viewed as an attempt to reduce ANS arousal, while rational-emotive therapy and "cognitive restructuring" techniques aim at the cognitive-interpretation variable. If it is the case that for many individuals the arousal-interpretation cycle depends in part upon the cognitive orientation to the public-speaking task, then therapy aimed at the cognitive orientation should provide effective additional or alternative techniques. (Or, conversely, if therapy aimed simply at shifting high PSA subjects from a performance to a communication orientation were to be successful, this would lend support to the suggestion of a cognitive-orientation variable within PSA models.)

Outlined below is a therapy technique based primarily on replacing a performance orientation with a communication orientation in high PSA subjects. While private counseling is the preferred mode, the technique can be administered to groups of high PSA subjects, or can be incorporated into public-speaking classes of typical PSA distributions. In one-on-one situations, the procedure, at least as performed by the author, usually takes place during a single three-hour session. The following description is merely a synopsis of the primary *goals* of the therapy. With the understanding that there is probably considerable latitude in the details of accomplishing these goals, the suggestions given here should be understood to reflect the idiosyncrasies of the author.[3]

The essential goals of therapy involve providing persuasive alternatives to counter the presumed anxiety-arousing cognitions constituting the performing orientation. That is to say, the theoretical rationale for the approach considers the performance orientation to constitute an underlying causal variable in most PSA situations. This cognitive orientation is considered to contain several underlying components which constitute its anxiety-instigating dimensions. The therapy, as practiced by the author, initially attacks these components equally, and then attempts to adjust to the idiosyncrasies of the subject in sometimes concentrating

---

[3] *A book-length description of the procedure is forthcoming from the author.*

efforts on certain components more than others. These components of the performance orientation include perceptions that: a) the public-speaking situation is novel and constitutes an unfamiliar situation; b) it requires unusually formal, artificial, and unfamiliar behaviors; c) the audience scrutinizes the speaker for adherence to delivery rules; d) that success depends on a perfect delivery according to these vague criteria; and e) that success is therefore unlikely.

1. *Information on the nature of PSA.* Although not critical to the theoretical perspective discussed above, the therapy includes a description of the PSA phenomenon. This is done in the spirit of helping the subject to understand the nature of his/her problem and the perspective of the therapy. Information on the frequency of PSA within the general population probably provides some consolation, as does the discounting of misconceptions about PSA being correlated with negative personality traits. Most important perhaps, is a description of ANS patterns in high, medium, and low PSA individuals (e.g., Behnke & Carlile 1971; Clevenger, Motley, & Carlile, 1967). That is to say, subjects should have a clear understanding of what constitutes a reasonable target of the therapy (i.e., the patterns of low PSA speakers), including the expectation of an ANS "confrontation" reaction (Clevenger et al., 1967) despite substantially reduced PSA.

2. *Persuasion to a communicative goal of public speaking.* By far the major effort in this therapy approach is persuading the subject that the audience's post-speech reflection on the speech content is more important than its post-speech reflection on the speaker. The fact of the matter is, of course, that a positive reflection on the content makes for a positive reflection on the speaker, and vice versa. But where the latter concern dominates the subject's attention—as it so often does in high PSA individuals—it may be better not to concede the interaction until very late in the session. It often seems strategically helpful to persuade the subject toward an exaggerated preoccupation with pragmatic communicative goals at the expense of a nearly total disinterest in the audience impression of the speaker. Residual preoccupation with audience evaluation of the speaker is likely to linger anyway. That is to say, the subject is persuaded toward believing that (within reason) the *only* thing that matters in a speech is whether the audience understands the message and the speaker's point of view.[4]

As for accomplishing this most difficult phase of the communication-orientation shift, it is usually helpful to make several contrasts.

---

[4] *"Entertaining" speeches are a special case in this regard, of course, and are discussed as including secondary goals with the few subjects who are concerned with them.*

These include contrasting the expectations of adult audiences in "real life" speech situations with those of the less mature audiences in the subject's earlier classroom experiences, contrasting a mature audience's listening behaviors with stereotypic evaluation behaviors of relevant classroom teachers and audiences, and contrasting the speaker-expertise dimension of stereotypic classroom speaking assignments with those of typical adult speaking opportunities. In other words, it is helpful for the performance-oriented high PSA subject to disassociate future speech objectives from past objectives featuring real or imagined skills evaluation. Thus, for example, a "cognitive-restructuring" response to the subject who claims consistent failure in public speaking is basically that he/she in fact has no frame of reference because past efforts have been non-realistic performances rather than communicatively-oriented speeches. Very important also, is elaboration on the notion that within a communication orientation, the objectives of public speaking become very similar to those of everyday serious conversation—with which the subject is already experienced, and usually reasonably accomplished.

3. *Persuasion toward naturalness in delivery.* Along with the notion that the objectives of public speaking parallel those of many interpersonal communication situations, the therapy emphasizes that the delivery behaviors of public speaking should be the familiar behaviors of everyday communication. That is to say, gesture, facial expression, vocal inflection, and so forth, do not need to be especially formal or otherwise foreign, but may be (or should be) essentially the same as those already in the subject's repertoire. In short, the approach promotes an extemporaneous style, emphasizing the preferred style to be natural rather than artificial. And just as the paralinguistic and other nonverbal accompaniments to speech are performed unconsciously in most communication—indeed often become negatively distorted if conscious—so should they be unconscious in public speaking. The primary objective here is to eliminate the performance-orientation notion that some unspecified set of special oratorical techniques must be employed for effective public speaking, and to emphasize again that one set of imagined inadequacies is in fact a set of already *familiar* and (usually) competent spontaneous behaviors.[5] To put it another way, the theme is that the only differences between public speaking and everyday-conversation are found in 1) the number of

---

[5] *Eye contact and projection are notable exceptions, of course. These may be dealt with separately toward the end of the therapy session after the general extemporaneous and natural style has been accepted as a target. Moreover, in cases where the subject manifests natural communicative idiosyncrasies judged by the therapist as likely to impair public speaking efforts, these may be addressed separately as well.*

people present (which may be viewed positively as an increase in efficiency), 2) the amount of advance time to plan the content (which may be viewed positively as an improved opportunity to prepare a communicative strategy), and 3) the amount of time one speaks before his/her "turn" is up (which may be viewed an optimal opportunity to fulfill one's communicative objectives).

4. *Miscellaneous additional information.* A variety of additional topics invariably arise, the details depending upon the subject and the circumstances. The main point for the present discussion is that virtually all additional discussion may be framed within a pragmatic communication perspective and may be presented in an effort to further allay the subject's PSA concerns. Thus, for example, discussion of audience perceptions of the speaker may focus on the audience's general inability to detect PSA. Discussion of additional "tips" for effective public speaking may focus on content preparation and organization. Subjects' articulated fears may be answered with standard rational-emotive-therapy responses, and so forth.

Preliminary Evidence

Both the above therapy technique and the suggested modification of the Schacterian model are offered here more as the considered impressions of an experienced PSA counselor than as the empirically tested claims of a PSA researcher. Rigorous experimental testing of various kinds remains to be done, and is invited by the present discussion. Nevertheless, a few empirical observations—mostly informal—are available to shed light on some of the relevant issues. These preliminary data generally support the hypotheses implied above, but at questionable levels of confidence.

Effectiveness of the therapy technique. The author's case file contains detailed records in several data categories for 82 private-consultation subjects (70 males, 12 females) of the above PSA-therapy technique, covering a period of about eight years. Summaries of these records provide a tentative gauge of effectiveness for the therapy technique outlined above, as all 82 subjects were treated accordingly.

All subjects were adults (most over the age of 25). Nineteen were students referred to the author by instructors of public-speaking courses. (None were students of the author's public-speaking classes, as these constitute a separate group.) Of the remaining 63 subjects, 27 are known to have been directed to the consultation by their employers or spouses. All subjects except some enrolled students had completed at least two years of college education. Represented vocations cover a wide range. All subjects acknowledged high PSA, acknowledged a high probability of future public-speaking tasks, and acknowledged a desire to reduce their level of PSA. PSA was measured before therapy for some subjects (via the PRPSA of McCroskey, 1970), though not for others, and high trait PSA was confirmed for all subjects tested (n = 34, mean = 138.94, range = 115-153, s.d. = 7.28). Therapy in all cases was basically as outlined above, with some variations and refinements occurring across time and across individual subjects.

It is not unusual for my therapy subjects to report back on their progress, or for employers, spouses, or instructors to report on the subject's behalf. And when unsolicited reports are not provided, I usually try to make contact and solicit a report. These reports are recorded, and the records constitute the only available information on the success of the therapy.[6] Unsolicited reports generally occurred within three days to two weeks of the therapy session. Solicited reports were generally obtained between three and four weeks after the therapy. These reports are almost uniformly positive accounts of a dramatic reduction in PSA. The typical report is that the results are viewed as somewhat "miraculous" given the severity of the original problem and the relative simplicity of its solution. When the report has included an evaluation of public-speaking ability as well, that report invariably has been one of observable improvement. A summary of these reports is provided in Table 1. The validity of these reports, especially the solicited ones, should not be trusted completely, of course, since possible sources of bias are obvious. Nevertheless, the available data, preliminary and questionable as they may be, are a tentative indicator that the therapy technique is a successful one.

I know of only one case among the 82 that should probably be considered a failure. The subject, although not measured formally, appeared to be very high in reticence and general communication apprehension. Although the case file includes about seven others who probably would be similarly diagnosed and who were the source of positive reports, the exceptional subject seemed to have unusual difficulty identifying with the notion that serious communication often occurs without a primary listener focus on evaluation of the speaker. The eventual recommendation was that this subject try other therapy methods, but as of this writing that advice has not been followed.

It remains possible that whatever success the subjects of this therapy enjoy should be attributed not so much to the "communication versus performance" aspects of the therapy, but rather to the various other kinds of information shared during a typical session. Tentative evidence

---

[6] *Reports from persons who instigated the counseling invariably include second-hand accounts of the subject's statements about the therapy and its effects, and often include personal observations by the person reporting.*

TABLE 1 Reports on Post-Therapy PSA (and Public Speaking Ability) of Author's Subjects. "Positive" indicates a report of substantially reduced PSA (or improved speaking ability)

	REPORTS			
	On PSA		On Speech(es)	
	Positive	Neutral or Negative	Positive	Neutral or Negative
Subjects Referred by Public Speaking Instructors (n=19)				
Unsolicited report by Instructor	19	0	19	0
Unsolicited report by Subject	7	0	2	9
(Subjects unaccounted for: n=0)				
Subjects Referred by Employers (n=19)				
Unsolicited report by Employer	7	0	4	0
Unsolicited report by Subject	12	0	2	0
Solicited report by Employer	5	0	3	0
Solicited report by Subject	3	0	0	0
*(Subjects unaccounted for: n=4)				
Subjects Referred by Spouses (n=8)				
Unsolicited report by Spouse	2	0	1	0
Unsolicited report by Subject	5	0	0	0
Solicited report by Spouse	0	0	0	0
Solicited report by Subject	2	0	0	0
*(Subjects unaccounted for: n=1)				
Other Subjects (n=36)				
Unsolicited report by Subject	16	0	3	0
Solicited report by Subject	10	1	1	0
*(Subjects unaccounted for: n=9)				

*Contact efforts unsuccessful.

against this rival hypothesis may be found in a small number of very informal but nevertheless serious sessions in which time was limited to less than thirty minutes. The case files reflect eight such cases, six of whom reported back, all of these positively. (These are not included in the group discussed above.) The point here is that the counseling effort in these cases consisted almost exclusively of admonitions against a cognitive orientation toward the speech as performance, and of directives toward a pragmatic-communication orientation, as there was little time to do much else. This supports, albeit very tentatively, the notion that the cognitive-orientation component of the more complete therapy technique is a critical component, if not the most critical component.

Modifying the Schacterian model. If, as suggested above, the ANS and cognitive-interpretation cycle of high PSA depends in part upon an initial cognitive orientation toward public speaking as more "performance" than "communication," then a measure of the performance orientation should be moderately and positively correlated with measures of PSA. To provide a preliminary test of this hypothesis, a preliminary instrument to measure cognitive orientation toward public speaking was devised and administered. Figure 1 represents and explains the instrument. The cognitive orientation instrument and the PRPSA (McCroskey, 1970) were administered to 27 students of a lower-division small-group-communication course at the author's institution. The presentation of the two instruments was such that the 34 items of one and the 16 items of the other were randomly ordered, presented as a single instrument, and later separated for analysis. For the PRPSA, mean = 111.1, s.d. = 20.5, coefficient alpha = .93. For the cognitive-orientation instrument, mean = 45.5, s.d. = 7.2, coefficient alpha = .97. More importantly, $r(25)$ = .71, $p < .01$, supporting the prediction of a moderate positive correlation between PSA and performance orientation. Given that the only test of the instrument itself is one of face-validity by the author, the support is again most tentative, however.

DISCUSSION

The model suggested by this report is represented in Figure 2. Presumably, one's general cognitive orientation to public-speaking tasks interacts with both the ANS and cognitive-interpretation variables of the Behnke and Beatty (1981) Schacterian model to determine one's level of PSA. A performance orientation is expected both to activate high ANS arousal (since ANS arousal accompanies tasks considered especially "formal," "novel," "evaluative," etc. in general contexts), and to activate interpretations consistent with high PSA. Notice the parallels between performance-orientation concerns, as described above, and the "fears" articulated by high PSA subjects of rational-emotive therapy. A communication orientation, on the other hand, should result in less ANS arousal (because the event is seen as less novel, formal, evaluative, etc.), and the accompanying interpretations should center on the content dimensions and pragmatic objectives of the speech task.

There is a difference, of course, between saying that preliminary evidence on the effects of a given cognitive orientation supports the Schacterian model, and saying that it fits the model. The latter implication is the more accurate in this case, and the distinction is important since the jury is still out, so to speak, on the Schacterian model, per se. The pure version of the Schacterian conceptualization (Schacter &

FIGURE 1 Performance/Communication Orientation Measure

CURRENT ATTITUDES TOWARD PUBLIC SPEAKING

DIRECTIONS: This instrument is composed of several statements concerning feelings about public speaking. Please indicate the degree to which the statements apply to you by marking whether you (SA) strongly agree, (A) agree, (U) are undecided, (D) disagree, or (SD) strongly disagree with each statement. Please work quickly and just record your first impression.

1. Memorizing a speech is a good idea for most speakers.
2. It is difficult to "be yourself" when giving a speech.
3. The main objective in a speech is to prove to the audience that you are a good speaker.
4. During a speech, the audience mentally "keeps score" of the speaker's mistakes.
5. Speaking style—gestures, vocabulary, expressiveness, etc.—should be much different during a speech than during everyday conversation.
6. One or two mistakes during a speech can make the speech a bad one.
7. A good way to get ready for a speech is to practice in front of a mirror.
8. In most ways, giving a speech is more like being in a play than like conversing casually with a friend.
9. The main thing an audience wants from a speech is a flawless delivery.
10. To give a good speech, one's style must be fairly formal and unnatural.
11. Losing your place, slips of the tongue, and similar mistakes can ruin a speech.
12. For a good speech, it is more important that the audience be impressed with the message than with the speaker.
13. The way one talks in everyday conversation is basically the way he/she should talk during a speech.
14. Except for talking longer, talking to more people, and preparing the content, giving a speech is the same as conversing.
15. In giving a speech, what you say is more important than how you say it.
16. All that matters for a speech to be good is that the audience understands the message.

Notes: Instructions were as shown. Questionnaire items were randomly mixed with those of the PRPSA, and later separated for analysis. Response columns (SA, A, U, D, SD) were provided. For scoring, responses SA to SD score 5 to 1 points, respectively, except on items shown above as numbers 12-16, for which scoring is reversed. Thus, total scores may range from 16-80, with higher scores presumed to indicate greater "performance" orientation.

COGNITIVE
ORIENTATION

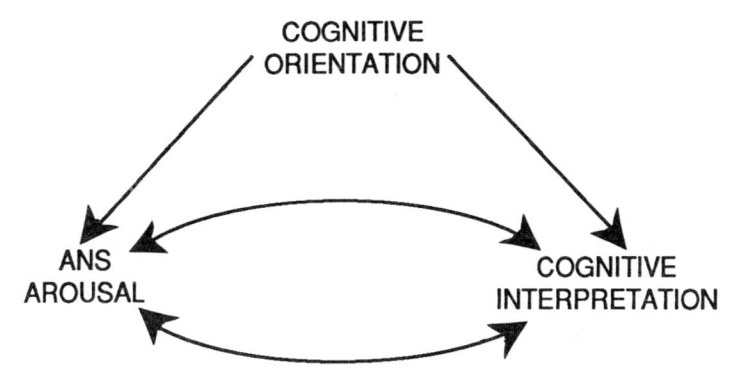

ANS AROUSAL ⇌ COGNITIVE INTERPRETATION

FIGURE 2   A Revised Schacterian Model of PSA

Singer, 1962) has been difficult to operationalize, since realistic sources of initially unexplained anxiety (or other emotion) have been difficult to establish in controlled conditions (see the discussion in Zimbardo, Ebbesen, & Maslach, 1977, for example). The original data presented in support of the model (Schacter & Singer, 1962) have been subsequently interpreted as less supportive than purported (e.g., Plutchik & Ax, 1967; Maslach, 1979).

A liberal interpretation of the more recent data (e.g., Maslach, 1979) would assert that the Schacterian model seems inappropriate as an explanation for positive affect, but might still be applicable to negatively interpreted arousal (such as high PSA, perhaps). In any case, the present report adds nothing to the question of whether PSA is, in fact, the result of labeling and rationalizing initially unexplained physiological arousal in the strict Schacterian sense.

Indeed, there are alternative models into which the cognitive variable discussed in this report might fit nicely as well, and these alternative models should be acknowledged. Schlenker and Leary (1982) have, for example, presented a model based upon the notion that social anxiety results from negative expectations regarding the desired outcome of an interaction. They point to the audience's positive impression of the communicator as one of the primary desired outcomes of the interaction. This notion is paralleled by the above discussion of PSA levels as depending in part upon whether the speaker centers attention on audience response to the message or on audience impression of the speaker. Other parallels may be found as well, especially in that both discussions view the communicator's concern over audience evaluation as a primary component of the anxiety.

Similarly, Greene and Sparks (1983) have presented a model in which communication apprehension is seen as the result of expected outcomes. When desired communication outcomes are seen by the subject as unrealistic or unlikely, increased anxiety follows. The implication for the above discussion would be that a performance orientation would not produce anxiety in speakers who (because of past practice and success, for example) are confident that they can satisfy performance-oriented criteria. Conversely, a communication orientation would not suffice in reducing the anxiety of speakers uncertain of their ability to achieve basic communication goals (such as speakers with inadequate preparation time, for example). The implication seems almost certainly correct.

Parallels may be found also between the focus of the present report and a model provided by Carver (1979) in which humans "test" (in the cybernetic sense of Miller, Galanter, & Pribram, 1960) their own behaviors against their hypothetical standard for appropriate behaviors in the corresponding context. A resulting mismatch determines (among other things) their psychological withdrawal from the situation. Adapting this model to the present discussion, the implication would be that a public speaker's test against performance-oriented behaviors is likely to be counter-productive since the standards are artificial and unfamiliar behaviors. The test against communication-oriented behaviors is more likely to produce "matches" since the standards are those already familiar to, and practiced by, the speaker.

On the whole, disagreements between the position presented in this paper and those of the various earlier models are minor. The Schlenker and Leary (1982) model suggests therapy aimed at teaching new skills, while the present approach concentrates on optimizing existing skills. The Carver (1979) model suggests a level of self-monitoring that seems inappropriate for most otherwise unconscious speech behaviors. Compatibility between the above discussion and the Greene and Sparks (1983) model is very high in that the present position represents an argument for restructuring public speakers' expectations for success via replacement of the more risky performance orientation. Moreover, where the expectancy model "begs the question of the expectation-formation processes" (Greene & Sparks, 1983, p.219), the above discussion concerning classroom origins of the performance orientation for public speaking may shed some light, at least for PSA.

In any case, it seems completely sensible that, as the Greene and Sparks model would claim, a speaker's prediction of success would play a major role in determining his or her anxiety level regardless of the success criteria employed. Thus, for example, low PSA despite a performance orientation should occur in speakers confident of their performance success. Intuitively, however, this would seem to characterize speakers with considerable performance-oriented experience. so the novelty variable often associated with PSA may be operating as well (or instead) in these cases. The therapy discussed above attempts to promote more optimistic outcome expectations by focusing on pragmatic communication objectives, but it also attempts to associate the public-speaking task with familiar behaviors and experiences by encouraging a natural, conversational, style. One of these concerns is represented in the Greene and Sparks (1983) model, while the other is not. Whether it ought to be is testable, it seems.

The point is that while the above discussion of the effects of cognitive orientation upon PSA is presented as an addition to the Schacterian model, that presentation is meant to imply neither support for that model nor dissatisfaction with alternative models. The major advantage of the Schacterian focus is in the therapeutic implications for the tentative identification of a relationship between PSA and one's cognitive orientation to the public-speaking task. The Schacterian model has been popular as a parsimonious representation of two well-known components of high PSA (physiological arousal and psychological interpretation) as clearly-identifiable targets of opposing but successful therapy techniques (systematic desensitization and rational emotive therapy). To the extent that the present discussion has identified an additional component of PSA, and to the extent that the corresponding therapy technique is successfully replicated and validated, the therapeutic implications of the Schacterian model may be advanced.

As for the generalizability of the revised Schacterian model to anxieties other than PSA, no claims are implied. We might hypothesize that the model should account for other "performance anxieties," but the appropriate alternative cognitive orientation and the corresponding therapy would of course be different in these cases. I do not feel qualified to speculate on what these alternative orientations or therapies should be, and indeed routinely refer subjects to other therapies in these situations.

Given the earlier claims of success with PSA therapy aimed at replacing the performance orientation, it is appropriate to recognize clearly that there are performance situations for which the technique is not effective, at least as practiced by the author. Very simply, these are situations in which the therapist cannot in good faith deny the legitimacy of the performance-oriented concerns, and cannot in good faith persuade toward an alternate orientation. Thus, for example, I do not employ this therapy technique with anxious concert musicians or stage actors, since I cannot in good faith deny the legitimacy of the performance-oriented concerns.[7]

With public-speaking situations, it is rare that the therapy seems inappropriate, but it is occasionally precluded by unusually artificial performance demands. The therapy did not seem appropriate, for example, in a recent case involving a student's anxiety in an oral interpretation class because her drama instructor had made it clear that grading was to be based on performance criteria requiring elocutionary behaviors.[8] Another exceptional case provides a particularly nice example. The speaker was one of several public-relations lecturers for a firm that tries to solicit recruits through lectures to high-school seniors. She had been giving these lectures successfully and without uncomfortable anxiety for several years (according to self report), and had done so as well in introducing new lectures to the lecturer team. Nevertheless, unusually high anxiety accompanied a unique situation in which she was to present a model lecture to newly hired lecturers who had already learned the same lecture themselves. The idea was to provide the Trainer with a model to dissect for the new lecturers, which put the focus on performance-oriented concerns. And the fact that the audience already knew the information served to negate pragmatic communication concerns. Clearly, the therapy technique discussed above could not be applied (and was not attempted) in this situation. In short, the therapy depends upon a clearly identifiable and arguably superior alternative to the performance orientation. Where that alternative and its rationale are not available, the therapy is inappropriate.

As for whether the advice contained in the therapy promotes effective public speaking, opinions will reflect the performance/communication orientation of the opinion source. The primary assumption of the therapy in this regard is that reduction of PSA in high-PSA cases should precede a concern with polishing the speech, lest there be no speech to polish. Moreover, the suggested approach to delivery—directness, naturalness, and conversationality in an extemporaneous style—is consistent with contemporary pedagogy and with empirical studies on speech effectiveness (e.g., Dietrich, 1946; Diehl, White, & Salz, 1961).

As for additional research on relevant issues, an obvious next step is a study in the comparative-therapies genre (e.g., Ayres & Hopf, 1985) to

---

[7] *This is not to say that a viable alternative to the performance orientation—some sort of analog to the communication orientation to public speaking—does not exist for these situations. I can hypothesize a few possibilities, but do not feel sufficiently qualified in the areas of acting, music, etc. to promote them to therapy subjects.*

[8] *Informal suggestions to focus attention on "communicating the mood" of the text were reported to have been of some help in this case, nevertheless.*

test the above claims of the suggested therapy technique. To some extent, evidence supporting the effectiveness of the therapy would support the model as well, although research on the effects of isolated therapy components would be required to more precisely confirm the role of the performance perspective. More ideally, rigorous simultaneous examination of all three components of the suggested model is in order.

In any case, the present report suggests an additional component for a Schacterian model of PSA, but is not intended to suggest its final component. Behnke and Beatty (1981) ended their discussion of the two-variable Schacterian model by highlighting the need to find determinants and sources of the arousal-interpretation interaction. This report has attempted to identify one of the instigating variables as the individual's cognitive orientation to the task. Almost undoubtedly, there are additional cognitive-orientation categories and/or additional cognitive variables operating similarly in PSA and in other forms of communication apprehension. Their discovery deserves attention.

REFERENCES

Ayres, J., & Hopf, T.S. (1985). Visualization, systematic desensitization, and rational emotive therapy: A comparative evaluation. *Communication Education, 36,* 246-240.

Behnke, R.R. & Beatty, M.J. (1981). A cognitive-physiological model of speech anxiety. *Communication Monographs, 48,* 158-163.

Behnke, R.R., & Carlile, L.W. (1971). Heart rate as an index of speech anxiety. *Speech Monographs, 38,* 65-69.

Buck, R. (1988). *Temperament, special skills, and the communication of emotion: A developmental-interactionist view.* Unpublished manuscript, Oxford University.

Carver, C.S. (1979). A cybernetic model of self-attention processes. *Journal of Personality and Social Psychology, 37,* 1251-1281.

Clevenger, T. (1984). An analysis of research on the social anxieties. In J.A. Daly & J.C. McCroskey (Eds.), *Avoiding communication: Shyness, reticence, and communication apprehension* (pp. 219-236). Beverly Hills: Sage.

Clevenger, T., Motley, M., & Carlile, L. (1967). *Changes in heart rate during classroom public speaking. Unpublished manuscript,* University of Texas, Austin.

Daly, J.A. (1978). The assessment of social-communication anxiety via self-reports: A comparison of measures. *Communication Monographs, 45,* 204-218.

Daly, A., & Buss, A.H. (1984). The transitory causes of audience anxiety. In J. A. Daly & J.C. McCroskey (Eds.), *Avoiding communication: Shyness, reticence, and communication apprehension* (pp. 67-78). Beverly Hills: Sage.

Daly, J.A., & McCroskey, J.C. (1984). *Avoiding communication: Shyness, reticence, and communication apprehension.* Beverly Hills: Sage.

Deitrich, J.E. (1946). The relative effectiveness of two modes of radio delivery in influencing attitudes. *Speech Monographs, 13,* 58-65.

Diehl, C.F., White, R.C., & Salz, P.H. (1962). Pitch change and comprehension. *Speech Monographs, 28*, 65-68.

Fremouw, W.J. (1984). Cognitive-behavioral therapies for modification of communication apprehension. In J.A. Daly, & J.C. McCroskey (Eds.), *Avoiding communication: Shyness, reticence, and communication apprehension* (pp. 209-215). Beverly Hills: Sage.

Greene, J.O., & Sparks, G.G. (1983). The role of outcome expectations in the experience of a state of communication apprehension. *Communication Quarterly, 31*, 212-219.

Maslach, C. (1979). The emotional consequences of arousal without reason. In C.E. Izard (Ed.), *Emotions in personality and psychopathology* (pp. 565-590). New York: Plenum Press.

McCroskey, J.C. (1970). Measures of communication-bound anxiety. *Speech Monographs, 37*, 269-277.

McCroskey, J.C. (1977). Oral communication apprehension: A summary of recent theory and research. *Human Communication Research, 4*, 78-96.

McCroskey, J.C. (1978). Validity of the PRCA as an index of oral communication apprehension. *Communication Monographs, 45*, 192-203.

Miller, G.A., Galanter, E., & Pribram, K.H. (1960). *Plans and the structure of behavior*. New York: Holt, Rinehart & Winston.

Motley, M. T. (1988). Taking the terror out of talk. *Psychology Today, 22*,(1), 46-49.

Plutchik, R., & Ax, A.F. (1967). A critique of "determinants of emotional state" by Schacter and Singer (1962). *Psychophysiology, 4*, 79-82.

Richmond, V.P., & McCroskey, J.C. (1985). *Communication apprehension avoidance, and effectiveness.* Scottsdale, AZ: Gorsuch Scarisbrick.

Schacter, S., & Singer, J.F. (1962). Cognitive, social and physiological determinants of emotional state. *Psychological Review, 69*, 379-399.

Schlenker, B.R., & Leary, M.R. (1982). Social anxiety and self-presentation: A conceptualization and model. *Psychological Bulletin, 92*, 641-669.

Zimbardo, P.G., Ebbesen, E.B., & Maslach, C. (1977). *Influencing attitudes and changing behavior.* Philipines: Addison-Wesley.

Decision Rule Orientation and Public Speaking Apprehension

Michael J. Beatty
Robyn P. Clair
Department of Communication
Cleveland State University, Cleveland, OH 44115

The present study examined the relationship between rule orientation and communication apprehension (CA) in a public speaking context. Results indicated a general relationship between the constructs such that low CAs were either maximax or MEU in orientation and moderately apprehensive and highly apprehensive speakers tended to be MEU or random in decision rule orientation. Further, results indicated that, regardless of general decision rule orientation, highly apprehensive speakers abandoned their usual orientation in selecting speech introduction strategies. Low and moderately apprehensive speakers tended to select those strategies in a manner consistent with their decision rule orientation.

Communication apprehension (CA) refers to a predisposition to "avoid communication, if possible, or suffer a variety of anxiety-type feelings when forced to communicate" (McCroskey, Daly & Sorensen, 1976, p. 376). Several published studies indicate that, in public speaking contexts, apprehension about public speaking is predictive of state anxiety reactions (Beatty, 1987a, 1988b; Beatty & Andriate, 1985; Beatty & Behnke, 1980; Behnke & Beatty, 1981; McCroskey & Beatty, 1984). A few studies show that unless strong counter-motives are present, apprehensive students avoid and withdraw from public speaking (Beatty, 1987b; Beatty, Forst, & Stewart, 1986).

A recent research project indicates that the likelihood of committing at least one choice-making error in the selection of speech introduction strategies is dependent on speakers' levels of public speaking apprehension (Beatty, 1988c). In conjunction with the relationship between faulty decision making and coping with ego-threatening problems which has been described in the counseling literature (Horan, 1979; Janis, 1983;

© 1990 Select Press

Janis & Mann, 1976, 1977, 1982; Neufeld, 1982; Spivack, Platt & Shure, 1976; Wheeler & Janis, 1980), Beatty's (1988c) finding underscores the connection between CA and cognitive processes and implicates decision making as important in the explanation of the CA and performance. *Decision rule orientation* refers to the characteristic way individuals select among alternatives in choice making situations (Beatty, 1986, 1987a, 1988a, 1988b). The present study examined the relationship between public speaking apprehension and decision rule orientation.

Conceptual Framework

In a simple sense, a decision may be defined as a choice among alternatives (Brunsonn, 1982). However, in the formal sense, decision making, or more precisely choice making, requires: a list of options, a list of future conditions or contingencies relevant to the consequences of the options, likelihood estimates for each contingency, an estimate of expected payoffs for each option under each contingency, and a decision criterion or rule which is consistent with the choice maker's objective or philosophy. (For an excellent discussion of these components see Huber, 1980 or Miller & Starr, 1967.)

The extant literature on individual choice making has been interpreted as evidence that human beings are not rational choice makers (Tversky, 1977; March & Simon, 1958; Nisbett & Ross, 1980; Rachlin, et al., 1986; Simon, 1957; Tversky & Kahneman, 1974, 1981). This conclusion is not universally accepted (Cohen, 1981; Peterson & Beach, 1967). Underlying the skeptical view of human rationality is the assumption of a single normative choice making criterion. Scenarios offering two choices, one presumed as correct, are administered to participants. Choices which deviate from those suggested by the normative model are viewed as irrational.

An examination of the *prescriptive* choice making literature, however, reveals a variety of *rational* decision criteria (e.g., Huber, 1980; Miller & Starr, 1967). As Miller and Starr (1967) conclude "decision theory provides no one best criterion for selecting a strategy under conditions of uncertainty. Instead, there are a number of different criteria, each of which has a perfectly good rationale to justify it. The choice among these criteria is determined by organizational policy and/or the attitude of the decision-maker" (p. 115).

The maximin (originally termed minimax) approach was the first criterion advocated in the decision science literature (Wald, 1939, 1947, 1949, 1950). The maximin criterion is conservative and minimizes losses even at the expense of large gains. In his analysis of decision criteria, Wald (1950) maintains that "It seems reasonable to judge the merit of any given decision function for purposes of inductive behavior entirely on the basis of the risk function" (p. 12). Philosophically, Wald suggested that it was prudent to assume that nature is always malevolent. Thus, the option which ensures the best payoff assuming a worst case scenario is selected. For this reason, the maximin rule is also known as the *criterion of pessimism*.

The maximax rule, also known as the *criterion of optimism* was formulated by Leonid Hurwicz (1951). In its original form, a coefficient of optimism was calculated by subtracting the payoff under the worst case scenario from that under the best case scenario. The option posting the largest coefficient was selected. In the contemporary literature, the maximax decision rule merely identifies the alternative that provides the largest potential payoff under a best case scenario (Huber, 1980). In application, the decision maker locates the cell in the matrix which offers the most positive outcome and selects the solution associated with that cell.

The criterion most widely recommended by contemporary decision scientists (e.g., Huber, 1980, p. 94) is the *maximum expected utility* (MEU) rule. According to this rule, the alternative that provides the highest average payoff across all future conditions should be selected. Underlying the MEU rule is the assumption that such a choice making strategy optimizes decisional consistency and stability. The rule is calculated by summing the weighted utilities (utility value x probability of occurrence) across future conditions for each option. The option producing the highest value (assuming utilities are scaled in a positive direction) is selected. The MEU rule may be represented algebraically as follows: where U_o represents the utility value of option 0, pF_i equals the probability of some future condition or contingency and U_i stands for the estimated utility value for option 0 under that contingency.

$$U_o = \sum_{I}^{N} pF_i U_i$$

The resemblance to the general linear model is not coincidental. The MEU rule was formulated and grew in prominence as linear regression analysis was developed. Moreover, Feather (1959) points to the influence of the MEU concept in the conceptualization of human behavior. The influence of the MEU decision criterion is conspicuous in theoretical perspectives advanced since the publication of Feather's paper. Notable in this category because it is algebraically identical to the MEU rule is Fishbein's (1967) formula depicting attitude toward a particular object.

Although the maximin philosophy dominated the conception of rational behavior in uncertain situations for slightly over two decades, the MEU perspective currently is in vogue among decision scientists. It has been argued, however, that tenacity concerning the normative value of any particular rule amounts to wishful thinking about how humans ought to use information in decision analysis (e.g., Peterson & Beach, 1967; Rapoport, 1966, 1970). Rather, as noted, the criterion "is determined by organizational policy and/or the attitude of the decision-maker" (Miller & Starr, 1967, p. 115). In discussing observations concerning human behavior in prisoners dilemma-type games, Rapoport (1970) concluded that "The lesson to be derived is that many of our cherished notions about every problem having an 'answer', about the existence of a 'best' choice among a set of courses of action...must be relegated to the growing collection of shattered illusions..." (p. 214). Rapoport (1970) further concludes that final decisions represent "choices which we make because of the way we view ourselves, and the world, including the other players" (p. 214). More recently, Beatty (1988a) argued that "decision rules should simply be the manifestation of one's goals, philosophy and intent" (p. 103). Thus, rationality in choice making as viewed from a decision theory perspective amounts to congruity between goals and decision criterion or rules.

A stream of research indicates that while many undergraduates who are untrained in the use of decision rules are inconsistent in choice making, a substantial number are moderately to highly consistent in selecting options that would have been identified through specific decision rule calculation (Beatty, 1986, 1987a, 1988a). In these studies six separate decision making cases featuring three alternative courses of action, three future conditions (equal likelihoods were assumed) and utility values for each option under each future condition were presented to subjects in written paragraph form. Each alternative represented exclusively the appropriate choice based on decision rules. Between one-third and one-half of the subjects, depending on the sample, selected at least four out of six times the option that would have been determined via MEU rule calculation. Approximately ten percent of the subjects selected maximin options and a small percentage consistently chose maximax alternatives. Moreover, ninety percent of consistent choice makers identified as generally descriptive of their philosophy specific maxims that are consistent with their choices (e.g., those selecting maximax options believe that, in general, one should try for large payoffs, nothing ventured nothing gained, etc.).

Student levels of consistency can be increased through training in decision matrix construction and rule selection and calculation (Beatty, 1988b). Even after training, however, students vary in their tendency to apply specific rules. This tendency to select choices indicative of particular decision criteria has been termed *decision rule orientation* (Beatty, 1988a,b). As mentioned, as many as fifty percent of subjects are inconsistent in their selections. Research findings suggest that the inconsistency can not be attributed to the type of utilities or nature of the decision task (for a review see Beatty, 1988b).

In Tversky and Kahneman's (1981) view "irrationality is inconsistency" (p. 458). Therefore, while many subjects demonstrate inconsistent choice making patterns, the decision rule orientation studies suggest that a substantial number of subjects make rational choices when the concept of rationality is broadened to include multiple decision criteria rather than assuming a single normative model. Conceptualized as an individual difference variable, the decision rule orientation construct represents a combination of prescriptive decision science principles concerning criteria and individual choice making.

Research Questions

A rationale for examining the relationship between communication apprehension and decision making in a broad range of situations can be reasoned from the theoretical underpinnings of decision counseling (Horan, 1979; Janis, 1983; Janis & Mann, 1976, 1977, 1982; Neufeld, 1982; Spivack, Platt & Shure, 1976; Wheeler and Janis, 1980). This literature suggests that apprehensive persons typically demonstrate deficiencies in decision making. A link between communication apprehension and communication strategy selection can be derived from the developmental literature. That is, similar antecedent conditions, namely family atmospheres in which communication is punished or at least devalued, contribute to both the development of CA and inadequate approaches to interpersonal decision making (for a review of this literature see, Beatty, 1988c,. pp. 297-298). Although the relationship between most of the dimensions of decision making (e.g., generating options, listing future conditions) and CA in a public speaking context has been studied (for a review see Beatty, 1988c, pp. 299-301), the relationship between CA and decision rule orientation has not been examined. The present study extends Beatty's (1988c) research which focused on the decision making characteristics of persons who are apprehensive about public speaking.

In essence, decision rules specify the criteria for processing relevant information regarding a proposed course of action. Specifically, they dictate what information is used, how it is weighted and how it is merged in the evaluation of options. Decision rule orientation captures individual differences in these respects. One question that emerges concerns whether there is a relationship between apprehension and decision rule orientation. An affirmative answer would implicate decision rule orientation, a broad construct, as an antecedent to apprehension by suggesting that particular rule orientations are more prone than others to apprehension.

The literature is equivocal concerning specific predictions. Findings link random rule application and cognitive backlog (Beatty, 1987a), a construct related to anxiety. The connection between CA and faulty decision making in the selection of speech introduction strategies would seem to imply that random choice makers are most likely prone to apprehension. However, literature also shows that socially anxious communicators tend to evaluate feedback as less positive than do nonanxious persons (Smith & Sarason, 1975). And the studies indicating that CAs report lower perceived chances of success in public speaking situations (Beatty, 1988c; Greene & Sparks, 1983; Miller, 1987) suggest that CAs are pessimistic. Since CA measures correlate with general personality factors such as introversion-extroversion and self-esteem (McCroskey, Daly, Richmond & Falcione, 1977; McCroskey, Daly, & Sorensen, 1976) it would appear that CAs would be maximin in orientation. Further complicating the matter, Beatty (1988c) reported that the introduction speech strategies selected by apprehensive speakers were maximax and MEU in nature. The frequency of errors in the production of those choices, however, mitigates against the likelihood of these rules being indicative of the the speakers' general decision rule orientation. This line of reasoning leads to a second research question regarding whether individuals at various levels of CA make choices related to public speaking which are consistent with their decision rule orientation.

METHOD

The public speaking component of McCroskey's (1982) PRCA-24 was employed as the measure of apprehension in the present study. This instrument consists of six Likert-type items (three reversed to avoid response bias) assessing apprehension in a public speaking context. In previous research, this instrument has yielded results consistent with theoretical expectations concerning CA and its consequences in performance situations (Beatty, 1987b; 1988c,d; Beatty, Forst, & Stewart, 1986; McCroskey & Beatty, 1984). When operationalized as a categorical variable, Beatty's (1987b, p. 209) recommendation was followed. Specifically, participants scoring 24 or greater were classified as highly apprehensive (HCA), scores of 12 or less were considered low apprehensives (LCA) and scores between 24 and 12 were classified as moderates (MCA). In the present study, the mean was 18.71, the standard deviation was 5.92 and the alpha reliability was .83.

Decision rule orientation was assessed in a manner similar to that employed in previous decision rule orientation research (Beatty, 1986, 1987a, 1988b). Six separate decision making cases featuring three alternatives, three future conditions and utility values for each alternative under each future condition were used. These cases required participants to make choices in civil defense, military, mountain climbing, cross-country driving, real estate and oil investment situations. Consequences or outcomes of choices included human lives, time-saved and money earned. The future conditions and utility values were arranged such that each alternative represented exclusively one decision rule. Participants were classified as having decision rule orientations if at least four of the six choices were representative of one decision rule. Participants were considered random decision makers if no such pattern was observed.

A public speaking case, parallel in format to those above, requiring participants to choose among three introduction strategies (i.e., humor, startling fact or statistic, and topic preview) was constructed. The three contingencies were described as various audience reactions, (i.e. positive, neutral, and negative). The case presented the participants with estimates of the effectiveness of each strategy given each possible outcome. Equal probabilities were assigned to each audience reaction.

Forty-one undergraduates enrolled in an upper level communication theory course participated in the present study. Early in the quarter, the apprehension measure was administered. Approximately five weeks later, the participants responded to the seven decision making scenarios. Communication apprehension and decision making were not discussed in the textbook. Neither topic was discussed by the instructor until after the data were collected.

RESULTS

Is there a relationship between decision rule orientation and public speaking apprehension?

The data were arranged in a three (HCA, MCA, LCA) by four (Maximax, MEU, maximin, random) contingency table. The frequencies for each cell and percentages of those frequencies for rows and columns are reported in Table 1. Results of a chi-square test, corrected for continuity, indicated an affirmative answer to the research question (X^2 = 11.78, df = 6, p < .05). Although HCAs were not significantly different from MCAs (X^2 = 1.20, df = 3), MCAs were significantly different from LCAs (X^2 = 8.32, df = 3, p < .05) and HCAs were different from LCAs at the .10 level of confidence (X^2 = 7.11, df = 3, p < .075). CA means and standard deviations for decision rule groups classified by rule orientation were as follows: max, n = 6, M = 13.83, sd = 6.52; MEU, n = 16, M = 18.38, sd = 5.62; min n = 7, M = 18.43, sd = 5.35; Randoms, n = 12, M =

TABLE 1 Frequencies and Percentages for Decision Rule Orientations by CA Level

Decision Rule Orientation	HCA f	C%	R%	MCA f	C%	R%	LCA f	C%	R%	T
Max	1	7	17	1	6	17	4	44	66	6
Meu	5	36	31	7	39	44	4	44	25	16
Min	2	14	29	4	22	57	1	11	14	7
Random	6	43	50	6	33	50	0	0	0	12
Total	14			18			9			41

Note: f = frequency, C = column, R = row.

21.75, sd = 5.10. A one-way anova for unequal cell sizes indicated an overall difference in apprehension due to decision rule category (F = 2.93, df = 3/37, p < .05, eta^2 = .19). The only statistically significant difference among specific mean contrasts was for the max versus random contrast (t = 2.42, df = 16, p < .05). However, given the means observed in this report, increased statistical power probably would lead to statistically significant differences in CA between max orientated and the other two groups of participants. It is also possible that randoms could be further differentiated from MEU and Min participants. While the small sample greatly restricts the interpretation of the F and t tests, they were reported to supplement the primary analysis.

Are the decisions made in response to public speaking scenarios consistent with general rule orientation for speakers reporting various levels of public speaking apprehension?

The data were organized into a three (HCA, MCA, LCA) by two (Consistent, Inconsistent) contingency table. The frequencies and relevant percentages of participants who selected options which were consistent or inconsistent with their general decision rule orientations are reported, by CA level, in Table 2. Random participants were omitted from the analysis because it is not possible to determine "consistency" of a choice in light of general randomness. The results of a chi-square corrected for continuity, indicated a significant relationship between the two variables (X^2 = 12.72, df = 2, p < .01). Specific group comparisons showed that LCAs were more consistent than HCAs (X^2 = 10.01, df = 1, p < .001) as were MCAs (X^2 = 7.08, df = 1, p < .05). However, MCAs and LCAs were not different in consistency between general rule orientation and strategy choice in a public speaking context (X^2 = 1.96, df = 1, n.s.).

TABLE 2 Frequencies For Consistent and Inconsistent Speech Introduction Strategies by CA Level

CA Level	Consistent	Inconsistent
HCA	1	7
MCA	10	2
LCA	9	0
Total	20	9

The mean CA score for consistent speakers (M = 14.9, sd = 4.64) was significantly lower (t = 4.86, df = 27, p < .05) than that of inconsistent speakers (M = 23.11, sd = 4.01).

DISCUSSION

The results of the present study indicate a general relationship between decision rule orientation and public speaking apprehension. Any one particular decision rule does not appear to constitute a necessary or sufficient condition for apprehension. Specifically, the vast majority of those reporting low levels of communication apprehension were either maximax or MEU in rule orientation. Moderately apprehensive participants tended to be either MEU or random in rule orientation as were highly apprehensive speakers. The notion that apprehensive speakers are maximin in decision rule orientation was not supported by the present findings. Viewed from the decision rule perspective, most maximax oriented participants tended to be low in apprehension, MEU and maximin oriented participants tended to be moderately apprehensive, and random decision makers were either high or moderate in public speaking apprehension. Measurement error aside, these results suggest that perhaps decision rule orientation interacts with other variables in relation to apprehension. The identification and investigation of those variables is a matter for future research.

Regardless of general decision rule orientation, highly apprehensive speakers abandoned their usual orientation in selecting speech introduction strategies. All nonapprehensive speakers were consistent with their general rule orientation. Moderately apprehensive speakers are more like nonapprehensive speakers in this regard. When random decision makers are considered in conjunction with these results, it appears that most highly apprehensive speakers are (1) random decision makers in general *or* (2) they abandon their usual orientation in public speaking contexts.

Such a dichotomy suggests two types of CAs. Moderately apprehensive speakers are (1) random in general or (2) consistent with rule orientation in public speaking settings. Those scoring low in public speaking apprehension are MEU or maximax in orientation and are consistent in public speaking settings. These observations point to a systematic overlap in decision making tendencies for high and moderate apprehensives, and moderate and low apprehensives. Although further research is needed to explain the overlap, the results of the present study indicate that individual differences in the way people process decision making information in general are related to their levels of public speaking apprehension.

REFERENCES

Beatty, M.J. (1988a). Decision rule orientation as an intrapersonal communication construct. In C.V. Roberts & K.W. Watson (Eds.), *Intrapersonal communication processes: Original essays,* (pp. 467-480). New Orleans: SPECTRA- Scarsbrick.

Beatty, M.J. (1988b). Increasing students' choice-making consistency: The effects of decision rule use training. *Communication Education, 37,* 95-105.

Beatty, M.J. (1988c). Public speaking apprehension, decision- making errors in the selection of speech introduction strategies and adherence to strategy. *Communication Education, 37,* 297-311.

Beatty, M.J. (1988d). Situational and predispositional correlates of public speaking anxiety. *Communication Education, 37,* 28-39.

Beatty, M.J. (1987a). Cognitive backlog and decision rule use. *Communication Research Reports, 4,* 79-81.

Beatty, M.J. (1987b). Communication apprehension as a determinant of avoidance, withdrawal and performance anxiety. *Communication Quarterly, 35,* 202-217.

Beatty, M.J. (1986). An exploratory study of decision rule use among college students. *Communication Research Reports, 3,* 125-128.

Beatty, M.J., & Andriate, G.S. (1985). Communication apprehension and general anxiety in the prediction of public speaking anxiety. *Communication Quarterly, 33,* 174-184.

Beatty, M.J., & Behnke, R.R. (1980). An assimilation theory perspective of communication apprehension. *Human Communication Research, 6,* 319-325.

Beatty, M.J., Forst, E., & Stewart, R. (1986). Communication apprehension and motivation as predictors of public speaking duration. *Communication Education, 35,* 143-146.

Behnke, R.R., & Beatty, M.J. (1981). A cognitive-physiological model of speech anxiety. *Communication Monographs, 48,* 158-163.

Brunsonn, N. (1982). The irrationality of action and action rationality: Decisions, ideologies, and organizational actions. *Journal of Management, 19,* 29-42.

Cohen, L.J. (1981). Can human irrationality be experimentally demonstrated? *The Behavioral and Brain Sciences, 4,* 317-370.

Feather, N.T. (1959). Subjective probability and decision under uncertainty. *Psychological Review, 66,* 150-164.

Fishbein, M. (1967). A behavior theory approach to the relations between belief about an object and the attitude toward the object. In M. Fishbein (Ed.), *Readings in attitude theory and measurement* (pp. 389-400). New York: John Wiley & Sons.

Greene, J.O. & Sparks, G.S. (1983). The role of outcome expectations in the experience of a state of communication apprehension. *Communication Quarterly, 31,* 212-219.

Horan, J.J. (1979). *Counseling for effective decision making: A cognitive-behavioral perspective.* Belmont, CA: Wadsworth.

Huber, G.P. (1980). *Managerial decision making.* Glenview, IL: Scott, Foresman and Company.

Hurwicz, L. (1951). Optimality criteria for decision making under ignorance. Cowels Commission discussion paper, *Statistics, No. 370,* mimeographed.

Janis, I.L. (1983). *Short-term counseling: Guidelines based on recent research.* New Haven, CN: Yale University Press.

Janis, I.L. & Mann, L. (1982). A theoretical framework for decision counseling. In I.L. Janis (Ed.), *Counseling on personal decisions: Theory and research on short-term helping relationships* (pp. 47-72). New Haven, CN: Yale University Press.

Janis, I.L. & Mann, L. (1977). *Decision making: A psychological analysis of conflict, choice, and commitment.* New York: Free Press.

Janis, I.L. & Mann, L. (1976). Coping with decisional conflict: An analysis of how stress affects decision-making suggests interviews to improve the process. *American Scientist, 64,* 657-666.

March, J.G. & Simon, H.A. (1958). *Organizations.* New York: John Wiley and Sons.

McCroskey, J.C. (1982). *Introduction to rhetorical communication* (4th ed.). New Brunswick, NJ: Prentice-Hall.

McCroskey, J.C. & Beatty, M.J. (1984). Communication apprehension and accumulated communication state anxiety experiences: A research note. *Communication Monographs, 51,* 79-84.

McCroskey, J.C., Daly, J.A., Richmond, V.P., Falcione, R.L. (1977). Studies in the relationship between communication apprehension and self-esteem. *Human Communication Research, 3,* 269-277.

McCroskey, J.C., Daly, J.A., & Sorensen, G.A. (1976). Personality correlates of communication apprehension. *Human Communications Research, 2,* 376-380.

Miller, D.W., & Starr, M.K. (1967). The structure of human decisions. Englewood Cliffs, NJ: Prentice-Hall.

Miller, M.D. (1987). The relationship of communication reticence and negative expectations. *Communication Education, 36,* 228-235.

Neufeld, R.W.J. (1982). On decisional processes instigated by threat: Some possible implications for stress-related deviance. In R.W.J. Neufeld (Ed.), *Psychological stress and psychopathology* (pp. 240-270). New York: McGraw-Hill

Nisbett, R.E. & Ross, L. (1980). *Human inference: Strategies and shortcomings of social judgment.* Englewood Cliffg, NJ: Prentice Hall.

Peterson, C.R., & Beach, L.R. (1967). Man as an intuitive statistician. *Psychological Bulletin, 68,* 29-46.

Rachlin, H., Logue, A.W., Gibbon, J., & Frankel, M. (1986). Cognition and behavior in studies of choice. *Psychological Review, 93,* 33-45.

Rapoport, A. (1970). *N-Person game theory: Concepts and applications.* Ann Arbor, MI: University of Michigan Press.

Rapoport, A. (1966). *Two person game theory: The essential ideas.* Ann Arbor, MI: University of Michigan Press.

Simon, H.A. (1957). *Models of man.* New York: John Wiley and Sons.

Smith, R.E., & Sarason, I.G. (1975). Social anxiety and evaluation of negative interpersonal feedback. *Journal of Consulting and Clinical Psychology, 43,* 429.

Spivack, G., Platt, J.J., & Shure, M.B. (1976). *The problem solving approach to adjustment.* San Francisco, CA: Jossey-Bass.

Tversky, A. (1977). On the elicitation of preferences: Descriptive and prescriptive considerations. In D. Bell, R.L. Kenney, & H. Raiffa (Eds.). *Conflicting objectives in decisions: International series on applied analysis* (pp. 209-222). New York: Wiley.

Tversky, A. & Kahneman, D. (1981). Framing of decisions and the psychology of choice. *Science, 211,* 453-458.

Tversky, A. & Kahneman, D. (1974). Judgment under uncertainty: Heuristics and biases. *Science, 185,* 1124-1131.

Wald, A. (1950). *Statistical decision functions.* New York: Wiley

Wald, A. (1949). Statistical decision functions. *Annals of Mathematical Statistics, 20,* 165-205.

Wald, A. (1947). An essentially complete class of admissible decision functions. *Annals of Mathematical Statistics, 18,* 549-555.

Wald, A. (1939). Contributions to the theory of statistical estimation and testing hypotheses. *Annals of Mathematical Statistics, 10,* 229-326.

Wheeler, D. & Janis, I.L. (1980). *A practical guide for making decisions.* New York: Free Press.

Shyness and Anxious Self-Preoccupation During a Social Interaction

Lisa A. Melchior
The Measurement Group
6245 Bristol Parkway #242, Culver City, CA 90230

Jonathan M. Cheek
Department of Psychology
Wellesley College, Wellesley, MA 02181

This study examined the relationship between shyness and the extent and the content of self-focus during an interaction with a stranger. Fifty-eight college women completed the Shyness Scale, conversed with another subject for five minutes, and rated themselves and their partner immediately after the conversation ended. Shy subjects reported that they spent more time self-focusing and experienced more anxious thoughts and other shyness symptoms than did those who were not shy. In addition, the shy subjects who conversed with a socially self-confident partner tended to experience the greatest difficulties during the interaction, and they rated themselves more negatively than their partners rated them. These results were interpreted as supporting the distribution-of-attention model of shyness as a propensity for engaging in anxious self-preoccupation.

The recent emphasis on cognitive approaches to the study of social behavior is making an important impact on the psychology of shyness. The definition of shyness as the tendency to feel tense, worried, or awkward during social interactions with unfamiliar people reflects a three-component model of social anxiety: conditioned somatic anxiety, cognitive processes involving excessive self-consciousness and worry about receiving negative evaluations from others, and social skills deficits (Buss, 1984; Cheek & Watson, 1989; Hartman, 1983). Leary (1983) has argued that cognitive theories not only stand on their own as explanations of social anxiety, but "also appear to subsume both the classical conditioning and social skills models" (p.53). That is, shy persons'

Authors' Notes: This research was supported by a Brachman Hoffman Small Grant and a Wellesley College Faculty Research Award to the second author.

We thank Robin Akert, David Pillemer, the editor, and the two anonymous reviewers for their helpful advice.

Correspondence may be addressed to either author.

© 1990 Select Press

cognitions regarding their somatic anxiety symptoms and degree of social skill may be more consequential than their objectively assessed level of tension or awkwardness (Cheek, Melchior, & Carpentieri, 1986).

A variety of studies on cognitive aspects of shyness have demonstrated a wide range of significant effects. For example, shy people tend to use more negative adjectives to describe themselves (Cacioppo, Glass, & Merluzzi, 1979). They also make more self-blaming causal attributions (Arkin, Appelman, & Burger, 1980), recall more negative self-referent information (Breck & Smith, 1983), expect to be evaluated more negatively by others (Goldfried, Padawer, & Robins, 1984; Smith, Ingram, & Brehm, 1983), and write less creative poems when anticipating evaluative feedback (Cheek & Stahl, 1986) (for a recent review, see Cheek & Melchior, 1990). Furthermore, shyness is related to cognitive interference and distractibility as manifested by poor performance on the Stroop Color and Word Test (Arnold & Cheek, 1986).

Cognitive explanations of what shy people do during social interactions are based on a distribution-of-attention model. Shy people may spend so much time monitoring their own feelings and behavior and worrying about how they appear to others that they become anxiously self-preoccupied (Crozier, 1979). Yet, as Davis (1982) put it, "perhaps the most fundamental prerequisite for responsive interaction is attention to one's partner" (p. 91; see also, Feffer & Suchotliff, 1966; Goffman, 1967). Because self-focused attention interferes with the attention which should be paid to the other person, shy people are believed to suffer from a "selective attention deficit' that impairs their ability to participate effectively in social transactions (Hartman, 1983).

Although this distribution-of-attention model is consistent with the research findings on various cognitive aspects of shyness described above, Crozier (1979) has emphasized the need for direct experimental tests of the model. Self-preoccupation has been studied extensively in the test anxiety literature (e.g., Geen, 1985; Sarason, 1984), but Leary (1986a) has pointed out that "its role in shyness and social anxiety has not yet been adequately examined" (p.32). Asendorpf (1987) has argued against an attentional model, and in favor of a self-presentational model of shyness, although his experiment did not assess distribution of attention directly. Therefore, the first purpose of the present research was to test the hypotheses that shy subjects will report spending more time engaged in self-focused attention during an interaction with a stranger than will those who are not shy.

A second issue concerns the cognitive *content* of the self-focused attention that may occur during a social interaction. As indicated by the research findings on cognitive aspects of shyness cited above, shy people tend to exhibit a persistently negative bias in their self-perceptions (e.g., Cheek et al., 1986). Crozier's (1979) conceptualization of shyness as a propensity towards engaging in *anxious* self-preoccupation obviously assumes that the content of the shy person's self-focusing is negative. Although Asendorpf (1987) suggested that the amount of time engaged in self-focus need not be related to a negative bias in such thinking, we believe that time spent self-focusing and negative content will be correlated when assessed for a social encounter between strangers (cf. Buss, 1980). To examine this assumption, we included a state version of Hartman's (1984) Social Anxiety Thoughts Questionnaire in the present experimental design.

Another important topic in the psychology of shyness involves the degree of congruence obtained between shy people's self-ratings and ratings of them made by others. A number of experimental studies have found that observers rate shy people more positively than the shy people rate themselves (e.g., Clark & Arkowitz, 1975; see also, Gough & Thorne, 1986; Jones & Briggs, 1984). This finding may be explained by the tendency of shy people to judge themselves using excessively high standards for social comparison (Goldfried & Sobocinski, 1975; Gormally, Sipps, Raphael, Edwin, & Varvil-Weld, 1981; Leary, 1983). Because realistic social comparison presumably requires paying attention to other people, the self-other discrepancy in ratings of shy people may be one consequence of their tendency to be anxiously self-preoccupied. In the present research, we expected that shy subjects' self-ratings made following the social interaction would be more negative than the ratings of them made by their partners.

The reactions of the shy subjects also may vary in relation to the shyness level of their conversational partners. Talking with a stranger is clearly a shyness eliciting social situation (Zimbardo, 1977). More recent research on shyness situations has suggested that strangers who are successful or "impressive" are especially anxiety-provoking (Russell, Cutrona, & Jones, 1986). The shy person may make an invidious comparison between herself and the socially self-confident person. As a result, the perceived discrepancy between the shy person's own performance and his or her ideal standard of social competence may become painfully salient (Carver & Scheier, 1986). Therefore, we expected that shy subjects paired with nonshy subjects would experience the most difficulties during the social interaction. It should be noted that previous experiments involving dyadic interactions have paired shy subjects with confederates (e.g., Asendorpf, 1987; Pilkonis, 1977) or with other shy subjects (e.g., Cheek & Buss, 1981), so that the present design adds a dimension to this type of shyness research.

To summarize, the issues discussed above suggest three hypotheses that need to be tested:

1. Shy subjects will report spending more time engaged in self-focused attention during an interaction with a stranger than those who are not shy; the cognitive content of this self-focusing will indicate anxious self-preoccupation.
2. Shy subjects' self-ratings following an interaction with a stranger will be more negative than ratings of them made by their conversational partner.
3. Shy subjects who conversed with nonshy partners will experience more anxiety and inhibition during the interaction than shy subjects who conversed with shy partners.

METHOD

Subjects and Procedure

Sixty-four female first-year college students participated in the study. To obtain a full range of shyness scores and to minimize the possibility of previous acquaintance, participants were solicited by a campus mailing sent to freshmen chosen at random from the student directory. Each subject was paid $4.00 for one hour of participation in the study.

Subjects completed the shyness pretest, conversed with a stranger, and responded to the dependent measures all in one session. First, subjects completed a questionnaire packet containing the shyness measure (described below) and a variety of filler items from other personality inventories which were included to keep subjects from focusing their attention on shyness. During this phase of the procedure, subjects were located in separate rooms and did not know that they were about to engage in a social interaction.

After completion of the questionnaires, subjects were introduced to each other by a female experimenter. None were previously acquainted. The experimenter informed the subjects that they were to get acquainted and that they could discuss anything except the experiment itself. Subjects were left to converse for 5 minutes. The interaction ended upon the experimenter's return. At that time, subjects were asked to complete the dependent measures (described below) in separate rooms. Finally, subjects were paid, given a full explanation of the study and thanked for their participation.

Measures

Shyness. The Cheek & Buss (1981) Shyness Scale measures the degree of discomfort and inhibition an individual typically experiences during social interactions. In a laboratory study, high scorers on the scale talked less and reported more unpleasant feelings than did low scorers. In this study, a 20-item revision of the original 9-item scale was used to assess symptoms representing the somatic (e.g., "I feel tense when I'm with people I don't know well"), behavioral (e.g., "I am socially somewhat awkward"), and cognitive (e.g., "I feel painfully self-conscious when I'm around strangers") components of shyness (Cheek & Melchior, 1985). The 20-item scale has an alpha coefficient of .94 and correlates .96 with the original 9-item version. In a sample of 31 college women, the revised scale had a 45-day test-retest reliability of .91 and correlated .69 with aggregated ratings of shyness received from family members and close friends. The revised scale consists of 20 5-point self-ratings scaled from 1 (very uncharacteristic) to 5 (very characteristic).

Dependent Measures

Following the dyadic interaction, subjects were instructed to complete the following set of measures. Although only five minutes elapsed between completion of the pretest package and the post-session questionnaire, the two sets of measures were not redundant. The Shyness Scale is a reliable measure of dispositional shyness, as demonstrated by its 45-day test-retest reliability ($r=.91$). In addition, subjects' responses on the Shyness Scale were made without knowledge of the upcoming experimental interaction, whereas the dependent measures referred specifically to reactions to that conversation.

Self-focusing. Following the dyadic interaction, distribution of attention was measured by asking subjects to divide the focus of their thoughts during the conversation (i.e., "I spent ____ % of the time focusing on what my partner was saying or doing; I spent ____ % of the time thinking about what I was going to say next or about what kind of impression I was making.") This method has been used previously in self-consciousness research (Christensen, 1982).

Cognitive content during the interaction. Subjects completed an inventory designed to tap self-relevant thoughts during the interaction. This measure, Hartman's (1984) Social Anxiety Thoughts Questionnaire, was originally intended to be a trait measure of anxiety. In the present study, however, the instructions were adapted to measure self-focusing during the experimental interaction. The 21 items on this scale indicate thoughts about general psychological discomfort, social incompetence, concerns about others' awareness of the subject's anxiety, fear of negative evaluation, and self-perceptions of the subject's own anxiety symptoms. Possible scores on each item ranged from 1 (never) to 5 (always). The Social Anxiety Thoughts Scale has a reliability coefficient equal to .94.

Post-session composite rating of shyness symptoms. Additional items were complied to determine subjects' impressions of themselves and their partners during the conversation. Based on post-interaction ratings used by Cheek and Buss (1981) and Curran, Wallander, and Fischetti (1980), we asked subjects to rate how self-conscious, awkward, inhibited, confident (reverse-scored) and relaxed (reverse-scored) they felt during the interaction, as well as how they perceived their partners on the same dimensions. The possible range of scores on each item equals 1 (not at all) to 5 (extremely). The 5-item composite of self-ratings yielded an alpha coefficient of .89; its corresponding 5-item composite of partner ratings had an alpha of .87.

Directing the conversation. To measure a behavioral consequence of shyness, we asked subjects to rate themselves and their partners on the extent to which each person directed the conversation on the same 5-point scale as the post-session composite (1=not at all to 5=extremely; Miell & LeVoi, 1985).

Plan for analyses. Because subjects had been randomly assigned to dyads, shy and nonshy groups were defined by a median split on the shyness scale. The median score was 50. Three subjects scored exactly 50 on the shyness scale; therefore those subjects and the subjects with whom they conversed were excluded from the analysis. This yielded a final sample of 58 (29 shy and 29 nonshy). The mean shyness score for this sample was 53.6. When broken down by dyadic pairings, there were 18 shy subjects paired with shy partners (9 dyads), 11 shy subjects paired with nonshy partners (11 dyads), and 18 nonshy subjects paired with nonshy partners (9 dyads).

We expected that at least some of the dependent measures would correlate significantly with each other, so the first step in our plan for analyses was to create a correlation matrix for all measures employed in the study. Second, the entire set of dependent measures was subjected to a 2 x 2 MANOVA, with subject's level of shyness and partner's level of shyness serving as the classification factors. Third, to test the hypothesis that shy subjects would rate themselves more negatively than their partners would rate them, paired t-tests were planned to compare post-session self-ratings with ratings made by their partners for both groups of shy subjects. Finally, to test the third hypothesis that shy subjects paired with nonshy partners would experience more difficulties than shy subjects paired with shy partners, comparisons were planned between these two groups for all dependent measures (e.g., Hays, 1973, pp. 515-517, 581-612).

TABLE 1   Correlations Among All Measures

	1	2	3	4	5	6
1. Shyness Scale (pretest measure)	—					
2. Percentage of time self-focusing	.48**	—				
3. Social Anxiety Thoughts questionnaire	.68**	.57**	—			
4. Post-session composite self-rating of shyness symptoms	.68**	.65**	.73**	—		
5. Post-session composite rating by partner of shyness symptoms	.18	.16	.11	.20	—	
6. Directed the conversation (self-rating)	-.12	.03	-.10	-.19	-.12	—
7. Directed the conversation (rating by partner)	-.15	.00	-.01	-.11	-.33*	.33*

Note: $N = 58$.
**$p < .001$; *$p < .05$.

RESULTS

The correlations among all measures for the entire sample of subjects are presented in Table 1. The Shyness Scale pretest measure correlated significantly with three of the four post-session self-report dependent measures, but not with either of the partner's ratings. Three of the self-report dependent measures—percentage of time spent self-focusing, the Social Anxiety Thoughts Questionnaire, and post-session composite self-rating—had highly significant positive intercorrelations (see Table 1).

The cell means for the four experimental groups on each dependent measure are presented in Table 2. The Subject's Level of Shyness x Partner's Level of Shyness MANOVA yielded a significant overall main effect for Subject's Level of shyness (Pallais value = .28, approximate F = 3.19, $p < .05$), and no other significant effects. Results from the univariate ANOVAs for each dependent measure are reported in Table 2. Significant main effects for Subject's Level of Shyness were obtained on three dependent variables: shy subjects spent more time self-focusing, reported more socially anxious thoughts, and rated themselves higher on the post-session composite measure of shyness symptoms that did nonshy subjects. Their partners also tended to rate the shy subjects higher on the post-session composite measure of shyness symptoms and to say that the shy subjects did not direct the conversation (ps < .10). There was one significant main effect for Partner's Level of Shyness. As can be seen in Table 2, nonshy subjects who interacted with shy subjects were rated the highest by their partners on the dimension of having directed the conversation. Finally, there were no significant Subject's Level of Shyness x Partner's Level of Shyness interactions.

Concerning the second hypothesis, examination of the cell means in Table 2 for the post-session composite ratings of shyness symptoms indicates that shy subjects who conversed with nonshy partners tended to rate themselves more negatively (M = 13.36) than their partners rated them (M = 10.91, t(10) = 2.15, p < .05, one-tailed). This comparison did not approach statistical significance for shy subjects (M = 11.33) who were rated by shy partners (M = 10.44).

Planned comparisons on all dependent measures between shy subjects paired with nonshy partners and shy subjects paired with shy partners were non-significant (note all subscripts in Table 2, columns 6 and 7). However, the discrepancies between those two groups on all of the dependent measures are in the direction predicted by the third hypothesis. That is, shy subjects paired with nonshy subjects did seem to experience more anxiety and inhibition during the conversation than did shy subjects paired with other shy subjects. The p values for four of the six comparisons could be considered as trends (.10 < p < .25). A binomial test (p = .016) suggests that these small but consistent differences across all six dependent measures may be meaningful rather than random (cf. Tivnan & Pillemer, 1978).

DISCUSSION

The finding that shy subjects reported spending significantly more time self-focusing during a social interaction than those who were not shy confirms empirically a long-standing speculation in the shyness literature (e.g., Campbell, 1896; Roback, 1933). Moreover, the results from the post-session self-reports on Hartman's (1984) Social Anxiety Thoughts Questionnaire provide strong support for Crozier's (1979, 1982) more recently elaborated model of shyness as a propensity for engaging in *anxious* self-preoccupation. The strong correlations between time engaged in self-focus and both the Social Anxiety Thoughts Questionnaire (r = .57) and the post-session self-ratings of shyness symptoms (r = .65) suggest that Asendorpf (1987) may have been premature in his conclusion that only negative thinking, and not self-focus per se, is crucial for dispositional shyness.

It is important to note that the existing research evidence on shyness and anxious self-preoccupation is relatively situation specific. Shy people have been found to focus excessively on negative self-perceptions when anticipating a social interaction with a stranger (Cacioppo et al., 1979), during such an interaction (i.e., the present findings; see also Asendorpf, 1987; Bruch, Gorsky, Collins, & Berger, 1989; Greene &

TABLE 2 Means and Analyses of Variance for Dependent Measures

Measure	F-ratios			Cell Means			
	Subject's Level of Shyness	Partner's Level of Shyness	Subject X Partner	Nonshy with Nonshy (n = 18)	Nonshy with Shy (n = 11)	Shy with Nonshy (n = 11)	Shy with Shy (n = 18)
Percentage of time spent self-focusing	7.76**	.34	1.54	19.17$_a$	22.27$_a$	38.18$_b$	29.56$_{ab}$
Social Anxiety Thoughts Questionnaire	12.52**	.39	.93	28.83$_a$	29.91$_{ab}$	43.27$_c$	38.17$_{bc}$
Post-session composite self-rating of shyness symptoms	16.73***	.77	1.69	8.33$_a$	8.73$_{ab}$	13.36$_c$	11.33$_{bc}$
Post-session composite rating of subject's shyness symptoms by partner	3.56^t	.12	.02	9.00$_a$	8.82$_a$	10.91$_a$	10.44$_a$
Self-rating of extent to which subject directed the conversation	2.05	2.91	.54	3.17$_{ab}$	3.36$_a$	2.73$_b$	3.22$_{ab}$
Partner's rating of extent to which subject directed the conversation	3.41^t	6.68*	.25	2.67$_a$	3.36$_b$	2.36$_a$	2.83$_{ab}$

Note: Means not sharing the same subscript differ at the $p < .05$ level. The range of possible scores for each dependent measure is described in the method section.

* $p < .05$; ** $p < .01$; *** $p < .001$; $^t p < .10$.

Sparks, 1983; Leary, 1986b), and soon afterwards (Breck & Smith, 1983; Steffen & Reckman, 1978). However, shyness tends to have only weak to moderate correlations with more global, dispositional measures of self-attention, such as private and public self-consciousness (rs = .10 and .26, respectively; Cheek & Buss, 1981), the poor attentional control daydreaming style (r = .20, Melchior & Cheek, 1984), and Murray's Narcissism Scale (r = .29, Cheek & Melchior, 1985).

Some critics have questioned the emphasis that recent cognitive theories of social behavior place on the role of acute self-awareness and conscious planning during interpersonal interactions (cf. Goffman, 1967). For example, Berger (1980) argued that, "if such a model were to underlie much of everyday interaction, I suspect that little conversation would ever take place!" (p. 52). Yet this seems to be exactly the shy person's predicament. Shy individuals seem to be so acutely self-conscious that they literally find themselves unable to interact with others due to their inappropriate distribution of attention. The degree of self-focus during a social interaction may be an important factor in differentiating shy people from the socially self-confident. For individuals who are not shy, the processes underlying social behavior may be habitual and more or less automatic (Briggs & Cheek, 1988; Cheek & Hogan, 1983). For those who worry about evaluation or poor performance in social situations, however, the planning of interactional strategies may be an extremely self-conscious, and therefore, disruptive process (Schlenker & Leary, 1982).

The present study also investigated two potential consequences of the shy person's propensity for becoming anxiously self-preoccupied during social interactions with strangers. The second hypothesis predicted that, consistent with previous research (e.g., Clark & Arkowitz, 1975), shy subjects would rate themselves more negatively than their partners would rate them. As can be seen in Table 2, shy subjects did tend to rate themselves higher on the composite index of shyness symptoms than their partners rated them, but this difference only approached significance for the comparison involving shy subjects who conversed with a nonshy partner ($p < .06$, two-tailed). The shy subjects paired with nonshy subjects also tended to rate themselves lower, and to receive lower ratings from their partners, on the behavioral dimension of the extent to which the subject directed the conversation. This pattern is congruent with previous research on the self-presentational strategy of shy people (Arkin, Lake, & Baumgardner, 1986).

The existing literature on ratings of shy people does contain some unresolved ambiguities. Ratings made by observers usually tend to be negative, but the degree and generality of these negative perceptions seem to vary with the *role* of the observer (e.g., experimenter's confederate or research assistant, co-participant in an experiment, college roommate, friend, parent, spouse, or professional counselor: Cheek et al., 1986; Gough & Thorne, 1986; Jones & Briggs, 1984). The self-ratings of shy people are, however, consistently and strongly negative. Moreover, shy people seem to cling to their negative self-perceptions by expressing doubts about the accuracy of positive feedback when it is given to them by friends or strangers (Asendorpf, 1987; Franzoi, 1983). The self-defeating cognitions and cautious self-presentation style of shy individuals creates a "vicious cycle" that deprives them of opportunities for experiencing social success and receiving approval from others (Arkin et al., 1986; Cheek et al., 1986).

The third hypothesis predicted that shy subjects who were paired with nonshy subjects would experience more anxiety and inhibition during interaction than shy subjects who were paired with shy partners. Although the results from all six dependent measures were in the expected direction, none of the comparisons reached the .05 level of significance. This pattern of findings does suggest that conversing with a socially self-confident partner may be a somewhat stronger shyness-eliciting situation than interacting with another shy person. Of course, all of the subjects in the present experiment were women. Interacting with a self-confident member of the opposite sex may be a more powerful shyness-eliciting manipulation and, presumably, would be more likely to produce statistically significant results (Russell et al., 1986; Zimbardo, 1977). We believe that future research should investigate the various possible combinations of shyness level and gender for both members of an interacting dyad because the personality characteristics of individuals involved in an interaction are a major determinant of the "situation" (e.g., Holland, 1985; Thorne, 1987).

One implication of the results of this study is that cognitive approaches to therapy may be appropriate for shy people who are excessively and painfully self-conscious. Techniques such as active listening, empathic responding, and decentering help shy people to shift their attention away from their distorted self-perceptions and anxious self-preoccupation and toward the demands of skillful interaction (Alden & Cappe, 1986; Hartman, 1986). Another method, cognitive restructuring, attempts to replace the shy individual's negative, self defeating thoughts with more positive cognitions (Glass & Shea, 1986). The most promising new direction for therapy appears to be developing combinations of cognitive, systematic desensitization, and social skills treatments, especially the possibility of matching treatment strategies to the shy individual's specific pattern of shyness symptoms (Cheek & Cheek, 1989; Turner & Beidel, 1985; Watson, 1986).

REFERENCES

Alden, L., & Cappe, R. (1986). Interpersonal process training for shy clients. In W.H. Jones, J.M. Cheek, & S.R. Briggs (Eds.), *Shyness: Perspectives on research and treatment* (pp. 343-355). New York: Plenum.

Arkin, R.M., Appelman, A.J., & Burger, J.M. (1980). Social anxiety, self-presentation, and self-serving bias in causal attribution. *Journal of Personality and Social Psychology, 38,* 23-35.

Arkin, R.M., Lake, E.A. & Baumgardner, A.B. (1986). Shyness and self-presentation. In W.H. Jones, J.M. Cheek, & S.R. Briggs (Eds.), *Shyness: Perspectives on research and treatment* (pp. 189-203). New York: Plenum

Arnold, A.P., & Cheek, J.M. (1986). Shyness, self-preoccupation, and the Stroop color and word test. *Personality and Individual Differences, 7,* 571-573.

Asendorpf, J.B. (1987). Videotape reconstruction of emotions and cognitions related to shyness. *Journal of Personality and Social Psychology, 53,* 542-549.

Berger, C.R. (1980). Self-consciousness and the study of interpersonal interactions: Approaches and issues. In H. Giles, W.P. Robinson, & P. Smith (Eds.), *Language: Social Psychological Perspectives* (pp. 49-53). Oxford: Pergamon Press.

Breck, B.E., & Smith, S.H. (1983). Selective recall of self-descriptive traits by socially anxious and nonanxious females. *Social Behavior and Personality, 11,* 71-76.

Briggs, S.R., & Cheek, J.M. (1988). On the nature of self-monitoring: Problems with assessment, problems with validity. *Journal of Personality and Social Psychology, 54,* 663-678.

Bruch, M.A., Gorsky, J.M., Collins, T.M., & Berger, P.A. (1989). Shyness and sociability reexamined: A multicomponent analysis. *Journal of Personality and Social Psychology, 57,* 904-915.

Buss, A.H. (1980). *Self-consciousness and social anxiety.* San Francisco: Freeman.

Buss, A.H. (1984). A conception of shyness. In J.A. Daly & J.C. McCroskey (Eds.), *Avoiding Communication: Shyness, reticence, and communication apprehension* (pp. 39-49). Beverly Hills, CA: Sage.

Cacioppo, J.T., Glass, C.R., & Merluzzi, T.V. (1979). Self-statements and self-evaluation: A cognitive response analysis of heterosocial anxiety. *Cognitive Therapy and Research, 3,* 249-262.

Campbell, H. (1896). Morbid shyness. *British Medical Journal, 2,* 805-807.

Carver, C.S., & Scheier, M.F. (1986). Analyzing shyness: A specific application of broader self-regulatory principles. In W.H. Jones, J.M. Cheek, & S.R. Briggs (Eds.), *Shyness: Perspectives on research and treatment* (pp. 173-185). New York: Plenum.

Cheek, J.M., & Buss, A.H. (1981). Shyness and sociability. *Journal of Personality and Social Psychology, 41,* 330-339.

Cheek, J.M., & Cheek, B. (1989). *Conquering shyness.* New York: Putnam.

Cheek, J.M., & Hogan, R. (1983). Self-concepts, self-presentations, and moral judgments. In J. Suls & A.G. Greenwald (Eds.), *Psychological perspectives on the self* (vol. 2, pp. 249-273). Hillsdale, NJ: Erlbaum.

Cheek, J.M., & Melchior, L.A. (1985, August). *Measuring the three components of shyness.* Paper presented at the meeting of the American Psychological Association, Los Angeles.

Cheek, J.M., & Melchior, L.A. (1990). Shyness, self-esteem and self-consciousness. In H. Leitenberg (Ed.), *Handbook of social and evaluation anxiety* (pp. 47-82). New York: Plenum.

Cheek, J.M., Melchior, L.A., & Carpentieri, A.M. (1986). Shyness and self-concept. In L.M. Hartman & K.R. Blankstein (Eds.), *Perception of self in emotional disorder and psychotherapy* (pp. 113-131). New York: Plenum.

Cheek, J.M., & Stahl, S.S. (1986). Shyness and verbal creativity. *Journal of Research in Personality, 20*, 51-61.
Cheek, J.M., & Watson, A.K. (1989). The definition of shyness: Psychological Imperialism or construct validity? *Journal of Social Behavior and Personality, 4*, 85-95.
Christensen, D. (1982). The relationship between self-consciousness and interpersonal effectiveness and a new scale to measure individual differences in self-consciousness. *Personality and Individual Differences, 3*, 177-188.
Clark, J.V., & Arkowitz, H. (1975). Social anxiety and self-evaluation of interpersonal performance. *Psychological Reports, 36*, 211-221.
Crozier, W.R. (1979). Shyness as anxious self-preoccupation. *Psychological Reports, 44*, 959-962.
Crozier, W.R. (1982). Explanations of social shyness. *Current Psychological Reviews, 2*, 47-60.
Curran J.P., Wallander, J.L., & Fischetti, M. (1980). The importance of behavioral and cognitive factors in heterosexual-social anxiety. *Journal of Personality, 48*, 285-292.
Davis, D. (1982). Determinants of responsiveness in dyadic interaction. In W. Ickes & E.S. Knowles (Eds.), *Personality, roles, and social behavior* (pp. 85-139). New York: Springer-Verlag.
Feffer, M., & Suchotliff, L. (1966). Decentering implications of social interaction. *Journal of Personality and Social Psychology, 4*, 415-422.
Franzoi, S.L.,(1983). Self-concept differences as a function of private self-consciousness and social anxiety. *Journal of Research in Personality, 17*, 275-287.
Geen, R.G. (1985). Test anxiety and visual vigilance. *Journal of Personality and Social Psychology, 49*, 963-970.
Glass, C.R., & Shea, C.A. (1986). Cognitive therapy for shyness and social anxiety. In W.H. Jones, J.M. Cheek, & S.R. Briggs (Eds.), *Shyness: Perspectives on research and treatment* (pp. 315-327). New York: Plenum.
Goffman, E. (1967). *Interaction ritual.* Garden City, NY: Anchor Press.
Goldfried, M.R., Padawer, W., & Robins, C. (1984). Social anxiety and the semantic structure of heterosocial interactions. *Journal of Abnormal Psychology, 93*, 87-97.
Goldfried, M.R., & Sobocinski, D. (1975). Effect of irrational beliefs on emotional arousal. *Journal of Consulting and Clinical Psychology, 43*, 504-510.
Gormally, J., Sipps, G., Raphael, R., Edwin, D. & Varvil-Weld, D. (1981). The relationship between maladaptive cognitions and social anxiety. *Journal of Consulting and Clinical Psychology, 49*, 300-301.
Gough, H.G., & Thorne, A. (1986). Positive, negative, and balanced shyness: Self-definitions and the reactions of others. In W.H. Jones, J.M. Cheek, and S.R. Briggs (Eds.), *Shyness: Perspectives on research and treatment* (pp. 205-225). New York: Plenum.
Greene, J.O., & Sparks, G.S. (1983). Explication and test of a cognitive model of communication apprehension: A new look at an old construct. *Human Communication Research, 9*, 349-366.
Hartman, L.M. (1983). A metacognitive model of social anxiety: Implications for treatment. *Clinical Psychology Review, 3*, 435-456.
Hartman, L.M. (1984). Cognitive components of social anxiety. *Journal of Clinical Psychology, 40*, 137-139.
Hartman, L.M. (1986). Social anxiety, problem drinking, and self-awareness. In L.M. Hartman & K.R. Blankstein (Eds.), *Perception of self in emotional disorder and psychotherapy* (pp. 265-282). New York: Plenum.
Hays, W.L. (1973). *Statistics for the social sciences* (2nd ed.). New York: Holt, Rinehart & Winston.
Holland, J.L. (1985). *Making vocational choices* (2nd ed.). Englewood Cliffs, NJ: Prentice-Hall.
Jones, W.H., & Briggs, S.R. (1984). The self-other discrepancy in social shyness. In R. Schwarzer (Ed.), *The self in anxiety, stress, and depression* (pp. 93-107). Amsterdam: North Holland.

Leary, M.R. (1983). *Understanding social anxiety: Social, personality, and clinical Perspectives*. Beverly Hills, CA: Sage.
Leary, M.R. (1986a). Affective and behavioral components of shyness. In W.H. Jones, J.M. Cheek, & S.R. Briggs (Eds.), *Shyness: Perspectives on research and treatment* (pp. 27-38). New York: Plenum.
Leary, M.R. (1986b). The impact of interactional impediments on social anxiety and self-presentation. *Journal of Experimental Social Psychology, 22*, 22-135.
Melchior, L.A., & Cheek, J.M. (1984). *Shyness, self-consciousness, and daydreaming styles*. Unpublished manuscript, Wellesley College.
Miell, D. & LeVoi, M. (1985). Self-monitoring and control in dyadic interactions. *Journal of Personality and Social Psychology, 49*, 1652-1661.
Pilkonis, P.A. (1977). the behavioral consequences of shyness. *Journal of Personality, 45*, 596-611.
Roback, A.A. (1933). *Self-consciousness and its treatment*. Cambridge, MA: Sci-Art Publishers.
Russell, D., Cutrona, C. & Jones, W.H. (1986). A trait-situational analysis of shyness. In W.H. Jones, J.M. Cheek, & S.R. Briggs, (Eds.), *Shyness: Perspectives on research and treatment* (pp. 239-249). New York: Plenum.
Sarason, I.G. (1984). Stress, anxiety, and cognitive interference: Reactions to tests. *Journal of Personality and Social Psychology, 46*, 929-938.
Schlenker, B.R., & Leary, M.R. (1982). Social anxiety and self-presentation: A conceptualization and model. *Psychological Bulletin, 92*, 641-669.
Smith, T.W., Ingram, R.E., & Brehm, S.S. (1983). Social anxiety, anxious self-preoccupation, and recall of self-relevant information. *Journal of Personality and Social Psychology, 44*, 1276-1283.
Steffen, J.J., & Reckman, R.F. (1978). Selective perception and interpretation of interpersonal cues in dyadic interactions. *Journal of Psychology, 99*, 245-248.
Thorne, A. (1987). The press of personality: Conversations between introverts and extroverts. *Journal of Personality and Social Psychology, 53*, 718-726.
Tivnan, T., & Pillemer, D.B. (1978). The importance of small but consistent group differences on standardized tests. *Journal of Clinical Psychology, 34*, 443-445.
Turner, S.M., & Beidel, D.C. (1985). Empirically derived subtypes of social anxiety. *Behavior Therapy, 16*, 384-392.
Watson, A.K. (1986). Alleviation of communication apprehension: An individualized approach. *Texas Speech Communication Journal, 11*, 3-13.
Zimbardo, P.G. (1977). *Shyness*. Reading, MA: Addison-Wesley.

Self-Disclosure and Social Perception: The Impact of Private, Negative, and Extreme Communications

Linda E. Lazowski
*Department of Psychology, Indiana University
Bloomington, IN 47405*

Susan M. Andersen
*Department of Psychology, New York University
6 Washington Place, 4th Fl., New York, NY 10003*

This research assessed the impact of three properties of self-disclosure "depth" (Altman & Taylor, 1973) on the impressions and evaluative responses that listener-observers formulated about an individual speaker. Listeners were exposed to a videotaped communication that varied in terms of its privacy, negativity, and extremity. Listeners' dispositional inferences about the speaker, perceptions of the informativeness of the disclosure, and liking and predicted comfort in interacting with the speaker were then assessed. Based on a social-cognitive analysis, we predicted that observers' impressions would be more influenced by private (cognitive/affective) vs. public (behavioral), negative vs. positive, and extreme vs. moderate disclosures. An interaction between disclosure negativity and privacy was also predicted, based on the notion that negative behavioral disclosures may seem to have especially threatening implications for the listener. The data largely supported these predictions. Listeners were far more influenced by negative than positive disclosures, as indicated on all three measures, and clearly perceived disclosures of thoughts and feelings as more informative than behavioral disclosures. Their dispositional inferences yielded the predicted interaction, which showed that disclosures concerning negative behaviors led to stronger dispositional inferences than did those concerning positive behaviors, while disclosure valence had no significant impact on the strength of inferences drawn from disclosures of thoughts and feelings. Disclosures of negative thoughts and feelings, however, were no less impactful than were disclosures of negative behaviors. The probable social-perception consequences of engaging in "deep" self-disclosure are discussed, as are the mechanisms that may mediate these effects, and their potential boundary conditions.

Authors' Note: The authors would like to thank Tom Golbetz for his painstaking rehearsal and delivery of each disclosure protocol. Special thanks also go to David Heise, Wim Liebrand, David Schneider, Jim Sherman, Peggy Thoits, and anonymous reviewers for their helpful comments on an earlier draft of this manuscript. Address correspondence to either author.

© 1990 Select Press

To a large degree, the impressions we form of other people are based on the information they are willing to disclose to us about themselves. Self-disclosing communications are presumably those that listeners perceive as intimate and revealing about a speaker (Jourard & Jaffe, 1970). "Deep" self-disclosures (cf. Altman & Taylor, 1973) should allow listeners to come to know a speaker, or to form an elaborated impression of him or her. Self-disclosure research has yet to assess the properties of a communication that actually lead listeners to perceive it as disclosing and to form an impression of the speaker based upon it; prior research has tended to focus instead on interpersonal attraction (e.g., Berg & Archer, 1980; Chaikin & Derlega, 1974) and reciprocity (e.g., Archer & Berg, 1978; Brewer & Mittelman, 1980; Cozby, 1972; Derlega, Harris, & Chaikin, 1973). Thus, the broader social-perception consequences of intimate communication are not known.

One important social consequence of self-disclosing communications is the affective impact they have on listeners. For example, some self-disclosing communications may lead listeners to view the speaker as similar to themselves and therefore, as predictable and understandable. Because familiarity is associated with positive affect (Zajonc, 1980), these disclosures may reduce anxiety in listeners and generally increase comfort and interpersonal attraction (cf. Derlega, 1984). By contrast, some disclosures, especially those that disconfirm listeners' expectancies, may increase uncertainty rather than dispel it (Planalp & Honeycutt, 1985; Planalp, Rutherford, & Honeycutt, 1988), perhaps leading to increased anxiety and stress, and decreased interpersonal attraction (cf. Berger & Calabrese, 1975; Miller, 1980). Communications that increase uncertainty and unpredictability in social relationships may lead listeners to feel a greater need to make sense of the speaker by attributing personal motives and dispositions to him or her, without which he or she ultimately cannot be predicted or understood. Thus, although it has been suggested that engaging in "honest self-disclosure," which often entails revealing negative aspects of the self, encourages relationship development and intimacy (Derlega, 1984), it is important to assess the circumstances under which this is true by examining the consequences of such communications for the impressions that listeners ultimately form of the disclosing individual.

As an example, negative disclosures may be considered "deep," but if they communicate the speaker's hostility toward other individuals, they are also likely to be threatening to listeners. This may occur not only because these communications violate the expectancy that the speaker is a predictable individual, but also because listeners may become fearful or anxious about any anticipated harm that may befall them in interactions with the disclosing person (cf. Lazarus & Averill, 1972). Furthermore, such communications may even elicit the expectation of potentially having to respond to the speaker by fighting back or somehow defending oneself. Other types of negative disclosures, particularly those that involve personal vulnerabilities and problems rather than deliberate harm to others, may, in fact, promote interpersonal attraction (Lazowski, 1988). Research is clearly needed to systematically track the relationship between various types of disclosure content and listeners' impressions of disclosing individuals. The present study was designed to identify the qualities of self-disclosing communications that lead listeners to perceive communications as informative, to make inferences about the speaker's personal dispositions, and to predict liking and comfort in subsequent interactions with the speaker.

In Altman and Taylor's (1973) model of social penetration processes, the "depth" of a personal communication is defined by several factors. One such factor is the personal nature of the communication, i.e., the privacy of the information it conveys. Altman and Taylor (1973) proposed that "low visibility" aspects of the self such as motives, feelings, and fantasies are more revealing about the self than are public sources of information that are more readily available to observers, such as one's behaviors.

Interestingly, research in the area of *self*-perception suggests that private sources of information such as one's own thoughts and feelings have considerably more impact on self-judgments than do overt behaviors (Andersen, 1984; Andersen & Ross, 1984; Andersen, Lazowski, & Donisi, 1986; Andersen & Williams, 1985). That is, people seem to believe that their thoughts and feelings make up their "core" self, or that which is essential about their own character. Because we experience our thoughts and feelings as occurring "within" us, we may see them as inextricably linked to the self (Andersen, 1987; Andersen & Ross, 1984). Many conceivable mechanisms may contribute to this perception; one is the privacy dimension, i.e., the subjective assumption that one's thoughts and feelings stem from "within" and not from social pressures and constraints.

Research on the manner in which *observers* use cognitive/affective and behavioral information in social judgments has been quite sparse. In fact, most social perception research has tended to emphasize the manner in which perceivers evaluate an actor's overt *behaviors* rather than how they evaluate actors' *communications*, particularly communications of cognitions and affects. One potential reason for this focus on behaviors is that they are concrete and visible, observers can easily attend to them (cf. Jones & Nisbett, 1972; Nisbett & Ross, 1980), and experimenters can readily measure them. By contrast, thoughts and feelings are less accessible to outside observers and are often available only when the speaker communicates them. In a self-disclosure context, however, cognitions, affects, and behaviors can be examined while equalizing the differences that normally exist in how perceptually salient overt behavior is to an outside observer relative to cognitions and affects. Both types of information about the self are communicated rather than enacted *in vivo*. Hence, self-disclosure provides a unique context for assessing the role of cognitions, affects, and behaviors in *social perception*.

Given the demonstrated importance of thoughts and feelings in self-inference processes, it could be argued that observers might also feel convinced that they have access to a speaker's "core" self when the speaker discloses thoughts and feelings. In fact, listeners do perceive disclosed thoughts and feelings to be more intimate and informative than disclosed behaviors (Andersen, 1984; Andersen & Ross, 1984; Runge & Archer, 1981). Thus, although some evidence exists to suggest that people believe their own thoughts and feelings are more important and predominant in their self-conceptions than thoughts and feelings are in *others'* self-conceptions (cf. Andersen & Ross, 1984; Johnson, 1987), observers nonetheless do tend to consider an actor's cognitions and affects to be more informative about the actor than his or her behaviors. Disclosed thoughts and feelings are likely to give listeners information not easily obtained simply by observing the person. Thus they may seem particularly diagnostic and may play a crucial role in subsequent impressions.

It is still possible, however, that certain conditions may exist in which an actual reversal of this pattern can be found, i.e., a reversal in the greater perceived diagnosticity of disclosed thoughts and feelings over behaviors. In particular, communicating about negative acts may be more informative than communicating about negative thoughts and feelings, because "bad" deeds have greater social consequences than "bad" thoughts. Although thoughts and feelings may generally be viewed as more revealing of one's character than are overt behaviors (cf. Andersen, 1984), it is possible that when the disclosed information is negative, the greater consequentialness of negative deeds relative to negative thoughts and feelings may figure centrally in perceivers' judgments about the speaker's dispositions (cf. Fiske, 1980; Reeder, 1985). When a speaker discloses that he or she has engaged in behaviors that have harmful consequences for other individuals, for example, he or she is disclosing a particularly unexpected and unaccountable set of responses relative to positive behaviors. Because positive behaviors toward others are expected as part of the basic fabric of society and social interaction (Jones

& Davis, 1965), negative behaviors are particularly likely to challenge listeners' expectancies and to produce uncertainty. Hence communications about negative behaviors may be especially likely to invoke dispositional inquiry in an effort to reduce uncertainty and to gain a sense of predictability about the speaker. By contrast, most people recognize that they experience a great deal of unexpressed affect, particularly negative affect (Johnson, 1987). Hearing a disclosure that an individual has privately experienced *negative* affects may seem to be no more diagnostic than hearing that he or she has privately experienced positive affects. For these reasons, the relative impact of cognitive/affective and behavioral communications on social perception when varying affective valence, warrants further consideration.

Along these lines, Altman and Taylor (1973) also suggested that affective valence contributes independently to the "depth" of a communication. The communication of negative information is not common in day to day interactions; hence, it may always seem relevant and informative to listeners. Research in social cognition has demonstrated that information valence is crucial in shaping perceivers' impressions of and liking for target individuals (e.g., Asch, 1946; Hamilton & Zanna, 1972; Jones & Davis, 1965; Kanouse & Hanson, 1972; Ostrom & Davis, 1979; Skowronski & Carlston, 1987, 1989). Unfavorable information about an individual is attended to longer than is positive information. It has a disproportional impact on impressions (Fiske, 1980) and interpersonal attraction (Fiske, 1980; Hamilton & Zanna, 1972); and it creates impressions that are quite resistant to later improvement (Reeder & Coovert, 1986; Richey, Richey, & Theiman, 1972). Such negativity effects may extend into the domain of self-disclosure, in that although disclosing negative rather than positive information may be perceived as more intimate, it may still lead to less liking (Gilbert & Horenstein, 1975; Runge & Archer, 1981), particularly when the speaker seems responsible for the negative event disclosed (Wortman, Adesman, Herman, & Greenberg, 1976). Thus, contrary to cultural notions that listeners are (and should be) supportive and sympathetic when others disclose unfavorable information about themselves, research suggests that social perceivers may often come to dislike individuals who characterize themselves using their negative experiences or attributes.

In listening to at least some kinds of negative disclosure, listeners may come to feel threatened or anxious about the potential harm that they begin to anticipate might happen to them if they were to interact with the speaker (cf. Lazarus & Averill, 1972). Similarly, most negative disclosures are likely to violate expectancies and hence to produce uncertainty, unpredictability, and stress in the listener (Miller, 1980). In this sense, the communication of negative information in interpersonal relations should generally lead to stronger dispositional inferences about the speaker, to greater perceived informativeness, and to a greater sense of disliking and discomfort than the communication of positive information (see also Gilbert & Horenstein, 1975; Runge & Archer, 1981). Of course, the precise explanation for negativity effects is not clear in the literature. These effects may, in fact, be multiply determined by informational processes (e.g., salience) and by motivationally based processes (e.g., a desire to protect oneself). In the present study, we sought to examine the social-perception consequences of negative and positive communications, both independently and in interaction with the cognitive/affective versus behavioral nature of the communicated information.

Finally, the extremity or uniqueness of disclosed information has also been suggested as a facet of self-disclosure "depth." Information that distinguishes individuals from one another rather than information that points out commonalities is said to be particularly intimate and revealing (cf. Altman & Taylor, 1973). Research in social cognition suggests that atypical information, because it is unexpected, may stand out and be given disproportional weight. Such information may even be processed differently than is more typical or expected information (e.g., Bargh & Thein, 1985; Fiske, 1980; Hastie & Kumar, 1979; Heise & MacKinnon, 1987; Pyszczynski & Greenberg, 1981; Srull & Wyer, 1980; Warr & Jackson, 1975). Extreme information, in fact, may be especially likely to have an impact on social judgments when it is negative (Fiske, 1980; Kanouse & Hanson, 1972; Skowronski & Carlston, 1987, 1989; Warr, 1974; Warr & Jackson, 1975), just as negative information may be especially likely to have an impact when it is extreme. In this sense, negativity and extremity are related; both contribute to information salience (Fiske, 1980; Nisbett & Ross, 1980; Taylor & Fiske, 1978; see also Altman & Taylor, 1973). Extremity was examined in the present design, in part, because unexpected information ought to provoke dispositional inferences (cf. Jones & Davis, 1965; Pyszczynski & Greenberg, 1981), just as negative information ought to do so. In addition, social-cognition research suggests that the extremity and negativity of communicated information ought to interact in influencing listeners' inferences about the speaker.

In sum, the present study examined listeners' responses to three dimensions of self-disclosure content by measuring their dispositional inferences about the speaker, their perceptions of disclosure informativeness, and their predicted liking and comfort in interacting with the speaker. Our central measure of disclosure depth was listeners' willingness to go beyond the information given and make inferences about the speaker's personality. This measure is sensitive to subtle changes in listeners' trait-based impressions of the speaker, and is scored in a way that is far less obvious to subjects than are typical Likert-type rating scales. Assessing actual dispositional inferences is important because they reflect perceivers' judgments and expectations about the speaker and their likely future behavior toward him or her (cf. Averett & Heise, 1987; Jones & Davis, 1965; Lazowski, Heise, & Smith-Lovin, 1989; Snyder, 1984; Snyder & Swann, 1978). We also included direct informativeness ratings as a secondary measure of self-disclosure depth, and ratings of liking and predicted comfort in interacting with the speaker as an index of evaluative responses to the speaker and the potential for later social rejection.

METHOD

Overview

Subjects viewed 1 of 16 videotaped disclosure sessions in which a speaker offered a personal communication to an off-camera individual during an alleged "peer encounter session." Each disclosure had been constructed in advance from a generic set of situational events so that only the target's specific reactions to the situation varied. Two generic disclosure stories were constructed, each containing ten manipulated statements, all delivered by the same male confederate. Observer subjects were run in a 2 X 2 X 2 X 2 (Privacy X Negativity X Extremity X Disclosure Scenario) factorial design. After viewing the disclosure, subjects (a) assessed its informativeness; (b) made a series of trait ratings about the speaker reflecting both the number of dispositional inferences they felt they could make based on the disclosure and the strength of these inferences; and (c) assessed their liking for him.

Participants

Subjects were 144 undergraduates (48 men and 96 women) who received course credit for their participation in this study. (No significant gender differences emerged.) Subjects were randomly assigned to 1 of 16 experimental conditions in a 2 X 2 X 2 X 2 (Privacy X Negativity X Extremity X Scenario) factorial design.

Materials

Two sets of eight self-disclosure protocols were constructed in which a male speaker recounted either an experience he'd had with an elderly man on a fishing trip or an incident at home in which he was awakened three times during the night by his neighbor's dog. In the fishing trip scenario, the speaker met a man who owned a store on the dock of a lake and who rented out boats from the store. The speaker recounted meeting the man, renting a boat, going out onto the lake, and then returning the boat. In the alternative scenario, the speaker described his reactions to being awakened in the night by a barking dog.

In both scenarios, the speaker described reactions that varied in their privacy,[1] that is, in whether they consisted of cognitions and affects or overt behaviors. Disclosure statements in the thoughts and feelings conditions consisted of *wishes* to engage in certain overt behaviors; by contrast, the speaker disclosed that he had actually *performed* these same behaviors in the behavioral condition.[2] The reactions the speaker described also varied in their positivity or negativity, which we operationalized in this study as kindness or hostility. Finally, the speaker's reactions also differed in extremity, that is, in the degree to which they were typical and ordinary or were extreme and unusual. The generic content of all of these communications and the number of communicated statements was held constant across conditions. Table 1 presents two of the ten disclosure statements as they appeared in each condition for each scenario.

To investigate the role of these factors in disclosure-based social perception, we asked a male undergraduate to rehearse each disclosure extensively before delivering it while being recorded on videotape. In each of the 16 videotaped disclosures (8 for each scenario), the confederate wore the same clothing and sat at the same desk recounting his story to an alleged listener who made no comments and was not visible on camera.

Pretest

Each disclosure protocol was assessed in advance by pretest subjects who rated all eight protocols concerning the fishing trip (N = 22); or all eight protocols concerning the barking dog (N = 16). In each case, the protocols were presented to the judges in random order. Explicit cognitive/affective and behavioral terminology was used to manipulate the "privacy" of the disclosure statements, a technique that reliably produces differences in perceived "visibility" (cf. Andersen, Lazowski, & Donisi, 1986). Subjects' ratings of disclosure valence were made on a bipolar scale ranging from "-2" ("completely negative") to "+2" ("completely

---

[1] *We use the term privacy to refer to the fact that cognitions and affects tend to occur "within" the person whereas behaviors tend to occur "outside" the person, even though behaviors can clearly be performed privately, just as thoughts and feelings can be nonverbally leaked and verbally communicated.*

[2] *This provides for a conservative test of the cognitive/affective superiority hypothesis since thoughts and feelings in the form of behavioral intentions may have less impact on dispositional inferences than do more general perceptions and evaluations of events, people, and situations, at least for actors (Andersen, Lazowski & Donisi, 1986; Andersen & Williams, 1985); this definition of cognitions and affects may therefore decrease the likelihood of our obtaining cognitive/affective effects in the present study.*

TABLE 1 Two Sample Self-Disclosure Statements as they Appeared in Each Scenario

Scenario A: Reactions to an elderly man at a lake
PRIVATE DISCLOSURES

Negative Statements

Extreme Statements:
1. I felt like telling him that I practically hated him, that I disliked him more than anyone I'd met in a long time.
2. I wanted to climb in the boat, shove him aside, and start the engine myself.

Moderate Statements:
1. I felt like telling him that he was really a pretty weird guy.
2. I felt irritated at his fumbling and wanted to start the engine myself.

Positive Statements

Extreme Statements:
1. I felt like telling him that I practically loved him, that I liked him more than anyone I'd met in a long time.
2. I felt so concerned that he might hurt himself that I wanted to gently help him to sit down and start the engine for him.

Moderate Statements:
1. I felt like telling him that he was really a pretty nice guy.
2. I felt like I wanted to give him a hand.

PUBLIC DISCLOSURES

Negative Statements

Extreme Statements:
1. I told him that I practically hated him, that I disliked him more than anyone I'd met in a long time.
2. I climbed in the boat, shoved him aside, and started the engine myself.

Moderate Statements:
1. I told him that he was really a pretty weird guy.
2. I remarked on his fumbling and started the engine myself.

Positive Statements

Extreme Statements:
1. I told him that I practically loved him, that I liked him more than anyone I'd met in a long time.
2. I climbed in the boat, gently helped him to sit down, and started the engine for him.

Moderate Statements:
1. I told him that he was really a pretty nice guy.
2. I reassured him and started the engine for him.

Scenario B: Reactions to a barking dog late at night
PRIVATE DISCLOSURES

Negative Statements

Extreme Statements:
1. I've always hated their dog.
2. I felt so aggravated and hoped he was choking on his leash.

(continued)

TABLE 1 (continued)

Moderate Statements:
1. I don't really like their dog.
2. I felt sort of annoyed when I thought that he might be choking on his leash.

Positive Statements

Extreme Statements:
1. I've always loved their dog.
2. I felt really concerned that he might be choking on his leash.

Moderate Statements:
1. I've always liked their dog.
2. I began to wonder whether the dog was okay.

PUBLIC DISCLOSURES

Negative Statements

Extreme Statements:
1. I've told my neighbors how much I hate their dog.
2. I looked over the fence and laughed out loud when I saw that he was choking on his leash.

Moderate Statements:
1. I've told my neighbors that I don't really like their dog.
2. I glanced over the fence and saw that he was choking and then I just stared at him for a minute.

Positive Statements

Extreme Statements:
1. I've told my neighbors how much I love their dog.
2. When I saw he was choking, I jumped over the fence and ran to him to loosen his leash.

Moderate Statements:
1. I've told my neighbors that I like their dog.
2. I went next door to check if the dog was okay.

positive"). In addition, they rated the extremity or typicality of the disclosure on a scale ranging from "1" ("completely typical and average") to "4" ("completely atypical and extreme").

Findings from repeated-measures analyses of variance indicated that subjects perceived the negative disclosures as significantly more negative than the positive disclosures, both for the fishing trip, (M = -1.5 vs. M = 1.3), $F(1,21) = 126.3$, $p < .001$, and for the barking dog scenario, (M = -1.4 vs. M = 1.2), $F(1,15) = 135.3$, $p < .001$, and rated the extreme disclosures as significantly more extreme than the moderate disclosures, again both for the fishing trip, (M = 3.4 vs. M = 2.1), $F(1,21) = 94.3$, $p < .001$, and for the barking dog, (M = 2.9 vs. M = 1.9), $F(1,15) = 90.9$, $p < .001$. Replicating earlier work (e.g., Fiske, 1980; Kanouse & Hanson, 1972), the negative disclosures were also viewed as more extreme than the positive disclosures (M = 3.2 vs. M = 2.4), $F(1,21) = 41.9$, $p < .001$, fishing trip; (M = 2.7 vs. M = 2.2), $F(1,15) = 5.0$, $p < .04$, barking dog.

Procedure

Subjects arrived for the experiment in groups of 4 same-sex participants and were seated in individual rooms to view 1 of the 16 videotaped disclosures via a television monitor. The study was described as "an investigation of the ways in which people form impressions of each other" and react to "peer encounter sessions." Subjects were asked to put themselves in the position of the listener, with whom the speaker was allegedly interacting. In this way, it was expected that subjects would imagine being in the same room with the speaker and would thus react to the speaker as if actually meeting him.

After viewing the videotape, subjects completed three measures. First, they indicated their dispositional inferences about the speaker by rating him in terms of 20 bipolar trait adjectives (e.g., "sincere-insincere," "friendly-unfriendly") that ranged from "-5" to "+5." The average of the absolute values of all non-zero ratings was then calculated to reflect the strength of the dispositional inferences listeners were willing to make about the speaker (cf. Andersen & Ross, 1984).[3] Second, subjects rated the informativeness of the communication by assessing its intimacy, revealingness, accuracy, and completeness. Finally, they indicated their liking and predicted comfort in interacting with the speaker by rating their similarity to him, their interest in meeting him, and their predicted comfort in interacting with him socially.

As manipulation checks, subjects indicated how "negative," "positive," "typical," and "extreme" they perceived the videotaped disclosure to be using four 11-point scales. They also estimated the extent to which they believed the speaker had disclosed thoughts and feelings, and behaviors on separate 11-point scales. After completing these measures, subjects were thanked for their participation and excused.

RESULTS

All dependent measures were examined in 2 X 2 X 2 X 2 (Privacy X Negativity X Extremity X Disclosure Scenario) analyses of variance. Our hypotheses were fourfold. First, we predicted a main effect for privacy indicating that disclosed cognitions and affects lead to stronger dispositional inferences and greater perceived informativeness than do disclosed behaviors (cf. Andersen, 1987; but not to greater liking, Andersen & Ross, 1984; Runge & Archer, 1981). Second, we predicted a

---

3. *This analysis differs from the one conducted on listeners' trait inferences in Andersen and Ross (1984), by considering inferential strength for only those items on which listeners made an inference rather than calculating inferential strength across all items, even if given a "0" or "could not say" rating. We have found the present measure to assess dispositional inference strength more precisely.*

similar main effect for negativity indicating that negative versus positive communications lead to stronger dispositional inferences and greater perceived informativeness, as well as to less liking and predicted comfort. Third, we predicted that an interaction between negativity and privacy would emerge showing that negativity powerfully increases the diagnosticity of behavior relative to positivity, perhaps to such an extent that it actually reverses the cognitive/affective advantage in dispositional inferences and perceived informativeness that exists among largely positive communications. Finally, we predicted an interaction between negativity and extremity in which the consequences of negative communications become particularly pronounced when the communicated information is also extreme.

Manipulation Effectiveness

Privacy. Subjects reported that in the private disclosure conditions the speaker communicated significantly more about his thoughts and feelings, (Private M = 7.2 vs. Public M = 4.1), $F(1,128) = 71.3$, $p < .0001$, and significantly less about his behaviors (Private M = 5.7 vs. Public M = 7.9), $F(1,128) = 29.4$, $p < .0001$, than in the public disclosure conditions.

Negativity. As anticipated, subjects viewed the negative disclosures as significantly more "negative" (Negative M = 7.3 vs. Positive M = 3.1), $F(1,128) = 108.9$, $p < .0001$, and as significantly less "positive" (Negative M = 2.7 vs. Positive M = 5.3), $F(1,128) = 45.0$, $p < .0001$, than the positive disclosures. They also rated negative disclosures as more "extreme" (Negative M = 6.7 vs. Positive M = 4.5), $F(1,128) = 22.0$, $p < .0001$, and as less "typical" (Negative M = 3.2 vs. Positive M = 4.5), $F(1,128) = 11.8$, $p < .0001$, than positive disclosures.

Extremity. Analyses of subjects' perceptions of the "extremity" or "unusualness" of the disclosures showed that subjects perceived extreme disclosures as less "typical" (M = 3.4) than moderate disclosures (M = 4.3), $F(1,128) = 5.1$, $p < .02$, but not as significantly more "extreme," (Extreme M = 5.9 vs. Moderate M = 5.3), $F(1,128) = 1.2$, n.s.

Dispositional Inferences about the Speaker

Listeners' willingness to make inferences about the speaker's personality was assessed by selecting for examination those bipolar trait scales (from the 20 provided) on which the listener actually made a judgment about the speaker, i.e., by circling any rating except the zero-point which was labelled "cannot say." The *strength* of listeners' inferences was then analyzed by averaging the absolute value of all trait ratings for which a non-zero rating was given. This procedure for assessing dispositional inference strength corrects for variability in the number of experimenter-provided traits that listeners perceived were relevant to the speaker. Scores reflecting the average strength of listeners' dispositional inferences about the speaker in each condition are presented in Table 2.

The ANOVA examining this composite score failed to yield the predicted main effect for privacy, but it did yield the predicted main effect for negativity, $F(1,128) = 5.79$, $p < .02$. In general, listeners made stronger inferences on the basis of negative (M = 3.0) rather than positive disclosures (M = 2.6). In addition, this main effect was qualified by two significant interactions.

One of these was the predicted interaction between negativity and privacy, $F(1,128) = 4.24$, $p < .04$, which was largely consistent with our expectations. That is, communications consisting of behaviors led to greater dispositional inference strength when negative (M = 3.0) than when positive (M = 2.4), $F(1,70) = 11.15$, $p < .001$, while communications of thoughts and feelings led to equally strong inferences whether negative (M = 2.9) or positive (M = 2.8), $F < 1$. Hence, the data supported the prediction that behavioral disclosures become particularly important when they are negative. Further, it is clear that positive behaviors led to the least extreme inferences overall, ($p < .05$, Tukey).

Beyond this, however, the interaction did not support the notion that when negative, communications about behaviors might be even *more* influential than communications about thoughts and feelings. That is, the cognitive/affective advantage was not *reversed* in the negative condition, communications about behaviors simply became as influential as communications about thoughts and feelings. Consistent with the suggestions of prior research (Andersen, 1984; Andersen & Ross, 1984), the data clearly indicated that when the communications were positive, disclosed thoughts and feelings led to significantly stronger dispositional inferences (M = 2.8) than did disclosed behaviors (M = 2.4), $F(1,70) = 5.97$, $p < .02$. By contrast, when the communications were negative, disclosed thoughts and feelings had no greater impact on dispositional inference strength (M = 2.9) than did disclosed behaviors (M = 3.0), $F < 1$, indicating a likely boundary condition on the superiority of cognitions and affects in impression formation tasks.

The second interaction to emerge on this measure supported the predicted relationship between negativity and extremity, $F(1,128) = 5.84$, $p < .02$. In particular, it indicated that listeners made stronger inferences about the speaker on the basis of negative rather than positive information, but only when the information was extreme (M Negative = 3.2, M Positive = 2.6), $F(1,70) = 13.87$, $p < .001$ and not when it was moderate (M Negative = 2.7, M Positive = 2.7), $F < 1$. Similarly, listeners made stronger inferences based on extreme rather than moderate disclo-

TABLE 2 Mean Strength of Dispositional Inferences by
Experimental Condition[a]

Disclosure Content	Cognitive/ Affective Statements	Behavioral Statements	Marginals
Negative Statements			
Extreme Statements	3.2	3.3	3.2
Moderate Statements	2.7	2.8	2.7
Total	2.9	3.0	3.0
Positive Statements			
Extreme Statements	2.8	2.4	2.6
Moderate Statements	2.8	2.5	2.7
Total	2.8	2.4	2.6
Grand Total	2.9	2.7	

[a] Scores reflect the average of the absolute values of listeners' non-zero trait ratings, each of which was made on a bipolar scale ranging from "-5" to "+5."

sures only when the disclosures were also negative (M Extreme = 3.2, M Moderate = 2.7), $F(1,70) = 8.35$, $p < .005$ and not when they were positive (M Extreme = 2.6, M Moderate = 2.7), $F < 1$. Thus, disclosures that were both negative and extreme led to the strongest dispositional inferences, supporting other findings in social cognition research (cf. Fiske, 1980).

Perceptions of Informativeness

Subjects' ratings of how "intimate," "accurate," "revealing" and "complete" they perceived the disclosure to be were combined to form a composite measure of perceived informativeness. The intercorrelations among these items ranged from .33 to .64, (Cronbach's $\alpha = .80$). As shown in Table 3, the ANOVA examining this composite measure of perceived informativeness yielded the predicted main effects for privacy and negativity, but not the predicted interaction between privacy and negativity, nor that between negativity and extremity. In particular, the data supported the hypothesis that disclosures of thoughts and feelings are perceived as significantly more informative (M = 5.0) than behavioral disclosures (M = 4.3), $F(1,128) = 3.8$, $p < .05$. The hypothesis that negative communications are perceived as significantly more informative (M = 5.0) than are positive communications (M = 4.3) was also supported, $F(1,128) = 3.9$, $p < .05$. Interestingly, the means for representing the predicted negativity by privacy interaction conform to the predicted pattern, but the interaction was not significant, $F(1,128) = .27$, n.s. However, disclosures concerning positive behaviors were perceived as the least informative of all the disclosures ($p < .05$, Tukey).

TABLE 3 Mean Assessment of Perceived Informativeness by Experimental Condition[a]

Disclosure Content	Cognitive/ Affective Statements	Behavioral Statements	Marginals
Negative Statements			
Extreme Statements	5.4	4.8	5.1
Moderate Statements	5.3	4.5	4.9
Total	5.3	4.6	5.0
Positive Statements			
Extreme Statements	4.6	3.8	4.2
Moderate Statements	4.7	4.0	4.4
Total	4.7	3.9	4.3
Grand Total	5.0	4.3	

[a]These composite scores reflect the average rating given to four informativeness items, each rated on a scale ranging from "0" ("Not at all") to "10" ("Extremely").

Finally, a main effect for scenario emerged showing that listeners rated disclosures concerning the elderly man as significantly more informative ($M = 4.9$) than those concerning the barking dog ($M = 4.1$), $F(1,128) = 6.9$, $p < .01$, perhaps because social interactions are treated as more diagnostic than are solitary experiences (see Berger & Douglas, 1981). However, no interactions with scenario emerged; hence, the findings clearly generalized across scenario.

Perceptions of Liking

Subjects' ratings of their similarity to the speaker, their willingness to meet him, and their predicted comfort in interacting with him were combined to form a composite measure. Intercorrelations among these three measures ranged from .59 to .72, (Cronbach's $\alpha = .85$). The ANOVA examining this composite score showed, as in previous research, that the privacy dimension had no impact on liking independent of negativity (Andersen & Ross, 1984; Runge & Archer, 1981). In particular, as shown in Table 4, regardless of whether the communication consisted of thoughts and feelings or behaviors, negative disclosures led listeners to like the speaker significantly less and to expect to be less comfortable interacting with him ($M = 1.7$) than did positive disclosures ($M = 4.2$), $F(1,128) = 50.0$, $p < .001$. Thus, negative thoughts and feelings produced as much discomfort and disliking as did negative behaviors, and positive thoughts and feelings were just as beneficial in increasing social regard and comfort as were positive deeds. No effects for extremity or scenario emerged.

TABLE 4 Mean Assessment of Interpersonal Attraction by Experimental Condition[a]

Disclosure Content	Cognitive/ Affective Statements	Behavioral Statements	Marginals
Negative Statements			
Extreme Statements	1.6	1.4	1.5
Moderate Statements	2.2	1.3	1.8
Total	1.9	1.4	1.7
Positive Statements			
Extreme Statements	3.5	4.5	4.0
Moderate Statements	4.5	4.0	4.3
Total	4.0	4.3	4.2
Grand Total	3.0	2.8	

[a] *These composite scores reflect the average rating given to three liking items, each rated on a scale ranging from "0" ("Not at all") to "10" ("Extremely").*

DISCUSSION

The present data demonstrate that disclosing about one's thoughts and feelings is seen as more informative than is disclosing about one's behaviors. Moreover, the wishes or intentions disclosed in the thoughts and feelings condition were seen as very informative even though they were presumably not acted upon. For example, wishing to help the old man clean up the dock, wanting to adopt the neighbor's neglected dog, and wanting to react violently toward the old man or the dog were all perceived as more informative than was actually engaging in these behaviors in the absence of reported thoughts and feelings. The fact that these unenacted intentions actually led the private communications to be seen as more informative than the public communications provides support for the notion that it is access to otherwise hidden cognitions and affects that gives listeners the feeling that they have heard something significant about the speaker. Thus, it is not the hint a disclosure provides about a speaker's likely behaviors that makes the disclosure seem informative, but rather the hint it provides about otherwise private affects and cognitions.

From a different perspective, it should be noted that in the thoughts and feelings conditions no relevant behaviors were presented (e.g., actually pushing the old man aside). That is, behaviors were essentially represented as nonoccurrences in this condition, which research suggests people routinely fail to utilize in their assessments of others (cf. Fazio, Sherman, & Herr, 1982; Nisbett & Ross, 1980; Ross, 1977). Hence, it becomes less suprising that the lack of behavioral enactments in the thoughts and feelings conditions was somehow ignored or discounted by listeners. Using the same logic regarding nonoccurrences, however, listeners should also have ignored or discounted the lack of corresponding cognitions and affects in the behavioral disclosure conditions. That is, although the speaker did not mention feeling irritated while pushing the old man aside, for example, listeners should have given behaviors weight even in the absence of such supportive private "evidence." Yet this was clearly not the case; the lack of thoughts and feelings in this condition apparently led listeners to view the behavioral communications as less informative.

Another way to view these findings is that when communications focus on behavior (and thoughts and feelings are not disclosed), listeners may come to believe that the recounted behaviors were somehow caused by situational contraints and demands rather than by personal motivations. Without an understanding of relevant thoughts and feelings, recounted behaviors may seem to have stemmed not from within the person but from outside him or her. By contrast, when thoughts and feelings are disclosed, they appear to afford more direct access to the speaker's personal motivations and thus are likely to be viewed as diagnostic, even when not acted upon. Hence, it may be this motivational information about a speaker which listeners derive from cognitive/affective disclosures that makes these disclosures seem particularly relevant to the speaker's stable characteristics.

This explanation becomes even more applicable when the data from our dispositional inference measure are considered. As the more sensitive of the two measures of disclosure depth and impact, the measure of dispositional inferences suggested a boundary condition on the superiority of disclosed thoughts and feelings relative to disclosed behaviors in influencing listeners' impressions. Namely, only when the communication was positive did listeners characterize the speaker in more extreme dispositional terms based on cognitive/affective versus behavioral disclosures. Because positive social behaviors are perceived to be more normative and thus consistent with social constraints, they are both expected and assumed to be driven by circumstance (e.g., DeSoto & Keuthe, 1959; Jones & Davis, 1965; Skowronski & Carlston, 1987). Consistent with this, positive behaviors led to the least extreme inferences and were perceived as the least informative, relative to the other disclosures. By contrast thoughts and feelings, whether negative or positive, may not be seen as comparably subject to situational constraints. They appear to be produced by the individual, to occur "within" the person, which may account for their being given greater weight than behaviors, especially positive behaviors. Negative behaviors, on the other hand, tend to be unexpected and hence less likely to be construed as produced by situational forces. Because negative actions violate social norms, they invoke the search for explanatory dispositions (cf. Pyszczynski & Greenberg, 1981). Hence, it may be that negative behavioral disclosures come to rival cognitive/affective disclosures in their impact on subsequent impressions partly because they are assumed to have been personally motivated, i.e., that they are driven by or accompanied by consistent thoughts and feelings.

Nonetheless, when the disclosures were negative, self-disclosed acts were treated as no more revealing of one's character than were self-disclosed thoughts and feelings, and overall, were seen as less revealing (see also Andersen, 1984; Andersen & Ross, 1984). These findings suggest that actions do not speak louder than words when they are communicated in the context of self-disclosure. (For situations where actions do speak louder than words, see Amabile & Kabat, 1982; Gilbert & Krull, 1988.) In addition, these findings extend the available literature on cognitions, affects, and behaviors in social perception (Andersen, 1984; Andersen & Ross, 1984) by showing that thoughts and feelings are treated as equally diagnostic or as more diagnostic than are behaviors, even when negativity and extremity are controlled. Namely, when negative behaviors are communicated, they do not *exceed* communicated thoughts and feelings in their impact. However, our findings also suggest a positive communication boundary condition for the cognitive/affective *advantage* in impression formation.

The present findings also demonstrate powerful main effects of negativity in interpersonal communications, not only using our dispositional inference measure but the measures of perceived informativeness and predicted liking/comfort as well. These findings are consistent with the disproportional weight social perceivers tend to give to negative information in the form of trait adjectives (Hamilton & Zanna, 1972; Kanouse & Hanson, 1972) and overt behaviors (Fiske, 1980). Thus they extend the well-replicated negativity effects in social cognition (e.g., Fiske, 1980; Hamilton & Zanna, 1972; Kanouse & Hanson, 1972) into the domain of interpersonal communication and self-disclosure. Our findings may suggest, then, that disclosing negative information about oneself is impactful in much the same way as are third- person descriptions of one's undesirable behaviors or traits (e.g., Hamilton, Katz, & Leirer, 1980; Higgins, Rholes, & Jones, 1977; Reeder & Coovert, 1986; Skowronski & Carlston, 1987).

Negative information may have such a significant impact, in part, because it stands out in social interaction and in disclosure contexts as well, i.e., it is unexpected. People frequently present others with positive information about themselves in order to manage favorable impressions, which suggests that it is positive information that is typically available to us about other individuals (cf. Cantril, 1965; DeSoto & Keuthe, 1959; Fiske, 1980; Kanouse & Hanson, 1972). Positive expectations exist in personal relationships (cf. DeSoto & Kuethe, 1959), in predictions about personal happiness (cf. Cantril, 1965), and in norms about other people (cf. Jones & Davis, 1965). Negative information may therefore be particularly salient against this background of positive presentations and expectations (cf. Taylor & Fiske, 1978).

Beyond the increased salience of negative information, it could be argued that negative disclosures are likely to arouse negative affect in listeners. Such disclosures undoubtedly disconfirm listeners' positive expectations about social interactions, at least with individuals who occupy non-deviant social identities (cf. Smith-Lovin & Heise, 1988). Thus they are likely to produce uncertainty and unpredictability (cf. Planalp & Honeycutt, 1985; Planalp, Rutherford, & Honeycutt, 1988) which has been shown to be associated with stress (Lazarus & Averill, 1972; Miller, 1980). Partly for this reason, listeners may have been motivated to develop a dispositional portrait of the speaker in order to resolve the uncertainty the disclosure created. Especially strong dispositional inferences may thus serve to make the speaker seem predictable, even if also very negative.

Hearing disclosures about socially unacceptable thoughts, feelings, and behaviors may also be threatening in more direct ways such as by leading one to feel anxious about being harmed while interacting with the speaker. Along these lines, the data clearly showed that listeners expected to be far less comfortable in a future interaction with the speaker after he disclosed about negative versus positive responses.

The predicted interaction that emerged between disclosure negativity and privacy can also be explained in these terms. That is, if the disclosure of negative behaviors produces negative affect in the listener, this may account for the greater dispositional thinking in this condition relative to when positive behaviors were disclosed. Negative behavioral disclosures may have been given more inferential weight by listeners because such disclosures may suggest to listeners that they may be called upon to react in some way, i.e., to somehow defend themselves or fight back in response to negative behaviors in an interaction with the speaker. This would mobilize more anxiety in these listeners relative to those exposed to positive behavioral communications (in ways that did not occur in the shift between negative and positive cognitive/affective disclosures). As with increases in uncertainty, increases in anxiety imply a greater need to come to a dispositional understanding of the speaker.

In terms of Altman and Taylor's "uniqueness" dimension of disclosure depth, our findings suggest that uniqueness or extremity had no independent impact on listeners' impressions. However, when extreme communications also involved negative aspects of the self, listeners did make stronger dispositional inferences about the speaker. Thus, when extremity did have an impact, it did so by moderating the effects of negativity, in the case of dispositional inferences. Given perceivers' positive expectations for social relationships, extreme negative reactions may seem especially unwarranted and "uncalled for" (e.g., Cantril, 1965; DeSoto & Keuthe, 1959), and may therefore be easy to attribute to dispositional factors (Reeder, 1985). Here again, the disconfirmation of social norms elicited by such uncalled for responses may be particularly likely to lead to uncertainty about the speaker which listeners attempt to resolve by assuming the worst and making correspondent dispositional inferences.

Based on this argument, it seems likely that if obvious situational causes for the disclosed responses had been presented, this may have defined a boundary condition for some of the findings reported in this study (cf. Jones & Davis, 1965; Kelley, 1973). That is, it may be only when situational causes are vague or unlikely that extreme negative responses are viewed as dispositionally diagnostic and that personal attributes and motives can easily be inferred from negative behaviors. Hence obvious situational causes may well interfere with these phenomena.[4]

Finally, it should be noted that the type of negativity disclosed in the present study included negative reactions that were potentially harmful to others. Thus, the profoundly unfavorable impressions and diminished social attraction demonstrated in this work may apply primarily to instances involving harm, immorality, or a lack of social conscience (cf. Reeder & Coovert, 1986; Skowronski & Carlston, 1987), and not, for example, to the disclosure of personal vulnerabilities (cf. Lazowski, 1988) or lack of skill (cf. Skowronski & Carlston, 1987). Similarly, the speaker in the present study expressed no remorse about his harmful acts or intentions, which may otherwise have given listeners reason to "forgive" him and to discount his negative reactions, or to otherwise feel less threatened. Expressions of affect that accompany self-disclosures func-

---

[4] *On a different note, it should be acknowledged that like most negative information, the negative communications employed in this study were perceived as more extreme than were the positive communications, probably because negative communications are unexpected and counternormative (Fiske, 1980; Jones & Davis, 1965; Kanouse & Hanson, 1972; Warr, 1974; Warr & Jackson, 1975). Hence, the greater extremity and unusualness of negative self-disclosures relative to positive ones may well play an important role in their impact.*

tion as metacommunications about the speaker's self-perceptions and may enable listeners to discount disclosures of negative responses when such expressions convey that the speaker's identity has been disrupted by the event (cf. Lazowski, Heise, & Smith-Lovin, 1988). The speaker's failure to express any potentially mitigating feelings such as anxiety, guilt, or remorse while engaging in negative disclosure in this study, may have provided listeners with no relief from their negative affect and with no way out of assuming that the speaker was particularly reprehensible.

In summary, the present results have indicated that certain aspects of self-disclosure depth clearly impact upon social perception. Disclosures of one's private thoughts and feelings or "low visibility" aspects of the self (Altman & Taylor, 1973) do indeed seem to represent one dimension of "deep" self-disclosure. Our data clearly show that such communications are seen as very informative, even when their valence and extremity are controlled. That is, private self-disclosures provide a means of conveying a "deep" impression even when the communication is positive or typical. Revealing one's private thoughts and feelings *can* be a relatively "safe" means of making the self known to others because it allows one to achieve self- disclosure depth without communicating disreputable aspects of the self. The perceived informativeness of private self-disclosures, however, can be a double-edged sword. On one hand, speakers can convince others that they possess favorable characteristics by revealing positive thoughts and feelings without having to "prove" their worth via behavioral evidence. On the other hand, if negative thoughts and feelings are disclosed, they can be *as* indicting as the disclosure of negative deeds.

In addition, the data also suggest a boundary condition on the cognitive/affective *advantage* in social perception. Listeners' dispositional inferences about the speaker were more influenced by private disclosures than by public ones only when largely positive. When disclosures were negative, listeners' inferences were no more influenced by the private than by the public nature of the communication, in part due to a marked difference between negative and positive behavioral disclosures. Finally, disclosures of negative information (regardless of whether cognitive/affective or behavioral) were perceived as highly informative, led to stronger dispositional inferences, and led the listener to feel less liking for the speaker. Even in self- disclosure contexts, then, which encourage honest communication and intimacy as opposed to "selective" communications (Derlega, 1984), the communication of negative information leads to well-elaborated, unfavorable impressions, and may culminate in social rejection. Further research is needed to identify conditions under which intimate self-disclosures—involving either negative information or cognitive and affective experiences will actually be met with empathy and increased liking rather than with little favorable response or with outright social rejection.

REFERENCES

Altman, I., & Taylor, D. A. (1973). *Social penetration: The development of interpersonal relationships.* New York: Holt, Rinehart, and Winston.

Amabile, T. M., & Kabat, L. G. (1982). When self-descriptions contradict behavior: Actions speak louder than words. *Social Cognition, 1,* 311- 335.

Andersen, S. M. (1987). The role of cultural assumptions in self-concept development. In K. Yardley and T. Honess (Eds.), *Self and identity: Psychosocial perspectives* (pp. 231-246). N.Y.: John Wiley and Sons Ltd.

Andersen, S. M. (1984). Self-knowledge and social inference: II. The diagnosticity of cognitive/affective and behavioral data. *Journal of Personality and Social Psychology, 46,* 294-307.

Andersen, S. M., Lazowski, L. E., & Donisi, M. (1986). Salience and self- inference: The role of biased recollections in self-inference processes. *Social Cognition, 4,* 75-95.

Andersen, S. M., & Williams, M. (1985). Cognitive/affective reactions in the improvement of self-esteem: When thoughts and feelings make a difference. *Journal of Personality and Social Psychology, 49,* 1086- 1097.

Andersen, S. M., & Ross, L. (1984). Self-knowledge and social inference: I. The impact of cognitive/affective and behavioral data. *Journal of Personality and Social Psychology, 46,* 280-293.

Archer, R. L., & Berg, J. H. (1978). Disclosure reciprocity and its limits: A reactance analysis. *Journal of Experimental Social Psychology, 14,* 527-540.

Archer, R. L., & Burleson, J. A. (1980). The effects of timing of self- disclosure on attraction and reciprocity. *Journal of Personality and Social Psychology, 38,* 120-130.

Asch, S. E. (1946). Forming impressions of personality. *Journal of Abnormal and Social Psychology, 41,* 258-290.

Averett, C., & Heise, D. R. (1987). Modified social identities: Amalgamations, attributions, and emotions. *Journal of Mathematical Sociology, 13,* 103-132.

Bargh, J. A., & Thein, R. D. (1985). Individual construct accessibility, person memory, and the recall-judgment link: The case of information overload. *Journal of Personality and Social Psychology, 49,* 1129-1146.

Berg, J. H., & Archer, R. L. (1980). Disclosure or concern: A second look at liking for the norm-breaker. *Journal of Personality, 48,* 245-257.

Berger, C. R., & Calabrese, R.J. (1975). Some explorations in initail interaction and beyond: Toward a developmental theory of interpersonal communication. *Human Communication Research, 1,* 99-112.

Berger, C. R., & Douglas, W. (1981). Studies in interpersonal epistemology: III. Anticipated interaction, self-monitoring, and observational context selection. *Communication Monographs, 48,* 183-196.

Brewer, M. B., & Mittelman, J. (1980). Effects of normative control of self-disclosure on reciprocity. *Journal of Personality, 48,* 89-102.

Cantril, H. (1965). *The pattern of human concerns.* New Brunswick, N.J.: Rutgers University Press.

Chaikin, A. L., & Derlega, V. J. (1974). Liking for the norm-breaker in self-disclosure. *Journal of Personality, 42,* 117-129.

Cozby, P. C. (1972). Self-disclosure, reciprocity and liking. *Sociometry, 35,* 151-160.

Derlega, V. J. (1984). Self-disclosure and intimate relationships. In V. J. Derlega (Ed.) *Communication, intimacy, and close relationships* (pp. 1-9). New York: Academic Press.

Derlega, V. J., Harris, M. S., & Chaikin, A. L. (1973). Self-disclosure reciprocity, liking, and the deviant. *Journal of Experimental Social Psychology, 9,* 277-284.

DeSoto, C. B., & Kuethe, J. L. (1959). Subjective probabilities of interpersonal relations.

Journal of Abnormal and Social Psychology, 59, 290-294.
Fazio, R. H., Sherman, S. J., & Herr, P. M. (1982). The feature-positive effect in the self-perception process: Does not doing matter as much as doing? *Journal of Personality and Social Psychology, 42*, 404-411.
Fiske, S. T. (1980). Attention and weight in person perception: The impact of negative and extreme behavior. *Journal of Personality and Social Psychology, 38*, 889-906.
Gilbert, D. T., & Krull, D. S. (1988). Seeing less and knowing more: The benefits of perceptual ignorance. *Journal of Personality and Social Psychology, 54*, 193-201.
Gilbert, S. J., & Horenstein, D. (1975). The communication of self- disclosure: Level versus valence. *Human Communication Research, 1*, 316-322.
Hamilton, D. L., Katz, L., & Leirer, V. O. (1980). Cognitive representation of personality impressions: Organizational processes in first impression formation. *Journal of Personality and Social Psychology, 39*, 1050-1063.
Hamilton, D. L. & Zanna, M. P. (1972). Differential weighting of favorable and unfavorable attributes in impressions of personality. *Journal of Experimental Research in Personality, 6*, 204-212.
Hastie, R., & Kumar, P. A. (1979). Person memory: Personality traits as organizing principles in memory for behaviors. *Journal of Personality and Social Psychology, 37*, 25-38.
Heise, D. R., & MacKinnon, N. J. (1987). Affective bases of likelihood judgments. *Journal of Mathematical Sociology, 13*, 133-151.
Higgins, E. T., Rholes, W. S., & Jones, C. R. (1977). Category accessibility and impression formation. *Journal of Experimental Social Psychology, 13*, 141-154.
Johnson, J. (1987). The heart on the sleeve and the secret self: Estimations of hidden emotion in self and acquaintances. *Journal of Personality, 55*, 563-582.
Jones, E. E., & Davis, K. E. (1965). From acts to dispositions: The attribution process in person perception. In L. Berkowitz (Ed.), *Advances in experimental social psychology* (Vol. 2, pp. 219-266). New York: Academic Press.
Jones, E. E., & Nisbett, R. E. (1972). The actor and observer: Divergent perceptions of the causes of behavior. In E. E. Jones, D. E. Kanouse, H. H. Kelley, R. E. Nisbett, S. Valins & B. Weiner (Eds.), *Attribution: Perceiving the causes of behavior* (pp. 79-94). Morristown, N.J.: General Learning Press.
Jourard, S. M., & Jaffe, P. E. (1970). Influence of an interviewer's disclosure on the self-disclosing behavior of interviewees. *Journal of Counseling Psychology, 17*, 252-257.
Kanouse, D. E., & Hanson, L. R. (1972). Negativity in evaluations. In E. E. Jones, D. E. Kanouse, H. H. Kelley, R. E. Nisbett, S. Valins & B. Weiner (Eds.), *Attribution: Perceiving the causes of behavior* (pp. 47- 62). Morristown, N.J.: General Learning Press.
Kelley, H. H. (1973). The process of causal attribution. *American Psychologist, 28*, 107-128.
Lazarus, R. S., & Averill, J. R. (1972). Emotion and cognition with special reference to anxiety. In C. D. Spielberger (Ed.), *Anxiety: Current trends in theory and research* (Vol. 2, pp. 242-283). New York: Academic Press.
Lazowski, L. E. (1988). Speakers' nonverbal expressions of emotion as moderators of listeners' reactions to disclosures of self harm and social harm. (Doctoral dissertation, University of California, Santa Barbara, 1987). *Dissertation Abstracts International, 49*, 2821B.
Lazowski, L. E., Heise, D. R., & Smith-Lovin, L. (1989). *Emotion displays and social inference*. Unpublished paper, Indiana University.
Miller, S. M. (1980). Why having control reduces stress: If I can stop the roller coaster, I don't want to get off. In J. Garber & M. E. P. Seligman (Eds.), *Human helplessness* (pp. 71-95). New York: Academic Press.
Nisbett, R. E., & Ross, L. (1980). *Human inference: Strategies and shortcomings in social judgment*. Englewood Cliffs, NJ: Prentice-Hall.
Ostrom, T. M., & Davis, D. (1979). Idiosyncratic weighting of trait information in

impression formation. *Journal of Personality and Social Psychology, 37,* 2025-2043.

Planalp, S. & Honeycutt, J. M. (1985). Events that increase uncertainty in personal relationships. *Human Communication Research, 11,* 593-604.

Planalp, S., Rutherford, D. K., & Honeycutt, J. M. (1988). Events that increase uncertainty in personal relationships II: Replication and extension. *Human Communication Research, 14,* 516-547.

Pyszczynski, T. A., & Greenberg, J. (1981). Role of disconfirmed expectancies in the instigation of attributional processing. *Journal of Personality and Social Psychology, 40,* 31-38.

Reeder, G. D., & Coovert, M. D. (1986). Revising an impression of morality. *Social Cognition, 4,* 1-17.

Richey, M. H., Richey, H. W., & Thieman, G. (1972). Negative salience in impressions of character: Effects of new information on established relationships. *Psychonomic Science, 28,* 65-66.

Ross, L. (1977). The intuitive psychologist and his shortcomings: Distortions in the attribution process. In L. Berkowitz (Ed.), *Advances in experimental social psychology* (Vol. 10). New York: Academic Press.

Runge, T. E., & Archer, R. L. (1981). Reactions to the disclosure of public and private self-information. *Social Psychology Quarterly, 44,* 357-362.

Skowronski, J. J., & Carlston, D. E. (1987). Social judgment and social memory: The role of cue diagnosticity in negativity, positivity, and extremity biases. *Journal of Personality and Social Psychology, 52,* 689-699.

Skowronski, J. J., & Carlston, D. E. (1989). Negativity and extremity biases in impression formation: A review of explanations. *Psychological Bulletin, 105,* 131-142.

Smith-Lovin, L., & Heise, D. R. (1988). *Analyzing social interaction: Advances in affect control theory.* New York: Gordon and Breach Science Publishers.

Snyder, M. (1984). When belief creates reality. In L. Berkowitz (Ed.), *Advances in experimental social psychology* (Vol. 18, pp. 247-305). New York: Academic Press.

Snyder, M., & Swann, W. B., Jr. (1978). Hypothesis-testing processes in social interaction. *Journal of Personality and Social Psychology, 36,* 1202-1212.

Srull, T. K., & Wyer, R. S., Jr. (1980). Category accessibility and social perception: Some implications for the study of person memory and interpersonal judgments. *Journal of Personality and Social Psychology, 38,* 841-856.

Taylor, S. E., & Fiske, S. T. (1978). Salience, attention, and attribution: Top of the head phenomena. In L. Berkowitz (Ed.), *Advances in experimental social psychology* (Vol. 11, pp. 249-288). New York: Academic Press.

Warr, P. (1974). Inference magnitude, range, and evaluative direction as factors affecting relative importance of cues in impression formation. *Journal of Personality and Social Psychology, 30,* 191-197.

Warr, P., & Jackson, P. (1975). The importance of extremity. *Journal of Personality and Social Psychology, 32,* 278-282.

Wortman, C. B., Adesman, P., Herman, E., & Greenberg, R. (1976). Self-disclosure: An attributional perspective. *Journal of Personality and Social Psychology, 33,* 184-191.

Zajonc, R. B. (1980). Thinking and feeling: Preferences need no inferences. *American Psychologist, 35,* 151-175.

Potential Cognitive Processes and Consequences of Receiver Apprehension: A Meta-analytic Review

Raymond W. Preiss
Department of Communication & Theatre Arts
University of Puget Sound, Tacoma, WA 98416

Lawrence R. Wheeless
Department of Communication Studies
West Virginia University, Morgantown, WV 26506

Mike Allen
Department of Communication
University of Wisconsin at Milwaukee, Milwaukee, WI 53201

Receiver apprehension has been conceptualized as an anxiety related to message decoding and information processing. A substantial body of literature on this concept exists. A meta-analysis was conducted to assess the features of the receiver apprehension domain. The analysis indicated that receiver apprehension can be related to listening effectiveness, information processing anxiety, information processing complexity, information processing efficiency, and education level. Results are discussed in terms of the comparative magnitude of receiver apprehension relations to these five categories, the search for moderator variables, and suggestions for future research.

Communication-related anxieties appear to be salient for, if not central to, "day-to-day" cognitive processes. Communication outcomes, in terms of cognitive consequences, most likely are altered or modified by such phenomena. Moreover, these types of anxieties may be important mediators of information processing which potentially engender cognitive biases in thought processes. The degree of apprehension individuals have apparently makes them susceptible to differences in performance.

One such concept, receiver apprehension (Wheeless, 1975), appears to be closely allied to these notions. Conceptually, receiver apprehension

© 1990 Select Press

is a communication phenomenon related to anxiety and cognition. Drawing from literature on reticence (Phillips, 1968) and communication apprehension (McCroskey, 1970), Wheeless focused upon the reception and processing (decoding) of information rather than the encoding and sending of information which that previous literature base emphasized. He reasoned that fear or anxiety associated with an individual's communicative roles—source or receiver—were different concepts as a function of the differences in those roles. Specifically, he suggested that the fear of sending messages relates to social approval, while the fear of receiving messages relates to cognitive processing of information. Wheeless (1975, p. 263) initially defined receiver apprehension as "...the fear of misinterpreting, inadequately processing and/or not being able to adjust psychologically to messages sent by others."

Preiss and Wheeless (in press) refined that earlier conceptualization by identifying three subcomponents of receiver apprehension that contribute to the degree and type of stressful cognitive behavior. The first component is a situation-type anxiety associated with message reception in specific fear-evoking situations. An identifiable stimulus-situation triggers this "primary anxiety" component (McReynolds, 1976). The second component is a trait-like, anxious response set associated with message decoding across situations. This "secondary anxiety" approach is grounded in the concepts of assimilation theory (McReynolds, 1976) and cognitive complexity. The third component consists of a pattern of cognitive responses based on interpretive schemes individuals use in perspective-taking and in developing strategic repertoires of communication responses (Delia, O'Keefe, & O'Keefe, 1982). This subcomponent, then, is a unique pattern of "low-order" interpretive schemes and reactions to messages. Preiss and Wheeless (in press) have tied these explanatory concepts to specific sets of studies on receiver apprehension and assessed their meaningfulness. These components, however, do not provide a comprehensive meaningful typology for categorizing most of the research on receiver apprehension.

The purpose of this paper was to provide a comprehensive review of the research on receiver apprehension and to assess the relative strengths of relationships to cognitive criteria. The twenty-eight studies utilized two versions of the receiver apprehension test (Wheeless, 1975; Wheeless & Scott, 1976). Since the study of receiver apprehension appears to be in the seminal stage, we were interested in examining what cognitive processes and potential consequences appear to be related to receiver apprehension. Based on the analysis and cumulation of relevant research, we thought we might come to a better understanding of receiver apprehension, as well as its relationships to cognitive processes, moderator variables, and potential consequences.

Through examination of the literature, we were able to inductively derive a comprehensive typological classification based upon the types of tested criteria studied in relation to receiver apprehension. Five categories of studies were readily discernible. Listening effectiveness was the first category which used recall-type tests of aurally transmitted information. The second classification, processing anxiety, consisted of studies comparing receiver apprehension to other anxiety measures—e.g., communication apprehension, shyness, change in receiver apprehension, and so forth. A third category of studies, which we called information processing effectiveness used reasoning tasks, inferential judgments, comparative judgments, and so forth based upon what one read and/or heard. Information processing complexity, the fourth category of studies, relied upon paragraph completion tests, cognitive complexity tests, construct differentiation tests, and so forth, as criterial cognitive measures. The final category consisted of education level (year in school) comparisons with receiver apprehension. This latter category reflects cognitive development and achievement. Listening effectiveness and processing effectiveness clearly reflect cognitive consequences and outcomes of information processing. Processing complexity may reflect thought process biases and antecedents to those biases. Processing anxiety reflects the relation of receiver apprehension to other anxiety-based measures. Specific studies representing these categories (see Tables 1 & 2) are discussed in the results section.

METHOD

An appropriate tool for empirically summarizing the results of a research domain is meta-analysis (Hedges & Olkin, 1985; Hunter, Schmidt, & Jackson, 1982). By coding and transforming outcomes into a common metric, it is possible to combine results across studies, estimate an average effect size, and detect moderator variables. While meta-analysis is often used to resolve conflicting research findings, the technique is also very useful in quantifying the empirical features of a body of literature (Cooper, 1984; Glass, McGaw, & Smith, 1981; Light & Pillemer, 1984) such as receiver apprehension.

In this investigation, we cumulated all empirical studies employing the two instruments designed to measure receiver apprehension. The 20-item Receiver Apprehension Test (RAT; Wheeless, 1975) and the 16-item Revised Receiver Apprehension Test (RRAT; Wheeless & Scott, 1976) consist of Likert-type items inquiring about receiver-based apprehension in three ways consistent with the conceptual definition: (a) situations where messages are encountered (e.g., "I occasionally have difficulty listening in a group discussion because I am worried about adjusting and adapting to new ideas"), (b) generalized affective responses to categories of messages (e.g., "Receiving new information sometimes makes me feel somewhat afraid"), and (c) cognitive reactions to message-processing tasks (e.g., "At times, I have difficulty concentrating on instructions others give me"). Studies examining source-based anxiety (e.g., communication apprehension) apart from receiver-based anxiety were excluded from the meta-analysis.

We initiated an extensive search of the literature using four methods: (a) manual and computer searches of *Social Sciences Citation Index; Psychological Abstracts, Resources in Education, Dissertation Abstracts International,* and *Index to Journals in Speech Communication;* (b) manual searches of convention programs; (c) correspondence with authors conducting primary research; and (d) locating all receiver apprehension monographs cited in published studies and convention papers. These efforts resulted in the location of 28 manuscripts, including 15 published articles, 7 convention papers, and 6 master's theses and dissertations.[1] To insure that all features in the receiver apprehension literature domain were reflected in the meta-analysis, no studies were excluded on the basis of quality or publication date (Glass, 1977).[2] These procedures resulted in the identification of 25 tests of criterion variables[3] that were empirically cumulated.

---

[1] *Several receiver apprehension studies tested more than one hypothesis using a single set of subjects. Rosenthal (1978) noted that cumulating multiple significance tests drawn from the same subjects violates statistical assumptions of independence. Strube and Hartman (1983) observed that this problem involves several levels of non-independence, including multiple dependent variables, multiple correlated statistical tests, and similar subject pools (p. 21). Bangert-Drowns (1986) argued that the interdependence problem is insurmountable and concluded that multiple findings must not be used as the unit of study (p. 397). Consequently, the decision rule in this meta-analysis was to extract a single effect size for each independent test of a hypothesis.*

[2] *One convention paper (McDowell, McDowell, Hyerdahl, & Steil, 1978) and one article (Scott & Wheeless, 1977a) were excluded from the meta-analysis because they reported multiariate results that could not be converted to a common metric.*

[3] *Because several statistical tests were often reported in a single study, a decision rule was required for computing effect sizes. For this meta-analysis, a three tier decision rule was developed: (a) If the study involves a single dependent variable, the statistical test for that variable will be used in computing the effect size, (b) If the study contains several dependent variables, the statistical test for the variable most directly related to information processing will be used in computing the effect size, (c) If the study contains several dependent variables and if the variable most directly related to information processing cannot be determined, the median statistical test for that variable will be used in computing the effect size.*

TABLE 1 Variables Extracted from Receiver Apprehension Studies

Study	Conceptual Variable	Measurement Device
Beatty (1981)	Self-reports of unassimilated material	Assimilation Scales (McReynolds & Acker, 1966)
Beatty (1985)	Situational listening anxiety	Change in RAT scores after listening "complex material"
Beatty, Behnke, & Henderson (1980)	State listening anxiety	STAI (A-Trait) (Spielberger, Gorsuch, & Lushene, 1968)
Beatty & Payne (1981)	Cognitive complexity	Paragraph Completion Task (Schroder, Driver, & Struefert, 1961)
Bocchino (1984)	Cognitive complexity	Paragraph Completion Task (Schroder, Driver, &Struefert, 1961)
Bock & Bock (1984)	Leniency errors	Induced positional anxiety during the Rating Error Paradigm (Bock & Bock, 1977)
Borzi (1984)	Shyness	Shyness Scale (McCroskey & Richmond, 1982)
Buhr & Pryor (1988)	Enjoyment of cognitive activities	Need for Cognition (Cacioppo & Petty, 1982)
Daly, et al. (1988)	Conversational sensitivity	Conversational Sensitivity Scale (Daly, et al., 1988)
Daniels & Whitman (1979)	Message recall	Test for facts embedded in experimental messages
McDowell & McDowell (1978)	Communication apprehension	PRCA (McCroskey, 1970)
McDowell, et al. (1981)	Education level on the RAT	High school vs. college scores (Wheeless, 1975)
Paschall (1984)	Listening effectiveness	Sequential Test of Educational Progress—Listening Test (STEP) (McGraw-Hill)
Preiss (1987)	Logic of communication functions	Functional Integration of Communication Concepts (O'Keefe, 1985)
Preiss, et al. (1985)	Self-persuasion	Scales completed after encoding
Roach, et al. (1985), 1 & 2	Listening comprehension	Watson-Barker Listening Test (Watson & Barker, 1984)
Roberts (1984)	Psychophysiological arousal	Tympanic temperature (Patterson, 1976)
Roberts (1986)	Listening comprehension scores	Watson-Barker Listening Test (Watson & Barker, 1984).
Scott & Wheeless (1977b)	Academic achievement	Examination and project scores

(continued on next page)

TABLE 1   (continued)

Study	Conceptual Variable	Measurement Device
Sheahan (1976)	Perceived amount of election information	Likert-type scale
Wheeless (1975)	Communication apprehension	PRCA (McCroskey, 1970)
Wheeless & Scott (1976)	academic achievement	Grade point average and 3 examination scores
Wigley (1987)	Trait argumentativeness	Argumentativeness Scale (Infante & Rancer, 1982)
Williams (1976)	Information anxiety	Information Anxiety Scale (Williams, 1976)

RESULTS

The decision rules and meta-analytic procedures resulted in 25 data points that were categorized into groups based upon conceptual similarities. This process was quite straightforward, as the primary categories specified the conceptual variables of interest and there was little conceptual overlap.[4] Five categories were identified: (a) listening effectiveness; (b) processing anxiety; (c) information processing effectiveness; (d) information processing complexity; and (e) education level.

Results of the meta-analysis (Table 2) indicated consistent patterns when primary studies were grouped into these categories, summary statistics were converted to correlations, and the magnitudes of relationships (effect sizes) were displayed.

A final meta-analytic procedure involved determining the average effect size. Procedures required correcting study outcomes for attenu-

---

[4] *The decision rule for categorizing effect sizes required little interpretation. For example, the four studies grouped in the listening effectiveness category examined message recall as an index of comprehension and each of the six studies classified as processing anxiety employed a measure of state or trait anxiety or arousal as the criterion variable. Effect sizes were grouped in the information processing effectiveness category if the outcome involved experimentally induced judgment errors or performance on learning tasks. An effect size was classified as a processing complexity outcome if it corresponded to the content or structural components of Schroder, Driver, and Streufert's (1967) model of cognitive complexity. Studies were grouped in the complexity category due to the content decision rule (Daly, Vangelisti, & Daughton, 1988; O'Hair, 1986; Sheahan, 1976) if the effect size reflected the low-knowledge dimension of a cognition, and due to the structural decision rule (Beatty & Payne, 1981; Bocchino, 1984; Buhr & Pryor, 1988; Preiss, 1987; Wigley, 1987) if the effect size indicated low-order rules for combining or integrating cognitions. Finally, both studies in the education level outcome category correlated year in school with RAT scores.*

TABLE 2 Classification of Effect Size Metrics[a]

	r	d	z	r^2	N
Listening Effectiveness					
Daniels & Whitman (1979)	-.185	-.376	.185	.035	132
	-.203	*-.442*			
Paschall (1984)	-.034	-.068	.034	.001	167
	-.037	*-.074*			
Roach et al.(1985)					
Group 1	-.257	-.532	.262	.066	112
	-.282	*-.690*			
Group 2	-.173	-.351	.174	.030	59
	-.189	*-.385*			
Roberts (1986)	-.210	-.429	.213	.044	120
	-.231	*-.475*			
Processing Anxiety					
Beatty (1985)	.283	.590	.741	.398	50
	.311	*.655*			
Beatty, Behnke,	.410	.899	.632	.315	82
& Henderson (1980)	*.500*	*1.150*			
Borzi (1985)	.309	.650	.311	.095	153
	.332	*.704*			
Roberts (1984)	.300	.629	.310	.090	54
	.329	*.696*			
Wheeless (1975)	.200	.408	.200	.040	234
	.222	*.455*			
Williams (1976)	.300	.629	.632	.314	314
	.329	*.696*			
Information Processing Effectiveness					
Beatty (1981)	-.627	-1.610	.993	.537	84
	-.773	*-2.438*			
Bock & Bock (1984)	-.781	-2.499	1.045	.610	217
	-.848	*-3.200*			
Preiss et al. (1985)	-.403	-.880	.426	.163	40
	-.442	*-.986*			
Scott & Wheeless (1977b)	-.361	-.774	.376	.130	194
	-.440	*-.980*			
Wheeless &	-.400	-.872	.424	.160	256
Scott (1976)	*-.468*	*-1.060*			

(continued on next page)

TABLE 2 (continued)

	r	d	z	r²	N
Information-Processing Complexity					
Beatty & Payne (1981)	-.681 *-.783*	-1.861 *-2.518*	.290	.613	51
Bocchino (1984)	-.105 *-.115*	-.211 *-.232*	.105	.011	401
Buhr & Pryor (1988)	-.330 *-.369*	-.699 *-.794*	.342	.109	71
Daly et al. (1988)	-.220 *-.265*	-.451 *.550*	.224	.048	230
O'Hair (1986)	-.127 *-.151*	-.256 *-.306*	.127	.016	303
Preiss (1987)	-.380 *-.417*	-.822 *-.917*	.400	.144	66
Sheahan (1976)	-.426 *-.486*	-.941 *-1.112*	.497	.182	194
Wigley (1987)	-.360 *-.416*	-.772 *-.915*	.376	.130	67
Education Level					
McDowell & McDowell (1978)	-.056 *-.061*	-.112 *-.112*	.056	.003	297
McDowell et al. (1981)	-.192 *-.211*	-.391 *-.432*	.194	.037	694

[a] *The correlations and d scores in italics have been corrected for attenuation of measurement. Measures of the effect size associated with receiver apprehension include r (average correlation coefficient), d (difference in standard deviation units; Cohen, 1977), z (standard normal deviate of r), and r² (average variance accounted for).*

ation and searching for outliers. Table 3 displays the results of this process.

The benchmark for evaluating an effect size has been provided by Cohen (1977). He suggested that $r = .1$ be termed a "small effect"; $r = .3$ a "medium effect"; and $r = .5$ a "large effect." Of course, these standards are quite crude indices, and classification is made as a general frame of reference. Regardless of the evaluation standard, most of the effect sizes associated with receiver apprehension in Table 3 easily exceed minimum standards for meaningfulness.

TABLE 3   Receiver Apprehension Across Outcome Categories

	Average[a] r	Total N	Study K	sd(E)[b]	sd(O)[c]	% of[d] variance	X^{2d}	df
Listening effectiveness	-.18	590	5	.08	.09	89%	5.1[e]	4
Processing anxiety	.32	887	6	.07	.08	77%	7.0	5
Information processing effectiveness	-.59	791	5	.05	.18	8%	60.3*	4
Information processing complexity	-.26	1383	8	.07	.17	17%	35.1*	7
Education level	-.17	991	2	.04	.07	57%	4.9*	1

*indicates X^2 significant at .05 level.

[a] The average correlation represents the mean correlation after correction for attenuation of measurement.

[b] Expected standard deviation.

[c] Observed standard deviation.

[d] This percentage represents the portion of variance in observed correlations that can be attributed to sampling error. A figure of 100% would indicate that all variance in the observed correlations can be attributed to sampling error. If the percentage of variance due to sampling error is low, this indicates that some other feature may be responsible for the observed variance in correlations.

[e] This chi-square value indicates whether or not the observed variance is significantly greater than that expected by normal sampling error (Hunter, Schmidt, & Jackson, 1983). A significant chi-square indicates that moderator variables may be present in an outcome category. A nonsignificant chi-square does not preclude the existence of moderator variables.

DISCUSSION

The results of the meta-analysis indicate that receiver apprehension has practical and theoretical significance. Across conceptual variables, the relationships to receiver apprehension are apparently pervasive and salient. The categories of listening effectiveness, processing complexity, and education level warrant separate discussion.

Listening Effectiveness

The effect size for listening effectiveness (Table 3) is apparently consistent with the view that increases in receiver apprehension are related to diminishing listening outcomes. However, the average corrected correlation coefficient found (-.18) was "small" using Cohen's (1977) index. This slight, but definite effect is consistent in magnitude ($X^2 = 5.3$, df = 4, $p > 05$) and direction across criterion measures (message recall and scores from two listening assessment instruments). It is noteworthy that three of the five studies cumulated in the meta-analysis (Paschall, 1984; groups 1 and 2, Roach et al., 1985) did not detect statistically significant relationships between receiver apprehension and listening ability.

The study reporting the strongest effect size (Roberts, 1986) made the most direct test of the receiver apprehension-listening effectiveness relationship. Roberts' investigation detected a curvilinear effect between the variables, and he concluded that some arousal is necessary if receivers are to focus attention on a listening task. His analysis and interpretations are persuasive and may explain why other studies have not detected significant decrements in listening ability at some moderate to high levels of receiver apprehension. Conceptually, apprehensive receivers may be able to focus or concentrate on a single listening task (see Preiss & Wheeless, in press, for a discussion of this issue). Thus, the evidence from this meta-analysis indicated that lower listening effectiveness may not be the primary or most important cognitive outcome of receiver apprehension.

Information Processing Anxiety

The magnitude of the effect size for processing anxiety (Table 3) was "medium" using Cohen's (1977) system, and the results were compatible with Wheeless' view that receiver apprehension is a generalized fear-like response to message processing. The corrected average correlation (.32) was consistent in magnitude (X^2 = 7.0, df = 5, p > .05) and direction across measures of state anxiety. Wheeless argued that receiver apprehension is associated with a variety of decoding situations, and the meta-analysis was consistent with this assumption. Anxiety-type responses were observed when individuals interacted with others (Borzi, 1985), anticipated encountering new information (Williams, 1976), anticipated decoding messages (Beatty et al., 1980), or participated in a listening task (Beatty, 1985; Roberts, 1984).

Although anxiety is a central feature of the receiver apprehension literature, the theoretical bases for the relationship are not completely clear. This issue is important because the meta-analysis was unable to determine if anxiety results in reduced information processing consequences or if inefficient information processing leads apprehensive individuals to perform inappropriately in social and educational settings. Over time, the apprehensive receiver may learn to respond anxiously when placed in situations where message decoding/interpretation must be performed efficiently. Perhaps the effect size for processing anxiety should not be considered in tandem with the previous outcome, but with the next potential cognitive outcome of receiver apprehension, information processing effectiveness.

Information Processing Effectiveness

The effect size for effective information processing was "large" (Cohen, 1977). The direction of study effects resulting in the corrected average correlation (-.53) is consistent across criterion measures. However, the search for moderator variables indicated that variance in the magnitude of study effects cannot be explained by sampling error ($X^2 = 60.3$, df = 4, $p < .05$; see Table 3). The finding that all effect sizes were in the expected direction suggested that moderator variables may mediate the degree of association between receiver apprehension and information processing consequences. It appears that outlier data points (amount of assimilated information and accuracy in evaluations of speaker performance), may be different from other study effects in the category (critical evaluation of arguments, examination scores, and grade point average).

The category "information processing effectiveness" may include sub-processes that vary in sensitivity to anxiety or arousal. For example, the outlier study effects seem to involve perceiving the information within environmental contexts rather than merely processing information. A possible explanation for the outliers may involve the cue-utilization hypothesis (Mueller, 1976), where high-anxiety individuals perceive more cues than their low-anxiety counterparts, yet utilize fewer cues when processing information. Apprehensive receivers may perceive the environment to be laden with unassimilated information (Beatty, 1981), yet they apparently employ fewer cues when under stress (Bock & Bock, 1984). The cue-utilization hypothesis would account for the outlier study effects. Our reasoning here underscores the importance of examining mediating cognitive structures addressed in the next outcome category.

Information Processing Complexity

The effect size for information processing complexity was "small" (Cohen, 1977). The direction of the effects was consistent across criterion measures and the resulting corrected average correlation coefficient (-.26) approached the benchmark for a "medium" effect using Cohen's system. The search for moderator variables indicated that variance in the magnitude of study effects could not be explained by sampling error ($X^2 = 35.1$, df = 7, $p < .05$; see Table 3).

The variability among the study effect sizes may reflect the variety of indices included in the processing complexity category. Two studies found that receiver apprehension was negatively related to cognitive complexity (Beatty & Payne, 1981; Bocchino, 1984) and the investigations by Preiss (1987) and Wigley (1987) extended this reasoning to information-processing styles (integrated communication concepts and trait argumentativeness). Daly, Vangelisti, & Daughton (1988) found that apprehensive receivers did not understand the intricacies of incoming messages. This finding helps to explain O'Hair's (1986) results that apprehensive receivers prefer low information messages and Sheahan's (1976) observation that high-receiver apprehensives report less task-relevant information (cf. cue-utilization hypothesis). Buhr and Pryor's (1988) finding that apprehensive receivers report low need for cognition (Cacioppo & Petty, 1982) is particularly important when interpreting studies in this outcome category. Experiencing less enjoyment of effortful cognitive activity may mediate the motivation to process information or perhaps may bias the tendency to process peripheral versus central persuasive cues (Buhr & Pryor, 1988). This analysis would be consistent with the subcomponent of receiver apprehension involving "low order" interpretive schemes and reactions to messages. The inability to adopt others' perspectives and formulate a range of appropriate responses may bias cognitive processes. Additional research is needed, of course, to verify these possible moderator variables and specify how they alter information processing abilities.

Education Level

The effect size for receiver apprehension and education was "small" according to Cohen's system. The corrected average correlation coefficient (-.17) was based on two studies reporting negative relationships. The variance in data points was not attributable to sampling error ($X^2 = 3.6$, df = 1, $p < .05$; see Table 3), indicating that a search for moderator variables is warranted.

When conceptualized as year in school (junior high, high school, year in college), education appeared to be associated with a small, but definite decrease in receiver apprehension scores. Unfortunately, the studies included in this category did not identify the variables that account for decrements in receiver apprehension. Two explanations for the effect size seem reasonable: (a) Education may improve cognitive skills, thus reducing receiver apprehension and, (b) highly apprehensive receivers may leave the education system earlier than low-apprehensive receivers. While both explanations are probably operating, we believe that attrition may be the most logical, dominant force behind the effect size. The anxiety- and processing-related outcomes associated with receiver apprehension may well be an important factor in the decision to drop out of high school or not to attend college. Thus, the apparent decrease in receiver apprehension scores may be an artifact caused by excluding the most apprehensive individuals from the analysis.

CONCLUSIONS

The picture of the construct that emerges from 14 years of research is one of a broadly based information processing syndrome. Although the outcomes of receiver apprehension are pervasive, results from the meta-analysis were unable to identify the antecedents of receiver apprehension or support any one theoretical explanation for the variable. The search for moderator variables indicates that the relationships between receiver apprehension and the categories of listening ability and processing anxiety show no outliers, and the outcomes are consistent in direction across studies.

In our search for moderator variables in the processing effectiveness and processing complexity categories, we attempted to discover the reasons for variance among the data points. The cue-utilization hypothesis helps to explain why apprehensive receivers may perceive the environment to be information-dense, yet process information ineffectively. Apprehensive receivers could focus on style- and delivery-related features of communication in order to minimize content-processing anxiety (Bock & Bock, 1984). The finding that apprehensive receivers exhibited low need for cognition suggests possible differences in cue-utilization. Low enjoyment of cognitive tasks may divert attention to less substantive aspects of communication, resulting in ineffective processing.

The processing complexity category may be used to explain the large effect size for processing effectiveness. The diversity of conceptual variables included in this category, however, is of concern. We believe that an "average effect" based on diverse measures (e.g. cognitive complexity, integrated communication concepts, need for cognition, argumentativeness, etc.) does provide insight into the day-to-day experiences of apprehensive receivers. Wigley (1987) maintains that individuals experiencing high receiver apprehension are likely to develop related cognitive traits; the processing complexity category provides an index of this tendency.

The studies we clustered in the processing complexity category provide an interesting picture of apprehensive receivers. Apparently, receiver apprehension may serve as a source of bias in thought processes. When processing information, they appeared to be cognitively simple,[5] insensitive to cues (Daly et al., 1988), and unable to understand others' motives (Preiss, 1987). This may explain why apprehensive receivers apparently do not enjoy cognitive activity (Buhr & Pryor, 1988) or processing issues and arguments (Wigley, 1987). As a result, apprehen-

---

[5] We can find no conceptual or methodological explanation for the discrepancy in cognitive complexity data points (Beatty & Payne, 1981; Bocchino, 1984).

sive receivers may feel they have inadequate information (Sheahan, 1976), yet prefer messages with low information content (O'Hair, 1986). Low processing complexity is an appropriate description of apprehensive receivers.

Additional theory development and related research is required to better understand the causes of, and relationships between, receiver apprehension and the five categories. Receiver apprehension may well be the result of low confidence in information processing that is grounded in a processing deficit. Thus, poor information processors who do not recognize the deficit *would not* experience anxiety and adequate information processors who perceive a deficit *would* experience anxiety. This reasoning suggests that receiver apprehension transcends information processing ability and may be understood by focusing on the relationship between the receiver and the message environment. For apprehensive receivers, processing demands are perceived to exceed processing capacity in this conceptual framework.

We believe that a processing capacity/processing demands rationale may be understood in the context of self-references; e.g., "a person may assimilate certain inputs according to the conceptual schemata that he or she is intelligent..., or that people are untrustworthy, and so on" (McReynolds, 1976, pp. 42-43). For apprehensive receivers, information may be processed according to the conceptual schemata of low confidence in judgments and low self-expectancies—variables we equate with low psychological self-approval. This notion is important because part of the definition of receiver apprehension involves the fear of adjusting psychologically to messages sent by others. Low psychological self-approval may be associated with bewilderment at the amount of available information, social alienation, and information avoidance. Low psychological self-approval and low self-expectancies may be an antecedent to anxiety and the conceptual schemata underlying receiver apprehension. Research has not yet addressed this issue related to underlying antecedents.

In summary, the meta-analysis revealed meaningful outcomes and processes associated with receiver apprehension in the areas of listening effectiveness, information processing anxiety, information processing effectiveness, information processing complexity, and education. Possible moderator variables for two of the outcome categories (processing effectiveness and complexity) include the cue-utilization hypothesis and motivation to engage in cognitive activity. The results of the investigation indicate that greater scholarly attention needs to be directed at the antecedents and cognitive processes related to receiver apprehension. To this end, we offer psychological self-approval as a possible antecedent to be examined in future research. With greater theory development, the construct may be unified conceptually and the relationships among anxiety, cognition, and communication may be more clearly understood.

REFERENCES

Bangert-Drowns, R.L. (1986). Review of developments in meta-analytic method. *Psychological Bulletin, 99,* 388-399.

Beatty, M.J. (1981). Receiver apprehension as a function of cognitive backlog. *Western Journal of Speech Communication, 45,* 277-281.

Beatty, M.J. (1985). The effects of anticipating listening (state) anxiety on the stability of receiver apprehension scores. *Central States Speech Journal, 36,* 72-76.

Beatty, M.J., Behnke, R.R., & Henderson, L.S. (1980). An empirical validation of the receiver apprehension test as a measure of trait listening anxiety. *Western Journal of Speech Communication, 44,* 132-136.

Beatty, M.J., & Payne, S.K. (1981). Receiver apprehension and cognitive complexity. *Western Journal of Speech Communication, 45,* 363-369.

Bocchino, I.L. (1984). An exploratory study of the relationship between listening comprehension, cognitive complexity, receiver apprehension, and mood state (Doctoral dissertation, University of Florida) *Dissertation Abstracts International, 45,* 2692-A.

Bock, D.G., & Bock, H.B. (1977). The effects of the sex of the rater on leniency, halo, and trait errors in speech rating behavior. *Communication Education, 26,* 298-306.

Bock, D.G., & Bock, H. B. (1984). The effects of positional stress and receiver apprehension on leniency errors in speech evaluation: A test of the rating error paradigm. *Communication Education, 33,* 337-341.

Borzi, M.G. (1985). A rose by any other name is not the same: An examination into the nature of shyness and other related constructs (Doctoral dissertation, University of Florida). *Dissertation Abstracts International, 47,* 344-A.

Buhr, T.A., & Pryor, B. (1988). Receivers' apprehension and need for cognition. *Psychological Reports, 62,* 995-996.

Cacioppo, J.T., & Petty, R.E. (1982). The need for cognition. *Journal of Personality and Social Psychology, 42,* 116-131.

Cohen, J. (1977). Statistical power analysis for the behavioral sciences (Revised edition). New York, NY: Academic Press.

Cooper, H.M. (1984). *The integrative literature review.* Beverly Hills, CA: Sage.

Daly, J.A., Vangelisti, A.L., & Daughton, S.M. (1988). The nature and correlates of conversational sensitivity. *Human Communication Research, 14,* 167-202.

Daniels, T.C., & Whitman, R.F. (1979). *The effects of message structure, required recall structure, and receiver apprehension upon recall of message information.* University of Wisconsin, Green Bay. (ERIC Document Reproduction Service No. ED 178 979).

Delia, J.G., O'Keefe, B.J., & O'Keefe, D.J. (1982). The constructivist approach to communication. In F. E. X Dance (Ed.), *Human communication theory: Comparative essays.* New York, NY: Harper & Row.

Glass, G.V. (1977). Integrating findings: The meta-analysis of research. *Review of research in education, 5,* 351-379.

Glass, G.V., McGaw, B., & Smith, M.L. (1981). *Meta-analysis in social research*. Beverly Hills, CA: Sage.

Hedges, L.V., & Olkin, I. (1985). *Statistical methods for meta-analysis*. Orlando, FL: Academic Press.

Hunter, J.E., Schmidt, F.L., & Jackson, G.B. (1982). *Advanced meta-analysis: Cumulating research findings across studies*. Beverly Hills, CA: Sage.

Infante, D.A., & Rancer, A.S. (1982). A conceptualization and measurement of argumentativeness. *Journal of Personality Assessment, 46*, 72-80.

Light, R.L., & Pillemer, D.B. (1984). *Summing up: The science of reviewing research*. Cambrige, MA: Harvard University Press.

McCroskey, J.C. (1970). Measures of Communication-bound anxiety. *Speech Monographs, 37*, 269-277.

McCroskey, J.C., & Richmond, V.P. (1982). Communication apprehension and shyness: Conceptual and operational distinctions. *Central States Speech Journal, 33*, 458-468.

McDowell, E.E., & McDowell, C.E. (1978). An investigation of source and receiver apprehension at the junior high, senior high and college levels. *Central States Speech Journal, 29*, 11-19.

McDowell, E.E., McDowell, C.E., Hyerdahl, J., & Steil, L.K. (1978, November). *A multivariate study of demographics, psychological sex-roles, and receiver apprehension*. Paper presented at the annual meeting of the International Communication Association, Minneapolis. (ERIC Document Reproduction Service No. ED 206 033).

McDowell, E.E., McDowell, C.E., Pullan, G., & Lindbergs, K. (1981, May). *An investigation of source and receiver apprehension between the United States and Australian students at the high school and college levels*. Paper presented at the annual meeting of the International Communication Association, Minneapolis. (ERIC Document Reproduction Service No. ED 206 033)

McReynolds, P. (1976). Assimilation and Anxiety. In M. Zuckerman and C.D. Spielberger (Eds.), *Emotions and anxiety: New concepts, methods, and applications* (pp. 35-86). New York, NY: John Wiley and Sons.

McReynolds, P., & Acker, M. (1966). On the assessment of anxiety: II. By a self-report inventory. *Psychological Reports, 19*, 231-237.

Mueller, J.H. (1976). Anxiety and cue utilization in human learning and memory. In M. Zuckerman and C.D. Spielberger (Eds.), *Emotions and anxiety: New concepts, methods, and applications* (pp. 197-229). New York, NY: John Wiley and Sons.

O'Hair, D. (1986). Patient preferences for physician persuasion strategies. *Theoretical Medicine, 7*, 147-164.

O'Keefe, B.J. (1985, November). *The functional integration of communication concepts: Evidence for individual differences in reasoning about communication*. Paper presented at the annual meeting of the Speech Communication Association, Denver.

Paschall, K.A. (1984). *The effect of receiver apprehension and source apprehension on listening comprehension*. (Doctoral dissertation, University of Florida), *Dissertation Abstracts International, 45*, 1917-A.

Patterson, M. (1976). An arousal model of interpersonal intimacy. *Psychological Review, 83*, 235-245.

Phillips, G.M. (1968). Reticence: Pathology of the normal speaker. *Speech Monographs, 35*, 39-49.

Preiss, R.W. (1987, February). *Cognitive consequences of receiver apprehension: Evidence of reasoning about communication and self-persuasion.* Paper presented at the meeting of the Western Speech Communication Association, Salt Lake City.

Preiss, R.W., Rindo, J., Fishfader, T., & Wickersham, T. (1985, May). *Receiver apprehension and self-persuasion following counterattitudinal advocacy.* Paper presented at the meeting of the Northwest Communication Association, Coeur D'Alene, ID.

Preiss, R.W., & Wheeless, L.R. (in press). Affective responses in listening: A meta-analysis of receiver apprehension outcomes. *Journal of the International Listening Association.*

Roach, D.A., Hauser, M.F., Jackson, J., & Hanna, M.S. (1985, March). *The effects of receiver apprehension and noise on listening comprehension..* Paper presented at the meeting of the International Listening Association, Orlando, FL.

Roberts, C.V. (1984). A physiological validation of the receiver apprehension test. *Communication Research Reports, 1,* 126-129.

Roberts, C.V. (1986). A validation of the Watson-Barker Listening Test. *Communication Research Report, 3,* 115-119.

Rosenthal, R. (1978). Combining the effects of independent studies. *Psychological Bulletin, 86,* 638-641.

Schroder, M.J., Driver, M.J., & Struefert, S. (1961). *Human information processing.* New York: John Wiley and Sons.

Schroder, M.J., Driver, M.J., & Struefert, S. (1967). *Human information processing: Individuals and groups functioning in complex social situations.* New York: Holt, Rinehart and Winston.

Scott, M.D., & Wheeless, L.R. (1977a) Communication apprehension, student attitudes, and levels of satisfaction. *Western Journal of Speech Communication, 41,* 188-198.

Scott, M.D., & Wheeless, L.R. (1977b). The relationship of three types of communication apprehension to classroom achievement. *The Southern Speech Communication Journal, 42,* 246-255.

Sheahan, M.E. (1976). *Communication apprehension and electoral participation.* Unpublished master's thesis, West Virginia University, Morgantown, WV.

Spielberger, C.D., Gorsuch, R.L., & Lushene, R.E. (1968). *The State-Trait Anxiety Inventory [STAI]: Preliminary test manual Form X.* Tallahassee, FL: Florida State University.

Strube, M.J., & Hartman, D.P. (1983). Meta-analysis: Techniques, applications, and functions. *Journal of Consulting and Clinical Psychology, 51,* 14-27.

Watson, K., & Barker, L. (1984). *Watson-Barker Listening Test.* New Orleans, LA: Spectra.

Wheeless, L.R. (1975). An investigation of receiver apprehension and social context dimensions of communication apprehension. *The Speech Teacher, 24,* 261-268.

Wheeless, L.R., & Scott, M.D. (1976, April). *The nature, measurement and potential effects of receiver apprehension.* Paper presented at the meeting of the International Communication Association, Portland, OR.

Wigley III, C.J. (1987). Student receiver apprehension as a correlate of trait argumentativeness. *Communication Research Reports, 4,* 51-53.

Williams, B.L. (1976). *The development of a construct of information anxiety and its relationship to receiver apprehension.* Unpublished master's these, West Virginia University, Morgantown, WV.

The Development and Validation of a Measure of Negative Affectivity

Joseph P. Stokes
Ira M. Levin

Department of Psychology, University of Illinois at Chicago
P.O. Box 4348, Chicago, IL 60680

Negative Affectivity (NA) is a dispositional trait characterized by a tendency to experience aversive emotional states. A 21-item self-report measure of NA is developed using factor analytic and other correlational methods (N=381). The scale development is cross validated with a second sample (N=323). The NA scale has high internal consistency and test-retest reliability. Three validity studies (total N=741) revealed that the scale correlated significantly with measures of anxiety, neuroticism, self-esteem, happiness, life satisfaction, job satisfaction, and experienced negative affect, but not with measures of creativity and intellectual achievement. The scale did not, however, show good discriminant validity with reports of positive affect. Having a measure of the global construct of NA may prove useful to researchers studying a variety of topics related to personality.

Watson and Clark (1984) reviewed studies using a number of apparently diverse personality scales and concluded that these scales measured the same stable and pervasive trait, which they called Negative Affectivity (NA). The consistently high intercorrelations among measures of trait anxiety, neuroticism, self esteem, ego strength, and maladjustment, to name a few, suggest that these measures tap a single construct. Watson and Clark defined Negative Affectivity as a dispositional trait characterized by a tendency to experience aversive emotional states. They considered 12 existing, highly intercorrelated measures as alternate measures of NA. Among these are measures of anxiety (e.g., Taylor, 1953), neuroticism (e.g., Eysenck, 1962; Eysenck & Eysenck, 1968), and several scales from the MMPI (e.g., Byrne, 1961; Edwards, 1957; Hathaway, 1956;

Authors' Notes: We gratefully acknowledge the assistance of Rebecca G. Burzette and Glen B. Warshauer in the data collection for the second validation study.

Requests for reprints should be sent to the first author.

© 1990 Select Press

McKinley & Hathaway, 1942). Other researchers and personality theorists have recognized the importance of a pervasive personality trait like NA (e.g. Costa & McCrae, 1980; Eysenck & Eysenck, 1968; McCrae & Costa, 1987; Tellegen, 1982). The influential five-factor model of personality developed by Fiske (1949), Tupes and Christal (1961), and Norman (1963), and supported by recent research (e.g. McCrae & Costa, 1985, 1987) includes NA, usually called neuroticism, as one of the five factors.

High- and low-NA individuals have quite dissimilar orientations to themselves, others, and the world around them. "High-NA individuals are more likely to report distress, discomfort, and dissatisfaction over time and regardless of the situation, even in the absence of any overt or objective source of stress" (Watson & Clark, 1984, p. 483). They tend to dwell on their mistakes, disappointments, and shortcomings, and to focus more on the negative aspects of others and the world in general. Compared to individuals with low levels of NA, those high in NA are more hostile and pessimistic, and they have poorer self images. In contrast, low-NA individuals appear to be more satisfied, secure, and calm, and to focus less on and to be more resilient in response to life's daily frustrations and irritations.

While NA represents subjective differences in temperament, ongoing mood, and cognitive orientation, Watson and Clark emphasized that it is not necessarily a measure of psychological health. By most definitions high-NA individuals would be more likely to be considered poorly adjusted; however, low- NA does not necessarily imply psychological health. Watson and Clark suggested that people low in NA may tend to distort information, to fail to recognize negative affect or to dissociate themselves from its experience. Although such defensiveness or repressiveness may be functional in that it allows one to maintain a favorable mood in the face of life's inevitable frustrations, disappointments, and problems, it does not follow that low-NA people are more objective assessors of their experience than high-NA people. In fact, high-NA people may make more realistic appraisals than do low-NA people. So the NA dimension is not synonymous with mental health or psychopathology. Nor does a high-NA level preclude an individual from experiencing positive emotional mood states (e.g., happiness, joy).

Watson and Clark described NA as a unitary dimension that has several aspects. One aspect involves ongoing feelings of nervousness and tension, although Watson and Clark cautioned that defining NA as trait anxiety is too narrow. Another aspect has as its central component negative attitudes about oneself and low self-esteem. Two other aspects focus on negative attitudes about other people and the world in general.

These aspects, respectively, might be described as cynicism or distrust of others and pessimism about the future. Each of these aspects of NA can be conceived as a bipolar continuum: nervous/calm, satisfied/dissatisfied with oneself, cynical/trusting of others, and pessimistic/optimistic about the future. Although these dimensions are distinguishable phenomenologically and in some clinical populations, we think they all reflect NA when they are measured by self report in nonclinical samples. Using these four aspects of NA as a conceptual base, then, we have developed a measure of the broader construct.

Each of these four aspects can be measured by existing instruments, although no single existing instrument taps all four aspects. We therefore set out to develop a measure of NA that would include the four conceptual dimensions described earlier. One of the points of the Watson and Clark (1984) article, of course, was that a variety of measures of NA already exists. We felt it would be useful, however, to have a single measure that was easy to administer and that focused specifically on the concept Watson and Clark described. Our ability to develop an internally consistent instrument that tapped various aspects of NA would provide further evidence of the legitimacy of the construct.

SCALE DEVELOPMENT

Subjects

The two samples used in the scale development (N=381 and N=323) were undergraduate students from an introductory psychology class whose participation in this research partially fulfilled a course requirement.

Procedures

We began with an initial pool of 28 items, seven for each of the four aspects of NA that we were considering: 1) nervous/calm (e.g., "I often feel restless and jittery for no apparent reason," "I rarely lose sleep over worrying about something"); 2) satisfied/dissatisfied with oneself (e.g., "I feel that I have a great deal to be proud of," "When things go wrong, I blame myself"); 3) cynical/trusting of others (e.g. "If you are not careful people will take advantage of you," "Human nature is basically good, kind, and caring"); 4) pessimistic/optimistic about the future (e.g. "I always expect the worst to happen," "I know that things will continually improve in my life"). The scale contained approximately an equal number of positively and negatively worded statements to minimize the effects of subjects' response sets.

This 28-item scale was administered to Development Sample 1 (N=381) as part of a larger questionnaire booklet which contained four or five other self-report scales unrelated to the research reported here.

Subjects rated their degree of agreement with each of the 28 items on a 6-point Likert Scale (disagree strongly, disagree, disagree slightly, agree slightly, agree, agree strongly).

We developed the NA scale by performing a principal components analysis on the ratings for the 28 items. Items that loaded .45 or greater on the first principal component were considered the core group of items measuring NA. We proceeded by correlating any items not in this core group with the sum of the core group. We selected the item that correlated highest with the core group and added it to the scale. We continued this iterative procedure until the addition of another item no longer increased coefficient alpha for the scale. This exact procedure of scale development was carried out on a second scale development sample (N=323) to cross validate the results.

Results

For Development Sample 1 the principal components analysis of the 28-item NA scale yielded 7 components with eigenvalues greater than one. However, the only large difference between eigenvalues occurred between Component One (eigenvalue = 6.4) and Component Two (eigenvalue = 2.5). Component Two comprised the seven cynical/trusting items. The 15 items loading .45 or greater on Component One represented a fairly equal mix of the other three NA aspects (nervous/calm, pessimistic/optimistic, self-dissatisfied/ self-satisfied). These 15 items were used as a core group from which a scale was developed. Each of the remaining 13 items was correlated with this 15-item core and the single item having the highest correlation was added to the scale. Coefficient alpha was computed each time an item was added. This procedure was continued until adding an item no longer increased alpha. This procedure produced a 21-item scale which did not include any of the cynical/trusting items.

Very similar results were obtained when the procedure was replicated with Development Sample 2. The components analysis again produced seven components with eigenvalues greater than 1.0. As in Sample 1, the only large difference in eigenvalues was between Component One (5.6) and Component Two (2.8). Component Two again included the seven cynical/trusting items. Fourteen of the 15 items that had loadings of .45 or greater on Component One in Development Sample 1 also had loadings of .45 or greater in Sample 2. The single item that failed to load .45 on Component One in Sample 2 was the first to be added to the core scale based on its correlation with the other 14 items. The scale-building procedure produced the same 21-item scale in Sample 2 as it had in Sample 1. The items themselves and the item-total correlations for various samples are shown in Table 1.

TABLE 1 Item-Scale Correlations for Various Samples

	Development Sample 1	Development Sample 2	Studies 1+2	Study 3
1. After an embarrassing experience I worry about it for days.	.46	.44	.39	.49
2. I know that things will continually improve in my life.	.54	.42	.46	.49
3. I feel that I have a great deal to be proud of.	.47	.45	.48	.58
4. I often feel restless and jittery for no apparent reason.	.47	.42	.36	.44
5. Things rarely work out the way I want them to.	.54	.51	.53	.64
6. I am not as well liked as most other people.	.48	.46	.43	.56
7. Everyday seems exciting, new, and different.	.40	.34	.32	.35
8. My feelings are more easily hurt than most other people.	.31	.36	.41	.51
9. I can easily concentrate on things for as long as I like.	.32	.24	.11	.23
10. Whenever someone criticizes me I think about it for days.	.51	.46	.48	.48
11. I am hopeful and optimistic about the future.	.60	.50	.37	.65
12. When things go wrong I blame myself.	.37	.36	.38	.28
13. I rarely lose sleep over worrying about something.	.29	.30	.26	.40
14. I am a person of worth, at least as good as other people.	.43	.31	.44	.36
15. I always expect the worst to happen.	.54	.51	.56	.55
16. I am more content and happy than most other people.	.36	.41	.52	.52
17. Happy endings only occur in the movies and in fairy tales.	.48	.42	.50	.54
18. I am not as self-confident as most other people.	.36	.46	.58	.55
19. When I meet people for the first time I am tense and uptight.	.44	.46	.40	.39
20. If I could live my life over I would do many things differently.	.34	.31	.43	.44
21. The future seems rather bleak and unpromising.	.63	.53	.68	.55

Note: Correlations reflect the relation between each item and the sum of all other items in the scale.

Coefficient alphas, a measure of internal consistency, were .87 and .84 for the 21-item scale for Samples 1 and 2, respectively. Eighty-five subjects from Sample 2 completed the 21-item scale six weeks after their original testing. The test-retest correlation was .88; the means from the first and second testings were not different (t=1.23). Mean scores for the 21-item NA Scale for the two development samples were 63.15 and 62.81; standard deviations were 17.12 and 15.96; ranges were 25-104 and 34-107.

VALIDATION STUDIES
Study 1

Convergent and discriminant validity are investigated by correlating the NA scale with measures of constructs hypothesized to be related/unrelated to NA based on prior research. Watson and Clark (1984) suggested that the Taylor Manifest Anxiety Scale (Taylor, 1953) and the neuroticism scale of the Eysenck Personality inventory (Eysenck & Eysenck, 1968) could be considered as alternate measures of NA due to their high correlations with various other measures of NA. They also reported significant covariation between measures of self-esteem/self-concept and NA. Other research Watson and Clark reviewed indicated that high-NA people were characterized as more introspective than low-NA people, while low-NA people were described as more gregarious and socially facile. As a result, we hypothesized that the 21-item NA scale would be positively correlated with the Taylor Manifest Anxiety Scale and the Eysenck Neuroticism Scale, and negatively correlated with the Rosenberg Self-Esteem Scale (Rosenberg, 1965) and the Eysenck Extraversion Scale. Since there was no theoretical or empirical basis for associating NA with creativity or intelligence, we hypothesized that the NA scale would not correlate with the Remote Associates Test (Mednick, 1962), a measure of creativity, or with the Shipley Institute of Living Scale vocabularly Test (Shipley, 1940), a measure of intellectual achievement.

Subjects and Procedure

Subjects were 211 introductory psychology students whose participation in the research partially fulfilled a course requirement. They met in groups of 15 to 20 and completed a questionnaire booklet containing the NA scale and a subset of the following measures: Rosenberg Self-Esteem Scale, Shipley Vocabularly Test, Remote Associates Test, Taylor Manifest Anxiety Scale, and Eysenck Personality Inventory.

Results

As hypothesized, the NA scale correlated significantly with the Taylor Manifest Anxiety Scale (r=.64, p<.001, N=100), the Eysenck Neuroticism Scale (r=.60, p<.0001, N=111), the Rosenberg Self-Esteem Scale (r=-.74, p<.0001, N=84), and the Eysenck Extraversion Scale (r=-.38, p<.0001, N=111). As expected no relation was found between the NA scale and the Remotes Associates Test (r=.001, N=105). However, a significant relation was found between the NA scale and the Shipley Vocabulary Test (r=-.30, p<.001, N=111).

Study 2

Study 2 was designed to provide additional information about the convergent and divergent validity of the NA scale. We were puzzled by the negative correlation of the NA scale with the Shipley Vocabularly Test and were interested in exploring further the relation of NA to other measures of intelligence and intellectual achievement. To this end we included both the Vocabulary Test and the Abstraction Test of the Shipley Institute of Living Scale (Shipley, 1940) in Study 2. We also included an antonym test and a mathematics test taken from old Scholastic Aptitude Tests (SAT; 10 SATS, 1986). Because we had no theoretical reason to expect scores on these tests to be correlated with NA scores and despite our previous finding that the Shipley Vocabulary Test was correlated with NA, we predicted that NA would not correlate with these measures.

In Study 2 we included other measures that we did expect to be correlated with NA. One was the Edwards Social Desirability Scale (Edwards, 1957), a scale derived from the MMPI that Watson and Clark suggested was a measure of NA. We think this scale is misnamed and is really more a measure of NA than of social desirability (see discussion later). We also included the Marlowe-Crowne Social Desirability Scale (Crowne & Marlowe, 1964) to examine the relation of NA scale scores to a tendency to respond in socially desirable ways.

Conceptually, NA should relate to overall reported happiness and life satisfaction, so we included single-item measures of happiness and life satisfaction taken from surveys of Gurin, Veroff, and Feld (1960). We asked "taking all things together, how would you say things are these days? Would you say you're ... not too happy, pretty happy, or very happy?" Respondents answered on a 5-point scale with points 1, 3, and 5 anchored by the descriptors. Using the same format, we also asked "In general, how satisfying do you find the way you're spending your life these days? Would you call it ... not very satisfying, pretty satisfying, or completely satisfying?"

Finally, we hypothesized that NA would correlate with reports of experienced affect. Drawing from Watson and Clark (1984) and from Watson and Tellegen's (1985) structure of mood, we chose seven descriptors of positive affect (active, alert, elated, enthusiastic, excited, peppy, and strong) and 12 descriptors of negative affect (angry, anxious, dissatisfied with myself, distressed, guilty, hostile, jittery, nervous, rejected, tense, upset, worried). For each descriptor, subjects rated the degree to which they had felt that feeling in the past week, using the following scale: definitely have not felt, may have felt a little, have felt somewhat, have felt quite a bit, have felt really a lot. Ratings for positive and negative affect descriptors were summed separately to create scores for experienced positive affect and for experienced negative affect. We predicted that NA scores would correlate positively with experienced negative affect and made no prediction concerning the relation of NA to experienced positive affect.

Subjects and Procedure

Subjects were 215 students from introductory psychology whose participation in this research partially fulfilled a course requirement. They met in groups of 8 to 15 and completed a questionnaire booklet containing the NA scale and one of two groups of other questionnaires: 1) Shipley Vocabulary Test, Shipley Abstraction Test, SAT antonyms, and SAT mathematics, or 2) Edwards Social Desirability Scale, Marlowe-Crowne Social Desirability Scale, happiness and life satisfaction ratings, and the experienced affect measure. The order of the measures within each packet was random, except that the NA scale came either first or last. Preliminary analyses revealed no effects attributable to whether the NA scale came first or last.

Results

None of the intellectual achievement measures correlated significantly with NA. The specific correlations with the NA scale were -.115 for the Shipley Vocabulary Test, .014 for the Shipley Abstraction Test, -.078 for the SAT antonyms, and .055 for the SAT mathematics (all Ns=107). Correlations of the NA scale with the other measures were as follows (all Ns=98, except for the Edwards, when N=84): Edwards, -.70, $p<.001$; Marlowe-Crowne, -.234, $p<.05$; happiness rating, -.509, $p<.001$; life satisfaction rating, -.455, $p<.001$, experienced positive affect, -.482, $p<.001$; and experienced negative affect, .625, $p<001$. Coefficient alpha for the NA scale for Validity Study 2 was .85.

Although we had made no prediction about the relation of NA to positive affect, we were disappointed that there was a substantial negative correlation. This relation is partially explained by the fact that reports of experienced positive and negative affect were themselves correlated in our data (r=-.284, N=98, p<.01). (The empirical relation of experienced positive and negative affect depends on the time-frame of the measures. See Diener & Emmons, 1985. Our results are typical for the one-week time period we used.) Experienced positive and negative affect together predict 49% of the variance in NA. Experienced positive affect accounts for about 10% of the variance in NA, above and beyond that accounted for by experienced negative affect.

Study 3

Because people high in NA tend to focus on negative aspects of themselves, others, and the world in general, we reasoned that they would be relatively dissatisfied with their jobs. In Study 3 we tested the ability of NA to predict job satisfaction. As measures of job satisfaction we used scales from both the Job Diagnostic Survey (JDS; Hackman & Oldham, 1980) and the Job Descriptive Index (JDI; Smith, Kendall, & Hulin, 1969). From the JDS we used a composite measure of satisfaction; from the JDI we used measures of satisfaction for each of five aspects of work: satisfaction with the work itself, pay, coworkers, supervision, and promotional opportunities. (See Levin & Stokes, in press, for a more thorough description of these measures.) We expected NA scores to correlate negatively with all these measures of job satisfaction.

Subjects and Procedures

The subjects for Validity Study 3 were 315 professional staff from a large international professional service firm. These professional staff represented four hierarchical job levels and had been with the organization an average of about three years (range of one to ten years). All had bachelor's degrees and about 30% had advanced degrees. Subjects met with the researcher in groups of 15 to 20 and individually completed the JDS, the JDI, and the NA scale.

Results

NA correlated negatively and significantly (p<.001, N=315) with five of the six measures of job satisfaction: JDS satisfaction (-.35), JDI satisfaction with work itself (-.29), JDI satisfaction with co-workers (-.22), JDI satisfaction with supervision (-.26), and JDI satisfaction with promotional opportunities (-.19). NA was not correlated with JDI satisfaction with pay (-.03).

DISCUSSION

The NA scale was developed as a self-report measure of negative affectivity, one of five factors of comprehensive models of personality. The 21-item NA scale has good psychometric properties. Coefficient alpha is consistently around .85, and the six-week test-retest reliability is .88. Although further research is needed to examine the scale's stability over longer time periods, the six-week interval is long enough to allow for normal mood changes and the occurrence of various life events.

Initially the NA construct was conceived of as representing four dimensions: nervous/calm, satisfied/dissatisfied with oneself, cynical/trusting of others, and pessimistic/optimistic about the future. Principal components analysis of the original items on two samples suggested that the cynical/trusting items formed a component separate from the other three dimensions, and these items were not included in the final version of the scale. The lower desire for social contact and affiliation that characterizes people high in NA seems to be more a function of their anxiety in social situations and of their lack of self confidence then of their cynicism or distrust of others. In the five-factor model of personality (cf. McCrae & Costa, 1985, 1987), cynicism or distrust of others is probably more central to the agreeableness factor than to NA.

Convergent validity was established by examining the relationship of NA to a variety of constructs mentioned by Watson and Clark (1984) as alternate measures of NA. People low in NA were found to have lower scores on measures of anxiety and neuroticism; those lower in NA scored higher on measures of self esteem and extraversion. NA scores also were related to scores on the Edwards Social Desirability Scale, a scale that is probably misnamed. Watson and Clark (1984) considered the Edwards as one of the alternate measures of NA because of its high correlation with other measures that are related to NA. Of the 39 MMPI items that make up the Edwards, 25 also contribute to one of the clinical scales, although they are scored in the opposite direction of the clinical scales. In the data reported here, the Edwards correlated with the more widely-used Marlowe-Crowne Social Desirability Scale at a statistically significant but low level ($r=.233$, $N=84$, $p<.05$).

The NA scale developed here also was related to self ratings of happiness and life satisfaction, and to the experience of negative affect. These findings are consistent with our conception of NA. They also support the model of subjective well-being presented by Costa and McCrae (1980), where personality characteristics that reflect NA (neuroticism, anxiety, hostility, etc.) partially determine happiness, morale, and life satisfaction.

As evidence of divergent validity, the NA scale was not related to a variety of measures of academic achievement, intellectual ability, and creativity. The NA scale was related weakly but significantly to the Marlowe-Crowne Social Desirability Scale ($r=-.234$). People who are trying to present themselves in a favorable light tend to report lower levels of NA. The relation of NA to social desirability makes conceptual sense, even though it is a limitation. It is not surprising that a measure of NA or one of its components is influenced by social desirability.

The measure of NA developed here did not show good discriminant validity with reports of experienced positive affect. Several of our items, in fact, focus on states (e.g., "I feel I have a great deal to be proud of," "I am hopeful and optimistic about the future") that reflect positive rather than negative affect in a two-factor model (Watson & Tellegen, 1985). Given our conceptualization of NA (and our reading of Watson and Clark's conceptualization), it is not surprising that NA correlates with reports of experienced positive affect. Of the three dimensions we used in our final concept of NA, only one (nervous/calm) can reasonably be considered independent of positive affect. The other two (satisfied/dissatisfied with self and pessimistic/optimistic) imply low levels of experienced positive affect. Certainly "I am hopeful and optimistic about the future" is face valid as an item measuring pessimism/optimism. Someone who disagrees with this item, however, probably experiences lower levels of positive emotions like enthusiasm than one who agrees with the item. In fact the construct we set out to measure, and the scale we developed, appear to tap a combination of positive and negative affect.

This lack of discriminant validity is a limitation of the current instrument. Our scale is not a good measure of NA to use in situations where discriminating negative and positive affect is important. In fact, data we have collected suggest that none of the alternate measures of NA mentioned in Watson and Clark (1984) fare particularly well when it comes to discriminant validity with positive affect. For a measure of NA to be independent of positive affect, it would probably have to be limited to the nervous/calm dimension from our concept of NA. Probably the best choice of an existing trait measure for research where such discrimination is critical is the Negative Emotionality Scale of Tellegen's (1982) Multidimensional Personality Questionnaire.

The NA scale reported here may, however, be helpful to researchers at both conceptual and methodological levels. Conceptually, NA may be important in explaining the relations of other variables. Rice, Near, and Hunt (1980) noted a positive relation between job and life satisfaction had been found in over 90 percent of the studies they reviewed. Over the years there has been considerable debate, speculation, and research concerning whether job satisfaction caused life satisfaction or vice versa. Research by Keon and McDonald (1982) indicated that job and life satisfaction were jointly determined with the level of one mutually influencing the level of the other. Years ago Kornhauser (1965) astutely speculated that personality variables may affect both job and life satisfaction. NA may be a common source of variance. More than likely the negative emotionality, dissatisfaction, and pessimism of high-NA people generalize to a variety of contexts. Such people may report themselves as discontented, regardless of what aspect of their lives they are asked to evaluate.

In certain research areas, a measure of NA will be a helpful methodological tool. For example, a lot of research in the last decade has focused on the relation of social support to measures of adjustment. Not surprisingly, more subjective measures of support bear a stronger relationship to adjustment and psychological disorders than do more objective measures (Billings & Moos, 1982; Henderson, Byrne, & Duncan-Jones, 1981; Hirsch, 1980; Hobfoll & Stokes, in 1988; Schaefer, Coyne, & Lazarus, 1981). One explanation for the relation between subjective measures of support and adjustment is that individual differences control perceptions of both (Levin & Stokes, 1986; Sarason, Sarason, & Shearin, 1986). In many studies measures of support may be confounded with measures of adjustment (see Dohrenwend, Dohrenwend, Dodson, & Shrout, 1984 and Thoits, 1982) because both are caused, at least in part, by NA (see Stokes & McKirnan, 1989, for a more thorough discussion of this point). Having a measure of NA would allow one to remove statistically the influence of NA on measures of support and adjustment, and would provide for a rigorous test of hypotheses relating the effects of social support and adjustment. .

REFERENCES

Billings, A.G., & Moos, R.H. (1981). The role of coping responses in attenuating the stress of life events. *Journal of Behavioral Medicine, 4,* 139-155.

Byrne, D. (1961). The Repression-Sensitization Scale: Rationale, reliability, and validity. *Journal of Personality, 29,* 334-349.

Costa, P.T., Jr., & McCrae, R.R. (1980). Influence of extraversion and neuroticism on subjective well-being: Happy and unhappy people. *Journal of Personality and Social Psychology, 38,* 668-678.

Crowne, D.P. & Marlowe, D. (1964). *The approval motive: Studies in evaluative dependence.* New York: Wiley.

Diener, E., & Emmons, R.A. (1985). The independence of positive and negative affects. *Journal of Personality and Social Psychology, 47,* 1105-1117.

Dohrenwend, B.S., Dohrenwend, B.P., Dodson, M. & Shrout, P.E. (1984). Symptoms, hassles, social supports and life events: Problems of confounded measures. *Journal of Abnormal Psychology, 93,* 222-230.

Edwards, A.L. (1957). *The social desirability variable in personality assessment and research.* New York: Dryden.

Eysenck, H.J. (1962). *The Maudsley Personality Inventory.* San Diego, CA: Educational and Industrial Testing Service.

Eysenck, H.J., & Eysenck, S.B.C. (1968). *Manual for the Eysenck Personality Inventory.* San Diego, CA: Educational and Industrial Testing Service.

Fiske, D.W. (1949). Consistency of the factorial structures of personality ratings from different sources. *Journal of Abnormal and Social Psychology, 44*, 329-344.

Gurin, G., Veroff, J., & Feld, S. (1960). *Americans view their mental health.* New York: Basic Books.

Hackman, J.R., & Oldham, G.R. (1980). *Work redesign.* Reading, Ma: Addison-Wesley.

Hathaway, S.R. (1956). Scales 5 (masculinity-femininity), 6 (paranoia), and 8 (schizophrenia). In G. S. Welsh & W.G. Dahlstrom (Eds.), *Basic readings on the MMPI in psychology and medicine* (pp. 104-111). Minneapolis, MN: University of Minnesota Press.

Henderson, S., Bryne, D.G., & Duncan-Jones, P. (1981). *Neurosis and the social environment.* Syndey: Academic Press.

Hirsch, B.J. (1980). Natural support systems and coping with major life changes. *American Journal of Community Psychology, 8*, 159-172.

Hobfoll, S.E., & Stokes, J.P. (1988). The process and mechanics of social support. In S. Duck, D.F. Hay, S.E. Hobfoll, W. Ickes, & B. Montogomery (Eds.), *Handbook of research in personal relationships.* London: Wiley.

Keon, T.L., & McDonald, B. (1982). Job satisfaction and life satisfaction: An empirical evaluation of their interrelationships. *Human Relations, 35*, 167-180.

Kornhauser, A.W. (1965). *Mental health of the industrial worker: A Detroit study.* New York: Wiley.

Levin, I.M., & Stokes, J.P. (1986). An examination of the relation of individual difference variables to loneliness. *Journal of Personality, 54*, 201-217.

Levin, I.M., & Stokes, J.P. (in press). A dispositional approach to job satisfaction: The role of negative affectivity. *Journal of Applied Psychology.*

McCrae, R.R., & Costa, P.T., Jr. (1985). Updating Norman's "adequate taxonomy:" Intelligence and personality dimensions in natural language and in questionnaires. *Journal of Personality and Social Psychology, 49*, 710-721.

McCrae, R.R., & Costa, P.T. Jr. (1987). Validation of the five-factor model of personality across instruments and observers. *Journal of Personality and Social Psychology, 52*, 81-90.

McKinley, J.C., & Hathaway, S.R. (1942). A multiphasic personality schedule (Minnesota): IV. Psychasthenia. *Journal of Applied Psychology, 26*, 614-624.

Mednick, S.A. (1962). The associative basis of the creative process. *Psychological Review, 69*, 220-232.

Norman, W.T. (1963). Toward an adequate taxonomy of personality attributes: Replicated factor structures in peer nominated personality ratings. *Journal of Abnormal and Social Psychology, 66*, 574-583.

Rice, R.W., Near, J.P., & Hunt, R.G. (1980). The job satisfaction - life satisfaction relationship: A review of empirical research. *Basic and Applied Social Psychology, 1*, 37-64.

Rosenberg, M. (1965). *Society and the adolescent image.* Princeton, NJ: Princeton University Press.

Sarason, I.G., Sarason, B.R., & Shearin, E.W. (1986). Social support as an individual differences variable: Its stability, origins,, and relational aspects. *Journal of Personality and Social Psychology, 50*, 845-855.

Schaefer, C.C., Coyne, J.C., & Lazarus, R.S. (1981). The health related functions of social support. *Journal of Behavioral Medicine, 4*, 381-406.

Shipley, W.C. (1940). A self administering scale for measuring intellectual impairment and deterioration. *Journal of Psychology, 9*, 371-377.

Smith, P.C., Kendall, L.M., & Hulin, C.L. (1969). *The measurement of satisfaction in work and retirement: A strategy for the study of attitudes.* Chicago, IL: Rand & McNally.

Stokes, J.P., & McKirnan, D.J. (1989). Affect and the social environment: The role of social support in depression and anxiety. In P. Kendall & D. Watson (Eds.), *Anxiety and depression: Distinctive and overlapping features.* Orlando, FL: Academic.

Taylor, J.A. (1953). A personality scale of manifest anxiety. *Journal of Abnormal and Social Psychology, 48*, 285-290.

Tellegen, A. (1982). *Brief manual for the Differential Personality Questionnaire.* Unpublished manuscript. University of Minnesota, Minneapolis. 10 SATS. (1986). New York: College Entrance Examination Board.

Thoits, P.A. (1982). Conceptual, methodological, and theoretical problems in studying social support as a buffer against life stress. *Journal of Health and Social Behavior, 23*, 145-159.

Tupes, E.C., & Christal, R.E. (1961). *Recurrent personality factors based on trait ratings* (USAF ASD Tech. Rep. No. 61-97). Washington, D.C.: U.S. Government Printing Office.

Watson, D., & Clark, L.A. (1984). Negative affectivity. The disposition to experience aversive emotional states. *Psychological Bulletin, 96*, 465-490.

Watson, D., & Tellegen, A. (1985). Toward a consensual structure of mood. *Psychological Bulletin, 98*, 219-235.

Cognitive Components of Test Anxiety: A Comparison of Assessment and Scoring Methods

Kirk R. Blankstein
Department of Psychology
Erindale College, University of Toronto
Mississauga, Ontario L5L 1C6, Canada

Gordon L. Flett
Department of Psychology, York University
4700 Keele Street, North York, Ontario M3J 1P3, Canada

The present study examined two issues pertaining to the unstructured cognitive assessment of test anxiety. Specifically, we investigated the results of unstructured cognitive assessments scored by the subject versus trained judges. In addition, we investigated the extent to which unstructured assessments (i.e., thought listings) and structured assessments (i.e., item endorsements) of cognition related to each other as well as to measures of test anxiety and performance. A sample of 54 male college students who differed in level of test anxiety attempted a relatively difficult anagram task. Subjects then listed their thoughts and provided item endorsement ratings. Comparison of the thought list scoring methods revealed that listed thoughts scored by the subjects were less reliably associated with test anxiety than the same thoughts scored by judges. As for the relation between unstructured and structured measures, comparable results were obtained from the experimenter-rated thought list and item endorsement data for thoughts involving the self: greater test anxiety was associated significantly with fewer positive self-referential thoughts and more negative self-referential thoughts. However, there was little relation between the structured and unstructured measures of task-related thinking. Overall, it is concluded that the findings constitute additional evidence for the role of cognitive factors involving the self in the experience of test anxiety.

Recent progress in the development of cognitive-behavioral strategies for the treatment of emotional disorders has led to heightened interest in cognitive assessment (e.g., Kendall, 1982; Kendall & Hollon, 1981). As a result, a variety of methods for obtaining and assessing

---

Authors' Note: Request reprints from the first author.

© 1990 Select Press

cognitions has emerged (see Merluzzi, Glass, & Genest, 1981). It has been suggested elsewhere that these measures of cognition can be grouped into several methodological categories: endorsement methods, production methods, recording methods, and sampling methods (Kendall & Hollon, 1981). Endorsement and production methods have been most widely used. Endorsement methods assess cognitions by instructing subjects to indicate whether a thought has occurred by responding to a predetermined series of items. In contrast, production methods such as the thought listing technique require that subjects retrospectively produce, typically in a written format, their thoughts from an immediately preceding interval. Although various innovative approaches to cognitive assessment have been available to practitioners and researchers alike, the most widely adopted strategy for assessing cognitions continues to be the structured endorsement questionnaire (see Clark, 1988, for a review).

Recently, concerns have been raised about the accuracy of structured self-statement questionnaires. For example, Glass and Arnkoff (1983) argued that item endorsements may not reflect actual thought content. Rather, subjects may be basing their responses to questionnaire items on having experienced similar but not identical thoughts. Furthermore, Hammen and Krantz (1985) posited that subjects may endorse items on the basis of implicit theories about their thoughts and feelings rather than on the actual occurrence of cognitions. Additionally, endorsement questionnaires rely on recognition rather than on recall processes and thus may be more susceptible to various response biases, rationalizations, inconsistent responses, and demand characteristics (Genest & Turk, 1981).

The potential usefulness of the thought listing procedure has been demonstrated recently in research examining individual differences in test anxiety. In two separate studies, Blankstein and his colleagues (Blankstein, Toner, & Flett, 1989; Blankstein, Flett, Boase, & Toner, in press) have administered an analogue test to subjects and shown that the frequency of negative self-referential thinking as assessed by a thought listing procedure is associated positively with test anxiety. This contrasts sharply with the results of past studies in this domain which have failed to detect a relation between test anxiety and unstructured cognitive assessments (Arnkoff & Smith, 1988; Galassi, Frierson, & Siegel, 1984; Glass & Arnkoff, 1983). However, these equivocal results can be attributed to differences in the methods and systems used to code listed thoughts. Studies which have not yielded the expected group differences have utilized a coding system that does not distinguish between thoughts involving the self and thoughts involving the task. The importance of making this distinction is signified by the growing body of research with other forms of assessment which confirms that a key element of test anxiety is the tendency to become self-focused when confronted with the threat of evaluation and to emit self-critical statements that may distract attention from the task at hand (e.g., Brown & Nelson, 1983; Deffenbacher & Hazaleus, 1985; Flett, Blankstein, & Boase, 1987; Hunsley, 1987; Sarason, Sarason, Keefe, Hayes, & Shearin, 1986).

Clearly, the thought-listing technique has the potential to provide a great deal of insight as to the nature of test anxiety. This possibility notwithstanding, there are several issues pertaining to unstructured assessments which remain to be investigated. The purpose of the present study was to examine some of these issues.

One important issue has to do with the scoring of the thought listings. Is it preferable to have participants or trained judges classify thoughts and assess their salience, facilitativeness, and so forth? Our past research has utilized ratings by trained judges. However, Tarico, Van Velsen, and Altmaier (1986) have outlined the merits of self-ratings: they are more economical and there are likely to be fewer unscoreable responses "... because subjects usually know what they meant by a brief or ambiguous phrase" (p.81). Although Tarico et al. (1986) reported that self-ratings by subjects and ratings by experts were not differentially effective as predictors of self-reported speech anxiety, Cacioppo, Glass, and Merluzzi (1979) reported a discrepancy between judge- and subjective ratings of thought-listings as a function of heterosocial anxiety. High socially anxious men generated more negative thoughts when these thoughts were rated by judges, whereas subject-rated thoughts were not correlated with social anxiety, despite the fact that subjects and judges were in general agreement as to what constituted positive, negative, and neutral thoughts. Given the obvious merits of subject-scored listed thoughts, and the inconsistency in reported findings, it appears important to conduct further comparisons of self- and expert- ratings of thought list protocols.

A second issue of importance involves the degree of overlap that exists between structured and unstructured methods of assessment. Are the same results obtained when the data are in the form of thought listings as opposed to item endorsement ratings? Existing research on this issue is equivocal. Some studies of phenomena other than test anxiety have found evidence that the two forms of assessment are related (Fichten, Amsel, & Robillard, 1988; Segal & Marshall, 1985). Other studies have found that structured and unstructured assessments are largely unrelated (Myszka, Galassi, & Ware, 1986). Similarly, the test anxiety studies that have been conducted thus far have provided evidence to suggest that the two forms of assessment are associated (Blankstein et al., in press;

Blankstein et al., 1989; Houston, Fox, & Forbes, 1984) but other research has detected no significant correlation between the types of measures (Arnkoff & Smith, 1988). One possible explanation for these conflicting findings is that, once again, the endorsement measures used in most previous test anxiety studies have not been constructed in a manner that allows researchers to distinguish between items pertaining to the self and items pertaining to other factors such as the testing context (e.g., Arnkoff & Smith, 1988). Consequently, in the present study, we constructed an endorsement measure that included separate subscales for positive and negative thoughts related to the self and the task. We expected that the advent of this measure would enable us to establish that there is indeed a relation between the results obtained with structured and unstructured methods.

In summary, the present study sought to further examine the utility of a thought list coding system in test anxiety by measuring the degree of overlap between thought listing and endorsement data and by comparing the results obtained with self-ratings and expert ratings of thought list assessments. Finally, the interrelationships among test anxiety, the measures of cognitions, actual performance and various ratings of self-expectation and evaluation were also examined to obtain a broader view of the role of cognitive factors in the experience of test anxiety.

METHOD

Subjects

The subjects were 54 male students enrolled in an undergraduate introductory psychology course at the University of Toronto. Subjects volunteered to participate and fulfilled a research participation requirement.

Procedure and Instruments

Participants were tested in small groups of 5 to 10 students in a seminar room structured to simulate an examination room. An "examination in progress" sign was attached to the door, a large wall clock was set for the time remaining in the exam, and students were seated by the experimenter in alternate seats and instructed not to communicate with each other. The experimenter walked around the examination table and occasionally peered over the shoulder of each participant during the test. The experimenter also periodically wrote the time remaining for the test on the blackboard.

Initially, subjects completed a consent form and the measure of test anxiety, Sarason's 37-item Test Anxiety Scale (TAS; Sarason, 1978). Respondents to the TAS are asked to agree or disagree with statements describing self-oriented, interfering, cognitive, "worry" reactions experienced in testing situations, and attitudes toward testing situations. Higher scores reflect greater test anxiety. Test-retest reliabilities over .80 have been obtained for intervals of several weeks and the scale has acceptable internal consistency (Sarason, 1978). Moreover, the scale is not influenced strongly by social desirability bias, particularly in male subjects (see Blankstein & Toner, 1987). It is for this reason that only male subjects were included in the current study. The mean TAS score in the present sample was 15.0 (SD = 6.3), a value that is consistent with the normative data for male subjects.

Subjects were advised to read the instructions for the test and to complete various pre-test ratings and then to await further instructions. In written instructions, subjects were informed that they were to perform an anagram test consisting of 20 anagrams of five letters each to be solved in 20 minutes. The instructions incorporated several factors used in past test anxiety research to elicit evaluative stress (e.g., Geen, 1984; Holroyd, Westbrook, Wolf, & Badhorn, 1978; Meichenbaum, 1972; Sarason, 1961). Stress-evaluation factors included: 1) the establishment of a relation between performance on the test, IQ, and college grades; 2) a suggestion that the test is easily done by peers; and 3) the pressure of a time limit for the test. Students were further instructed that they would be given feedback concerning their absolute score and relative group standing on the test.

Next, students completed several questions related to intelligence tests, awareness of actual IQ score, self-estimated IQ, estimate of IQ relative to other first-year psychology students, and predicted course grade. Subjects then indicated how they thought they would perform on the test (self-expectation) and how other students would perform on the test (other-expectation); how important it was for them to perform well on the test (self-importance) and how important it was for others to perform well on the test (other-performance) and self-ratings concerning the importance of good performance in introductory psychology and academic evaluations in general. These ratings were presented on seven-point scales ranging from very unsuccessful/not important to very successful/extremely important. Higher scores reflected a more positive expectation/high importance.

Anagram Test

Subjects were then given a sample anagram (OAPNR = APRON) and were instructed to begin the test. The experimenter initiated the countdown on the clock. The test contained 20 relatively difficult anagrams presented on a single long page with space to work on solutions. Subjects were instructed to use the space provided to work out their solutions and to underline their answers. The anagrams were selected from normative data of median solution times for five-lettered anagrams

(Tresselt & Mayzner, 1966). The median solution time for the anagrams was in excess of 2.5 minutes (M = 155.7 seconds) making it extremely difficult to score well in a 20-minute period. Anagrams were used because they minimize differences in experience or knowledge (Bourne, Ekstrand, & Dominowski, 1971). "Difficult" anagrams were chosen because there is evidence to suggest that high, relative to less, test-anxious students perform less well on difficult cognitive tasks (e.g., Wine, 1971).

Thought-Listing Procedure

Once the test was finished, students were instructed to turn the page and complete the thought-listing. The thought-listing instructions were as follows:

> Please list as many thoughts and feelings as you can recall having during the anagram test. Every thought and feeling that went through your mind during that time is important, i.e., thoughts and feelings about yourself, the situation or unrelated to the experiment. Be spontaneous. Ignore spelling, grammar, and punctuation. It is important that you list all thoughts and feelings as you experienced them. Therefore, do not choose your words as though you are writing an essay. Do not put the thoughts and feelings into well structured sentences if they were not experienced in that form. Please be completely honest. Your responses will be confidential. Do not feel that you have to use all the space that has been provided. Please put only one thought or feeling per number. Please list as many thoughts and feelings as you can recall having during the anagram test.

The instructions were taken from Petty and Cacioppo (1977) and modified for the present study. Numbering and space was provided for 27 listed thoughts.

On the next page, subjects were given the instructions for coding their listed thoughts and were asked to enter their ratings to the left of each thought listed on the preceding page. A coding system composed of two dimensions of response classification for listed thoughts suggested by Cacioppo and Petty (1981) was employed by both subjects and judges. The first dimension was the polarity dimension, which was divided into three subgroups: positive thoughts (+); negative thoughts (-); and neutral thoughts (0). The second was the referent dimension, which included thoughts referring to one's self (S), the task (T), and thoughts unrelated to one's self or the task (U). Using the three subgroups within each dimension, we constructed nine categories of thought classification.

Each thought was classified first by the subject and subsequently by an independent, trained rater (who was blind as to the subjects' test anxiety level and thought list ratings) as S+, S-, S0, T+, T-, T0, U+, U-, or U0. In the case of the judge's ratings, a sample of 10 thought-listing self-reports was selected randomly and scored independently by a second rater. An interjudge reliability of 93% was obtained. The number of thoughts in each category as well as the total number of reported thoughts were tabulated for each subject.

Next, subjects responded to an Anagram Task Self-Statement Test (ATSST; untitled in the test booklet) which was constructed by the present authors and designed to assess "the kinds of thoughts that go through people's heads while they are working on a test." The ATSST consists of 20 rationally derived items with five items for each of four subscales: a positive self-referential subscale (ATSST - S+), a negative self-referential subscale (ATSST - S-), a positive task-referential subscale (ATSST - T+), and a negative task-referential subscale (ATSST - T-).[1] Examples of items for the respective subscales are as follows: "I thought that I feel intelligent or smart" (S+); "I thought that I feel dumb or stupid" (S-); "I thought about looking for letter combinations that occur frequently in English" (T+); "I thought that I was randomly putting down letter combinations" (T-). These subscales represent the four primary categories of the thought-list coding system. Subjects indicated the frequency of occurrence of specific thoughts during the test on the ATSST by making five-point ratings ranging from "never" to "very often." Scores were the sum of endorsements. Internal consistency reliability coefficients for the ATSST subscales were higher for the self-referent scales and are acceptable for instruments in the initial stages of development. The respective alpha values were .62 and .82 for the positive-self and negative-self subscales. Unfortunately, the alpha values were somewhat lower for the positive-task (alpha = .55) and negative-task scales (alpha = .57), suggesting that the results for these scales should perhaps be interpreted with caution.

Finally, subjects completed a postexperiment questionnaire. It was used as a validity and manipulation check for several aspects of the study. It consisted of seven-point ratings of several variables including the perceptions of being test anxious in this test situation, how similar the test situation and the subject's behavior, thoughts, and bodily reactions were to a real-life test situation, and beliefs related to the relationships among anagram performance, IQ, and success in college. Following completion of the questionnaire, the experimenter gave each group a brief summary of the study and subjects were given feedback concerning their absolute score and relative group standing on the anagram test.

---

[1] *Copies of the ATSST and other stimulus materials are available from the first author.*

TABLE 1 Partial Correlations With Test Anxiety, Means, and Standard Deviations for Thought List Measures

Measure	r with anx	r with perf	M	SD
Experimenter-Scored				
Self-Positive	-.29**	.32**	1.2	1.3
Self-Negative	.33**	-.32**	3.3	2.1
Self-Neutral	-.04	.23*	0.4	0.7
Task-Positive	-.31**	.00	1.9	2.3
Task-Negative	.29**	-.10	1.4	2.6
Task-Neutral	-.24*	.26*	1.1	1.3
Subject-Scored				
Self-Positive	-.28**	.16	1.2	1.6
Self-Negative	.25*	-.26	2.4	1.9
Self-Neutral	-.05	.11	1.1	1.0
Task-Positive	-.16	.15	1.7	2.0
Task-Negative	.22	.08	2.0	2.1
Task-Neutral	-.21	-.04	1.0	1.3

**$p < .05$, *$p < .10$.

RESULTS

Intercorrelations among measures were computed using the Pearson product-moment method. All correlations involving the thought list measures were partial correlations that controlled for the total number of thoughts produced.

Intercorrelations Between Test Anxiety and Subjects' and Judge's Ratings of Listed Thoughts

The means and standard deviations for both the subjects' and the judge's ratings of the critical categories and total number of the listed thoughts and their correlations with test anxiety are presented in Table 1. Inspection reveals that both methods of scoring the thought listings—the subjects themselves and an independent judge—produced significant relations with test anxiety, although the relations tend to be stronger for the judge's ratings. Thus, the correlation between test anxiety and S+ listed thoughts was significant for both the judge ($r = -.29$, $p < .05$) and subjects ($r = -.28$, $p < .05$), indicating that more test anxious respondents were less likely to list positive thoughts about themselves. Relatively more test anxious subjects were also more likely to experience negative self-referential thoughts when listed thoughts were rated by the judge ($r = .33$, $p < .05$), although this effect was only marginally significant for the subjects' ratings ($r = .25$, $p < .10$). Similarly, the judge's ratings of

TABLE 2 Partial Correlations With Test Anxiety, Means, and Standard Deviations for ATSST Endorsement Measures

Measure	r with anx	r with perf	M	SD
Self-Positive	-.35***	.35***	9.9	3.1
Self-Negative	.54***	-.33**	12.8	4.4
Task-Positive	-.08	.27*	14.6	3.0
Task-Negative	.22	-.41**	12.8	3.7

*** $p < .01$, ** $p < .05$, * $p < .10$.

task thoughts were significantly related to test anxiety, irrespective of whether the thoughts were positive ($r = -.31$, $p < .05$) or negative ($r = .29$, $p < .05$). However, the subject-scored thoughts designated as task-related, whether positive or negative, were not significantly associated with test anxiety.[2] Thus, while the pattern of relations with test anxiety is similar for both judge-scored and subject-scored listed thoughts, the associations were strongest for ratings by the judge. It should be noted that both the judge and subjects rated in excess of 40% of the listed thoughts as negative thoughts about the self or the task.

Comparability of Subjects' and Judge's Ratings of Listed Thoughts

If subjects and judges were rating listed thoughts in an identical manner then the same number, on average, of thoughts would be listed in each of the critical categories and the correlations with test anxiety would be virtually identical. This was clearly not the case. Nonetheless, the findings do suggest considerable overlap. Correlations were calculated too among the judge- and subject-scored thought listings. The results showed that subjects and judges were in general agreement as to what constituted S+ thoughts ($r = .61$, $p < .001$), S- thoughts ($r = .60$, $p < .001$) and T+ thoughts ($r = .53$, $p < .001$). Agreement with respect to T- thoughts was less strong ($r = .31$, $p < .05$). Note that while three of these correlations are substantial, they display considerable discordance between judge's and subjects' ratings. Inspection of the actual records indicated that while the agreement was 100% between the judge and certain subjects, it was 0% between the judge and other subjects.

Intercorrelations Between Test Anxiety and the ATSST Endorsement Measure

The means, standard deviations, and correlations involving the ATSST endorsement measures are presented in Table 2. A relatively strong

---

[2] *The categories of unrelated thoughts scored by either method were not correlated significantly with test anxiety or performance.*

association exists between ATSST negative thoughts about the self and test anxiety (r = .54, p < .001). Furthermore, relatively more test anxious subjects are less likely to endorse positive self-thoughts (r = -.35, p < .001). However, significant correlations did not obtain for the task-related thoughts, although the correlation between test anxiety and negative task thoughts on the ATSST was marginally significant (r = .23, p < .10).

Comparability of Ratings of Listed Thoughts and Thought Endorsements

Partial correlations were computed between the values for the critical categories of listed thoughts and scores on the corresponding ATSST subscales to determine the comparability of data generated by thought listing and endorsement methods. Scores on the ATSST - S+ subscale were positively associated with the corresponding S+ thought list category ratings. This relationship held for judge-scored (r = .47, p < .001) and subject-scored (r = .42, p < .002) listed thoughts. Similarly, negative self-referential thoughts endorsed on the ATSST were positively correlated with both judge's (r = .53, p < .001) and subjects' (r = .31, p < .05) ratings of the negative self-referential listed thoughts. In contrast, there were no significant correlations for positive task thoughts as assessed by the ATSST with positive task thoughts from the thought listing or for negative task thoughts from the ATSST and T- thoughts from the thought listing, for both judge- and subject rated thoughts.

Interrelations Between Test Anxiety and Pretask Ratings and Actual Performance

Analyses of the various pre-task questionnaire ratings revealed that only one item was significantly related with test anxiety: relatively test anxious subjects expected to perform unsuccessfully on the task as assessed by the self-expectation item (r = -.33, p < .01). Anxiety was not related to the various importance ratings suggesting that level of test anxiety did not influence subjects' motivation to perform well. It is clear that the anagram task was extremely difficult for a majority of subjects (M performance = 5.6 items correct of a possible 20 or 28%; SD = 3.9). The correlation between test anxiety and performance approached significance (r = -.25, p < .10). Test anxious subjects tended to perform poorly on the test.

Interrelations Between Performance and Thought Listings, the Endorsement Measure and Pretask and Postexperiment Ratings

The judge's ratings of respondents' thought list protocols were related to actual performance on the anagram test only for the self-referential categories. Performance was associated positively with S+ listed thoughts (r = .32, p < .05) and was correlated negatively with S- thoughts (r = -.32, p < .05). Task-related thoughts, both positive and negative, were not correlated significantly with performance. Most important, none of the subjects' ratings of the thought listings, in any category, were related significantly to anagram test performance. In contrast, endorsement of subscales on the ATSST was significantly associated with performance. Positive self-referential statements correlated directly and significantly with actual performance (r = .35, p < .01). Endorsement of the negative self-referential items was correlated inversely and significantly with anagram performance (r = -.33, p < .02). Similar relationships were found for the T+ (r = .27, p < .05) and T- (r = -.41, p < .01) subscales.

It is interesting that while endorsement of ATSST task-related thoughts, both positive and negative, was unrelated to test anxiety, endorsement of these same subscale items was related to actual test performance. This suggests that factors other than test anxiety are predictive of test performance. In the present study, three pre-task ratings were also related to actual test performance: high perceived IQ (r = +.29, p < .05); the perception that other students are less intelligent (r = -.32, p < .02); and a positive performance self-expectancy (r = +.30, p < .05).

DISCUSSION

The results of the present study confirmed that the categories of a thought list scoring system that discriminates between self-focused and task-referential thoughts that are scored as negative, positive, or neutral are reliably associated with individual differences in the level of test anxiety. The findings for the judge-scored protocols are consistent with the results of similar studies conducted by Blankstein and his colleagues (Blankstein et al., in press; Blankstein et al., 1989). During an anagram task, relatively more test-anxious males recalled thoughts that were judged to be negative self-focused thoughts, listed fewer positive thoughts about themselves, recalled more negative thoughts about the task, and reported fewer thoughts judged by the expert to be facilitative of task performance. These results are consistent with predictions from cognitive-attentional theories of test anxiety (e.g., Meichenbaum & Butler, 1980; Sarason, 1972; 1988; Wine, 1980) and attest to the validity of the thought list method when an appropriate theory-based classification system is employed.

Regarding the question of whether it is preferable to have participants or trained judges classify thoughts, it is clear that thought listings coded by the subjects were less reliably associated with variations in test anxiety than the judge-scored listed thoughts. Although the pattern of relations was similar, for the subject-scored protocols only the correlation between test anxiety and positive self-referential thoughts attained an acceptable level of statistical significance: relatively more test anxious males listed fewer self-positive thoughts. Correlations calculated between the judge- and subject-scored thought listings showed that subjects and judges were in general agreement as to what constituted the critical categories of thoughts; however, there was still substantial discordance between their ratings.

Our results are similar to those reported by Cacioppo et al. (1979) for heterosocial anxiety but differ from the results of Tarico et al. (1986) who found that self- and judges' ratings were not differentially predictive of speech anxiety. Are judges' ratings more valid than self-ratings or are subjects' ratings the more valid of the two methods of rating listed thoughts? It is clear that judges' ratings, with few exceptions, can discriminate between dysfunctional groups. In each of several studies, the researchers have been careful to ensure that judges were blind as to the anxiety level of the participants and the results were consistent with theoretical predictions from past research on test anxiety. At present, we are inclined to conclude that the judges' ratings are more valid. However, we must reserve judgment on the question of the relative validity of subjects' ratings because there is no independent means of assessing this issue. Nevertheless, it does seem clear that the practice of having subjects score their own thoughts offers few advantages, at least in the context of test anxiety research. In fact, it can even be argued that it may be unethical to have subjects score their own thoughts in that certain individuals will be forced to once again acknowledge and confront negative attributes pertaining to the self.

Theoretically, subjects' ratings should be more economical in terms of time and subjects should be in a better position to judge their own thoughts. However, there are several sources of error that may contribute to the unreliability of scoring and thereby make the ratings less valid: misunderstanding of categories and criteria, carelessness, disruption due to anxiety, attribution biases, and deception. Expert raters are typically carefully trained in the classification system and criteria for coding thoughts and there is usually a check on the reliability of their scoring of thought list protocols. However, subjects receive minimal instructions and training and no study has assessed the test-retest reliability of subjects scoring the same thoughts. Perhaps the findings would be more comparable if subjects were given more intensive training. Although carelessness may be a factor in judges' scoring of protocols, it is more likely to be a problem with subjects' ratings since they are less likely to be dedicated to scientific rigor. There is also the possibility that the carryover of anxiety (or other emotional reactions) during the task to the rating period can interfere with performance of the rating task, especially in relatively more anxious subjects. Another possibility is that subjects deliberately attempt to manage the impressions that others have of them or engage in self-deception (Flett, Blankstein, Pliner, & Bator, 1988; Sackeim & Gur, 1979) by scoring their own thoughts more positively and less negatively than they were actually experienced during the anagram test. We are currently examining the validity of these alternative interpretations of our findings.

We constructed an endorsement measure of self-statements experienced during the anagram test (ATSST). The ATSST subscales corresponded to the four critical categories of our thought-list classification scheme. Consistent with our expectations, relatively more test anxious subjects endorsed more negative thoughts about the self and fewer positive self thoughts. The task related thoughts (both positive and negative) were not significantly associated with test anxiety. How comparable are the data generated by the thought listing and endorsement methods? For both negative and positive self-referential thoughts, the methods produced similar results, regardless of whether listed thoughts were scored by subjects or by a judge. That is, increased test anxiety and poorer performance were reliably associated with fewer positive thoughts, about the self and a greater number of negative thoughts about the self. However, a different pattern emerges when the various measures of task-related thinking are compared. Analyses of the thought list data scored by a rater other than the subject found that level of test anxiety but not performance was correlated with the number of task-positive and task-negative thoughts. In contrast, the analogous endorsement measures were not correlated with test anxiety but they were correlated with performance.

How can we account for these discrepancies? One likely explanation involves the relatively low frequency of task-related thoughts that were mentioned spontaneously by subjects. In general, thought list measures are characterized by a low frequency (Fichten et al., 1988) and this is especially true of task-related thoughts. These findings imply that the degree of task-related thinking manifested in these evaluative contexts is less important than other types of variables. Given that the majority of listed thoughts pertain to the self and the results involving the various measures of the self-referential thinking were more consistent, it would appear that future research should perhaps focus on the more critical role of self-referential thought in test anxiety.

The limitations of the current findings must be noted. First, the generalizability of our findings may be questioned on two grounds. Since our sample consisted of male subjects, the results may not generalize to female subjects. In addition, all subjects in the present study attempted relatively difficult anagrams. The possible role of task difficulty as a mediating factor in the link between anxiety and cognition needs to be examined. Second, the endorsement measure, the ATSST, was constructed for the purposes of the present research and there is need for additional reliability and validity data on this instrument. The relatively low internal consistency obtained with the task-referential subscales may be an indication that there is need for a revised thought endorsement measure. Third, we treated test anxiety as a unitary concept in the present study but recent formulations have focused on the multidimensional nature of test anxiety (e.g., Sarason, 1984). The extent to which cognitive assessments relate to various components of test anxiety (i.e., worry, tension, test-irrelevant thinking, and bodily symptoms) needs to be examined in future research. Finally, although the current findings have demonstrated that test anxiety is associated with greater negative self-referential cognitions and fewer positive self-referential cognitions, irrespective of method of assessment, the current findings do not address the causality issue. It is vital that subsequent research determines whether self-referential thoughts are a cause of, or are merely a correlate of, test anxiety.

In summary, the results of the present study corroborated past research by showing that both unstructured and structured cognitive assessments, particularly those involving the self, are related to test anxiety and level of performance. Greater test anxiety and poorer performance were associated with fewer positive thoughts about the self and a greater number of negative thoughts about the self. Moreover, the current findings extended past research by showing that the results are stronger when the scoring of thought listing is conducted by trained raters rather than by the subject. Taken together, the results of the present study suggest that additional research on the cognitive aspects of test anxiety with such measures is indeed warranted.

REFERENCES

Arnkoff, D.B., & Smith, R.J. (1988). Cognitive processes in test anxiety: An analysis of two assessment procedures in an actual test. *Cognitive Therapy and Research, 12,* 425-439.

Blankstein, K.R., Flett, G.L., Boase, P., & Toner, B. (in press). Thought listing versus endorsement measures of self-referential thinking in test anxiety. *Anxiety Research.*

Blankstein, K.R., & Toner, B.B. (1987). Influence of social-desirability responding on the Sarason Test Anxiety Scale: Implications for selection of subjects. *Psychological Reports, 61,* 63-69.

Blankstein, K.R., Toner, B.B., & Flett, G.L. (1989). Test anxiety and the contents of consciousness: Thought listing and endorsement measures. *Journal of Research in Personality, 23*, 269-286.

Bourne, L.E., Jr., Ekstrand, B.R., & Dominowski, R.L. (1971). *The psychology of thinking*. Englewood Cliffs, NJ: Prentice-Hall.

Brown, S.D., & Nelson, T.L. (1983). Beyond the uniformity myth: A comparison of academically successful and unsuccessful test anxious college students. *Journal of Counseling Psychology, 30*, 367-374.

Cacioppo, J.T., Glass, C.R., & Merluzzi, T.V. (1979). Self-statements and self-evaluations: A cognitive-response analysis of heterosexual anxiety. *Cognitive Therapy and Research, 3*, 249-262.

Clark, D.A. (1988). The validity of measures of cognition: A review of the literature. *Cognitive Therapy and Research, 12*, 1-20.

Deffenbacher, J.L., & Hazaleus, S.L. (1985). Cognitive, emotional, and physiological components of test anxiety. *Cognitive Therapy and Research, 9*, 169-180.

Fichten, C.S., Amsel, R., & Robillard, K. (1988). Issues in cognitive assessment: Task difficulty, reactivity of measurement, thought listing versus inventory approaches, and sequences versus frequency counts. *Behavioral Assessment, 10*, 399-425.

Flett, G.L., Blankstein, K.R., & Boase, P. (1987). Self-focused attention in test anxiety and depression. *Journal of Social Behavior and Personality, 2*, 259-266.

Flett, G.L., Blankstein, K.R., Pliner, P., & Bator, C. (1988). Impression-management and self-deception components of appraised emotional experience. *British Journal of Social Psychology, 27*, 67-77.

Galassi, J.P., Frierson, H.T. Jr. and Siegel, R.G. (1984). Cognitions, test anxiety and test performance: A closer look. *Journal of Consulting and Clinical Psychology, 52*, 319-320.

Geen, R.G. (1984). Test anxiety and visual vigilance. *Journal of Personality and Social Psychology, 49*, 963-970.

Genest, M., & Turk, D.C. (1981). Think-aloud approaches to cognitive assessment. In T. V. Merluzzi, C. R. Glass, & M. Genest (Eds.), *Cognitive assessment*. New York, NY: Guilford Press.

Glass, C.R. and Arnkoff, D.B. (1983). Cognitive set and level of test anxiety: Effects on thinking processes in problematic situations. *Cognitive Therapy and Research, 7*, 529-542.

Hammen, C., & Krantz, S.E. (1985). Measures of psychological processes in depression. In E. Beckham & W. Leber (Eds.), *Depression: Treatment, assessment, and research*. Homewood, IL: The Dorsey Press.

Holroyd, K.A., Westbrook, T., Wolf, M., & Badhorn, E. (1978). Performance, cognition, and physiological responding in test anxiety. *Journal of Abnormal Psychology, 87*, 442-451.

Houston, B.K., Fox, J.E., & Forbes, L. (1984). Trait anxiety and children's state anxiety, cognitive behaviors, and performance under stress. *Cognitive Therapy and Research, 8*, 631-641.

Hunsley, J. (1987). Cognitive processes in mathematics anxiety and test anxiety: The role of appraisals, internal dialogue, and attributions. *Journal of Educational Psychology, 79*, 388-392.

Kendall, P.C. (1982). Behavioral assessment and methodology. In C.M. Franks,

G.T. Wilson, P.C. Kendall, & K.D. Brownell (Eds.), *Annual review of behavior therapy, theory, and practice* (Vol. 8). New York, NY: Guilford Press.

Kendall, P.C., & Hollon, S.D. (1981). Assessing self-referent speech: Methods in the measurement of self-statements. In P.C. Kendall and S.D. Hollon (Eds.), *Assessment strategies for cognitive-behavioral interventions.* New York, NY: Academic Press.

Meichenbaum, D.H. (1972). Cognitive modification of test anxious college students. *Journal of Consulting and Clinical Psychology, 39,* 370-380.

Meichenbaum, D.H., & Butler, L. (1980). Toward a conceptual model for the treatment of test anxiety: Implications for research and treatment. In I.G. Sarason (Ed.), *Test anxiety: Theory, research and applications* (pp. 187-208). Hillsdale, NJ: Erlbaum.

Merluzzi, T.V., Glass, C.R., & Genest, M. (1981). *Cognitive assessment.* New York, NY: Guilford Press.

Myszka, M.T., Galassi, J.P., & Ware, W.B. (1986). Comparison of cognitive assessment methods with heterosexually anxious college women. *Journal of Counseling Psychology, 33,* 401-407.

Petty, R.E. and Cacioppo, J.T. (1977). Forewarning, cognitive responding, and resistance to persuasion. *Journal of Personality and Social Psychology, 35,* 645-655.

Sackeim, H.A., & Gur, R.C. (1979). Self-deception, other-deception and self-reported psychopathology. *Journal of Consulting and Clinical Psychology, 47,* 213-215.

Sarason, I.G. (1961). The effects of anxiety and threat on the solution of a difficult task. *Journal of Abnormal and Social Psychology, 62,* 165-168.

Sarason, I.G. (1972). Experimental approaches to test anxiety: Attention and the uses of information. In C.D. Spielberger (Ed.), *Anxiety: Current trends in theory and research,* Vol. 2 (pp. 383-403). New York, NY: Academic Press.

Sarason, I.G. (1978). The Test Anxiety Scale: Concept and research. In C. D. Spielberger and I. G. Sarason (Eds.), *Stress and anxiety,* Vol. 5 (pp. 193-216). Washington, DC: Hemisphere.

Sarason, I.G. (1984). Stress, anxiety and cognitive interference: reactions to tests. *Journal of Personality and Social Psychology, 46,* 929-938.

Sarason, I.G., Sarason, B.R., Keefe, D.E., Hayes, B.E., & Shearin, E.N. (1986). Cognitive interference: Situational determinants and traitlike characteristics. *Journal of Personality and Social Psychology, 31,* 215-226.

Segal, Z.V., & Marshall, W.L. (1985). Heterosexual social skills in a population of rapists and child molesters. *Journal of Consulting and Clinical Psychology, 53,* 55-63.

Tarico, V.S., Van Velzen, D.R., & Altmaier, E.M. (1986). Comparison of thought-listing rating methods. *Journal of Counseling Psychology, 33,* 81-83.

Tresselt, M.E., & Mayzner, M.S. (1966). Narrative solution times for a sample of 134 solution words and 378 associated anagrams. *Psychonomic Monograpy Supplements, 1,* 293-298.

Wine, J.D. (1971). Test anxiety and the direction of attention. *Psychological Bulletin, 76,* 92-104.

Wine, J.D. (1980). Cognitive-attentional theory of test anxiety. In I. G. Sarason (Ed.), *Test anxiety: Theory, research, and applications* (pp. 349-385). Hillsdale, NJ: Erlbaum.

Communication Apprehension and Rational Emotive Therapy: An Interview with Dr. Albert Ellis

Arden K. Watson
Department of Speech Communication
Pennsylvania State University, Delaware County Campus
Media, PA 19063

Carly H. Dodd
Department of Speech Communication
Abilene Christian University, Abilene, TX 79699

Communication Apprehension, an individual's level of fear or anxiety associated with either real or anticipated communication, is found to affect 20 percent of the college population, working adults, and senior citizens. Speech Communication educators have used and studied a variety of methods for alleviating this malady. From among those methods, rational emotive therapy shows promise for helping the communicatively apprehensive student in overcoming this debilitating anxiety. In order to better understand how rational emotive therapy is useful as a method for treating communication apprehension, the authors interviewed Dr. Albert Ellis at the Institute for Rational Emotive Therapy. The substance of this report includes a discussion of the causes of social anxiety, shyness, and speech anxiety. It also covers comparisons of systematic desensitization and skills training in the alleviation of communication apprehension; detailed explanation and benefits of the rational A-B-C model; appropriateness of using rational emotive therapy in the speech classroom; and how students can change their thinking to alleviate communication apprehension through replacing irrational beliefs with rational ones.

Communication apprehension (CA) in this discussion is defined as an individual's level of fear or anxiety, associated with either real or anticipated communication with another person or persons (McCroskey, 1970). CA has been reported to be America's number one fear (Wallechinsky, Wallace, & Wallace, 1978), and to be prevalent in approximately

---

Authors' Note: The authors are especially indebted to the faculty research fund at Western Kentucky University.

© 1990 Select Press

20% of the college student population (McCroskey, 1970). Research suggests that communication apprehension is related to negative personality traits (McCroskey, Daly, & Sorenson, 1976) and causes certain social withdrawal behaviors (McCroskey, 1977). As a result of these findings, speech educators have sought to develop methods of alleviating this malady in the speech classroom (Glaser, 1981). Among the methods used and studied, rational emotive therapy shows promise of helping the communication apprehensive student to overcome this debilitating anxiety (Kelly & Watson, 1986; Watson & Dodd, 1984; Fremouw & Scott, 1979; Meichenbaum, Gilmore, & Fedoravicius, 1971).

Psychologist Albert Ellis defines rational emotive therapy (RET) as a theory of personality and a method of psychotherapy (Ellis, 1962) which takes two forms. In its general form, rational emotive therapy employs a large variety of cognitive, affective, and behavioral methods of personality change. This method is synonymous with multimodal therapy and with broad-spectrum behavior therapy. In its more specific form, rational emotive therapy emphasizes cognitive restructuring, or philosophic disputing, in accordance with the A-B-C theory of emotional disturbance and personality change. The cognitive approach of the theory and practice may be briefly stated in A-B-C form. At point A, there is an Activating event about which the individual becomes concerned or anxious. At point B, the individual has a rational or irrational belief about the Activating event. As a result of point B or the Belief system, the individual experiences rational or irrational Consequences of desirable or undesirable emotions and behaviors. At point D, the individual can be taught to Dispute the irrational beliefs. As a result of the disputing, a new philosophy (effect), point E, can be affected which is more suitable and productive for the individual. Thus rational emotive therapy is cognitive, emotive, and behavioral. Through the use of the rational emotive A-B-C model (Ellis & Greiger, 1977), students may be able to give up their irrational beliefs (speech anxiety) and achieve increased self-confidence and effective communication.

To discuss the nature of communication apprehension and its treatment, the authors secured an appointment with Dr. Albert Ellis and recorded the following interview at the Institute for Rational Emotive Therapy on November 8, 1980.

Albert Ellis, Ph.D. in clinical psychology, Columbia University, has taught at Rutgers and at New York University and served as Chief Psychologist of the New Jersey Department of Institutions and Agencies. Presently he is the President of the Institute for Rational Emotive Therapy and practice psychotherapy and marriage and family counseling at its clinic in New York City.

Dr. Ellis has published over five hundred papers in professional journals and anthologies and is the author of over fifty books, including *Reason and Emotion in Psychotherapy and Humanistic Psychotherapy: The Rational-Emotive Approach*. His major works on the theory and technique of rational emotive psychotherapy are *A New Guide to Rational Living* (with Robert A. Harper), *The Practice of Rational-Emotive Therapy* (with Windy Dryden) and *Handbook of Rational Emotive Therapy* (with Russell Greiger).

INTERVIEW

Question: How would you define communication apprehension from a rational emotive therapy viewpoint?

Ellis: What is called social anxiety, shyness, or speech anxiety largely stems from the irrational belief, "I have to communicate well and make a good impression on others." These same people also have a rational or sensible belief, "I'd like to communicate well, but if I don't, I don't!" If they rigorously stayed with this rational idea of preference, they wouldn't all be great speakers, but they would usually do much better.

Question: Some people approach treating communication apprehension more from a skill training point of view, assuming that skill training provides a background for each social situation where communication is involved. There is another school of thought, among communication scholars, which argues that the basic cause is a kind of phobia dealing with speech anxiety. This assumption thus suggests a desensitization approach for treatment. How do you see those two lines of thought?

Ellis: Well, both skill training and desensitization are really doing the same thing, but their practitioners often don't realize it. Let's take the skill training approach. The skill training approach is taking what we call "A", (the Activating event) in the A-B-C's of RET and focusing on changing that event instead of mainly focusing on "B", (the person's Beliefs *about* that event). When "A" is the individual's poor skill at speaking and "C", (emotion Consequence) is this person's anxiety, helping him or her to become more skilled at "A" will partly reduce "C". The reason the skill training works is explained by Albert Bandura's self efficacy theory or the RET theory of self-rating since people often put themselves down when they are inefficacious. If you teach them to be more efficacious in anything—tennis, golf, speaking—they will put themselves down less but they won't give up the irrational Belief, "I *must* be efficacious." In fact, they will frequently reinforce this idea. So skill training 'works' but it offers an inelegant solution.

The elegant solution to almost all anxiety feelings is to accept yourself whether or not you are good at anything. Then you really have it made and you can go on to practice doing it better, and ordinarily you do improve. Skill training is inelegant because it teaches people to speak better; but most of those who improve, since they still hold the basic philosophy, "I must speak well or I am a worthless person," wrongly tell themselves, "Because I am not speaking more effectively, I am a great person." They are still as underlyingly anxious as they were before, and some are even more anxious. Pragmatically, they are temporarily improved. But as soon as they do poorly again at speech or anything else, they will most probably go back to condemning themselves.

Question: Are you saying that if the skills were improved, and we could demonstrate the skills that were, learned, *that* then would be the only concern?

Ellis: Well, RET actually does do both—skill training *and* help people to change their fundamental anxiety-provoking beliefs or philosophy. In RET-oriented communication training, we first go to "B," people's irrational beliefs—and particularly their absolutistic, perfectionistic mu*sts* about succeeding—and show them how to change these *musturbatory* ideas and reformulate them as preferences. If, as is usual, people with communication anxiety are telling themselves, "I *have* to speak well, else I am a rotten person," we would go on to "D" (Disputing), and ask, "Why *must* you speak adequately? What's *awful* if you don't? How does failing make you a rotten individual?" We would, by this kind of realistically-oriented, scientific method, try to help these anxious individuals to see that if one fails, it is highly unfortunate, but it is hardly the end of the world. As we showed them, how to change their irrational Beliefs (at point "B") we would also do skill training and help them change their Activating Experiences (their poor speech) at point "A." Skill training is really a cognitive method, since it is mainly under instruction. And RET, which in 1955 started the current trend in cognitive behavior therapy, naturally emphasizes several kinds of cognitive methods.

Question: Could classroom teachers, then, approach a speech class emphasizing both RET and skills training?

Ellis: Yes, they are both very compatible. People sometimes think the two are different, just like they wrongly think RET and Behavior Therapy are different. RET usually includes in vivo desensitization and is really a form of behavior therapy. It is cognitive, emotive, *and* behavioral. Skill training also is both cognitive teaching and behavioral homework. So, classroom teachers emphasizing RET and skills training ought to make clear that skill training is normally included in RET; they are not two different methods of treatment.

What we are really teaching with RET is a new way of thinking, so that people will learn to think scientifically, flexibly, to challenge their own assumptions. Suppose somebody is afraid to go up in an airplane and I say, "What are you afraid of?" and he or she says, "I'm afraid the airplane will fall. I'll get killed." I point out that only 300 people or less per year get killed in airplanes; moreover 60,000 people are killed and five times that many are maimed in automobiles. "Since you are not afraid of automobiles, why are you afraid of airplanes?" The quick answer will be, "Well yes, there is very little chance that the airplane will fall," but the airplane phobia remains because people who have it won't give up the idea because of their basic MUST—which is, "Under *no* condition must I get dramatically killed even though the probability is exceptionally *low*." As long as they have the *must*, they will foolishly believe that there *is* a good chance that their plane is going to fall—which is against reality. People's unrealistic statements largely come from their *musts*. If they never told themselves, "I *must* be able to control the plane and must not be killed in a crash, they would not hold to anti-empirical statements like, "There's a good chance this plane will fall." An implicit *must* is behind most unrealistic, overgeneralized predictions and is very frequently ignored. Therefore if you just simply question the prediction without finding and disputing this *must*, you are not doing elegant RET. Inelegantly, you can teach people coping statements like, "I won't die if I speak badly in public." But if you take college students, who are quite capable of seeing their *musts* and surrendering them and show them how to do this, you help them on a deeper level, particularly if you show them that they are master of their own emotional fate. They can be taught that emotionally they control their own destiny and that they never have to upset themselves about *anything* including speech. They can be helped to look at things philosophically to see that there aren't any absolutes in the universe and if people were really nonabsolutistic and stuck to reality, empirical reality, they would not disturb themselves. If they only had preferences rather than *musts* and *only* told themselves, "I desire to do well in speaking, but if I don't, I don't! I never *have to*, it is not *necessary* that I do well," they would minimize their public speaking anxiety and other kinds of anxiety, too. Our A-B-C-D-E rational self-help form will help them get to their mu*sts* and *shoulds* and change these grandiose commands. Those are the main things I would be concerned about clarifying in any academic RET based communication apprehension program.

Question: How does one distinguish between rational and irrational thinking?

Ellis: Let's consider "B" in our system. "B" is an irrational Belief such as, "I must do well. I must do well at public speaking. The audience must approve of me." That would be the basic "B." Once you get people to see this basic must, they you could ask, "Is it really true?" The must is often implicit because people will say, "I'd *like* to do well," but they really mean, "I *must*." Get them to acknowledge a *must*, then the question, "Is it really true?" would always produce "No" for an answer, because there are no musts, no absolutes as far as we can determine. As long as you help people to state their irrational idea clearly, all you have to do is put in 'why' in front of it. "*Why* must you do well at public speaking?" The answer is, "There is no real reason why I must, though it would be *preferable* if I did!" "*Why* is it awful if you do poorly?" Answer: "It is not a*wful*, only inconvenient." "*Why* can't you stand doing poorly?" Answer: "I can stand it, although I don't like it." And, "*Why* are you a worm if you act badly?" Answer: "I'm not a worm. I'm a human who acted wormily this time." You see, you help them to state their musts. *That* is the usual essence of their irrationality.

Then, the second question in deciding between rational or irrational thinking is, "Does it help protect my life and lead to a happier existence?"

Question: I assume that this protection refers more to physical things, either alcohol, drugs, or physical problems that one has, or does it refer possibly to choosing inappropriate behavior, such as speech anxiety?

Ellis: No, this may be wrong. Let's take anxiety. Sometimes anxiety would help protect your life, but at too great an expense. Suppose you have a great fear of elevators. Does it protect your life? Well, sure it does, since one out of a million times an elevator may fall. But it would be so disadvantageous not to go into them that you wouldn't want to live by continually walking up and down twenty flights of stairs!

Question: What is the next question to ask to distinguish rational from irrational beliefs?

Ellis: Well, If students have the irrational idea, "I must do well," the answer to, "Does it help me get what I want," is no. But their preference for speaking well will often get them what they want. So, again, the crucial irrational element is an overt or implicit *must*. Then ask, "Does it help me to avoid unwanted emotions?" This is a dangerous question because it is often a foolish goal to seek calmness and serenity when one is beset with problems. Thus, Epictetus wrongly said, "If my wife, whom I love, dies, I'd better be calm and serene," because calmness and serenity in the face of real problems is self-defeating. Instead, we'd better be sorry, frustrated, or annoyed when unwanted events occur—so we can go back and *change* the situation. We (RET) are often accused of being too unemotional but instead we encourage deep feelings of sorrow, annoyance, and determination when things go wrong. Being calm and serene under *all* conditions would not lead to a very happy life and wouldn't help us cope with or change many obnoxious conditions.

Question: Students who have completed an RET based communication apprehension reduction program have been described by other students as becoming less emotional. Some anxiety, as you say, is helpful especially in speaking. Can it cause the student to learn to be a better speaker?

Ellis: Well, it's good to be emotional but not despairing or hysterical. The goal of RET is to minimize emotional *disturbance* (such as overwhelming anxious, depression, and hostility) but not to remove *emotion*. We'd better be very involved, very emotional, or we're not going to enjoy life. So in RET we look carefully at 'unwanted emotions,' because it is easy to wrongly define sorrow and regret as 'unwanted.' Why are sorrow and regret often self-helping? Because they help us to take care of ourselves—but not to bring in *in*appropriate feelings of depression. Sorrow and depression are two different things. sorrow goes from 1 to 99 and depression goes from 101 to infinity. Depression stems from "Isn't that awful that this sorrow exists! I can't stand it! It *must* not exist!" But sorrow, meaning, "Isn't it very bad that this situation exists; let me try to change it!," is quite appropriate.

CONCLUSION

In conclusion, it appears from Dr. Ellis's remarks that RET is a viable alternative for helping students to understand their *irrational* thinking and to overcome communication anxiety. The RET process helps the subject to view the communication situation in a rational rather than irrational manner. The process focuses on the acceptance of self with evaluation only of the behavior, in this case, speaking skills. Not only is RET cognitive, emotive, and behavioral, but it includes in vivo desensitization as well as skill training. Moreover, RET proposes that we feel largely as we think, helps to challenge our own assumptions, and shows how unrealistic statements come from the use of *must* and *should*.

RET may be actualized by the use of an A-B-C-D-E model of personality and emotional disturbance and used with many types of individuals, including mild neurotics to severe psychotics. Briefly the model includes A, the activating experience; B, the belief about A; C, the upsetting emotional and behavioral consequences; D, the disputing of irrational ideas; and E, a new cognitive effect or conclusion. The subject considers A, a problem or circumstance ("I am about to give a speech in Speech class."); B, examines the self-talk ("I must give a perfect speech and make an A."); and consequences, C ("I feel anxious, nervous, and fearful.") said as a result of the A situation. The subject then D, attacks and challenges the irrational ideas ("Is it true that I must give a perfect speech? No, that is irrational and demands that I be perfect. Rationally, I will probably make some mistakes.") and sees that B (not A) caused the unwanted emotion. In E, ways are found to change irrational philosophies ("I will concentrate on improving my speaking skills and not demand that my speech or I be perfect") (Ellis, 1973).

The classroom method utilizing RET (which includes skills) also appears theoretically sound. Our challenge is to continually test our assumptions, using insights from various sources to refine our endeavors in assisting the high communication apprehensive student.

REFERENCES

Ellis, A. (1962). *Reason and emotion in psychotherapy*. New York: Citadel.
Ellis, A. (1973). *Humanistic psychotherapy*. New York: McGraw-Hill.
Ellis, A., & Dryden, W. (1987). *The practice of rational-emotive therapy*. New York: Springer.
Ellis, A. & Greiger, R. (1977). *Handbook for rational-emotive therapy*. New York: Springer.
Ellis, A., & Harper, R.A. (1975). *A new guide to rational living*. North Hollywood, CA: Wilshire Book Co.
Fremouw, W.J., & Scott, M.D. (1979). Cognitive restructuring: An alternative method of the treatment of communication apprehension. *Communication Education, 28,* 129-133.
Glaser, S.R. (1981). Oral communication and avoidance: The current status of treatment and research. *Communication Education, 30,* 321-341.
Kelly, L. & Watson, A.K. (1986). *Speaking with confidence and skill*. Lanham, MD. University Press of America.
McCroskey, J.C. (1970). Measures of communication bound anxiety. *Speech Monographs, 37,* 269-277.
McCroskey, J.C. (1972). Implementation of a large scale program of systematic desensitization for communication apprehension. *Speech Teacher, 21,* 255-264.
McCroskey, J.C. (1977). Oral communication apprehension: A summary of recent theory and research. *Human Communication Research, 4,* 78-89.
McCroskey, J.C., Daly, J.A., & Sorensen, G.A. (1976). Personality correlates of communication apprehension: A research note. *Human Communication Research, 2,* 376-380.
Meichenbaum, D.H., Gilmore, J.B., & Fedoravicius, A. (1971). Group insight versus group desensitization in treating speech anxiety. *Journal of Consulting and Clinical Psychology, 36,* 410-421.
Wallechinsky, D., Wallace, I., & Wallace, A. (1978). *The book of lists*. New York: Bantam Books.
Watson, A.K. & Dodd, C.H. (1984). Alleviating communication apprehension through rational emotive therapy: A comparative evaluation. *Communication Education, 33,* 257-266.

INDEX OF NAMES

A

Acker, M. 159, 170
Adesman, P. 135, 154
Alden, L. 127, 128
Allen, M. 155
Altmaier, E.M. 189, 202
Altman, I. 132, 133, 135, 136, 151, 152
Amabile, T.M. 148, 152
Amsel, R. 189, 201
Andersen, J.F. 48, 49, 57
Andersen, P.A. 46, 47, 48, 49, 50, 51, 53, 57, 59
Andersen, S.M. 131, 133, 134, 138, 141, 143, 145, 148, 152
Anderson, K. 56, 58
Andriate, G.S. 105, 114
Appelman, A.J. 118, 128
Apsler, R. 63, 83
Archer, R.L. 132, 134, 135, 136, 141, 145, 152, 154
Arensberg, C. M. 21, 35
Arkin 118, 126, 127
Arkowitz, H. 7, 17, 119, 126, 129
Arnkoff, D.B. 188, 190, 200, 201
Arnold, A.P. 118, 128
Arnston, P. H. 21, 37
Asch, S.E. 135, 152
Asendorpf, J.B. 118, 119, 124, 127, 128
Averett, C. 137, 152
Averill, J.R. 133, 135, 149, 153
Ax, A.F. 99, 104
Axsom, D. 62, 83
Ayres, J. 102, 103

B

Badhorn, E. 191, 201
Baer, J.E. 23, 24, 36
Bales, R. F. 21, 35
Bangert-Drowns, R.L. 158, 169
Bargh, J.A. 83, 136, 152
Barker, L. 159, 171
Barker, L.L. 48, 57
Barraclaugh, R.A. 31, 32, 35
Bator, C. 199, 201
Baumeister, R.F. 42, 44
Baumgardner, A.B. 126, 128
Beach, L.R. 106, 108, 115
Beaton, A. 54, 57

Beatty, M.J. 28, 35, 47, 58, 85, 86, 87, 97, 103, 105, 106, 108, 109, 110, 111, 114, 159, 160, 161, 162, 164, 165, 169
Beaumont, G. 54, 57
Beck, A.T. 2, 17
Beckham, E. 201
Behnke, R.R. 28, 35, 85, 86, 87, 92, 97, 103, 105, 114, 159, 161, 169
Beidel, D.C. 127, 130
Bell, D. 116
Benson, D.F. 57, 58, 59
Berg, J.H. 132, 152
Berger, C.R. 19, 35, 126, 128, 132, 145, 152
Berger, P.A. 124, 128
Berkowitz, L. 83, 84, 153, 154
Biggers, T. 57, 59
Biggs, S.R. 58
Billings, A.G. 184
Blackwell, R.T. 9, 17
Blank, A. 62, 84
Blankstein, K.R. 129, 130, 187, 188, 189, 191, 197, 199, 200, 201
Boase, P. 188, 189, 200, 201
Bocchino, I.L. 159, 160, 162, 165, 169
Bock, D.G. 159, 161, 165, 167, 169
Bock, H.B. 159, 161, 165, 167, 169
Bogen, J.E. 49, 57
Booth-Butterfield, S. 28, 35
Borden, G.A. 48, 57
Borg, W.R. 25, 35
Borgatta, E.F. 21, 35
Borzi, M.G. 159, 161, 164, 169
Bourne, L.E., Jr. 192, 201
Breck, B.E. 118, 124, 128
Brehm, S.S. 118, 130
Brewer, M.B. 132, 152
Briggs, S.R. 18, 44, 119, 126, 127, 128, 129, 130
Broadbent, D.E. 8, 17
Brown, S.D. 189, 201
Brownell, K.D. 202
Bruch, M.A. 124, 128
Brunsonn, N. 106, 114
Bryce, I.G. 54, 57
Buck, R. 55, 57, 87, 103
Buhr, T.A. 159, 160, 162, 166, 167, 169
Burger, J.M. 118, 128
Burgoon, J.K. 21, 30, 34, 35

211

Burleson, J.A. 152
Burns, M. 57
Burroughs, N.F. 31, 36
Buss, A.H. 30, 35, 89, 103, 117, 119, 120, 122, 126, 128
Butler, L. 197, 202
Byrne, D. 74, 83, 173, 184, 185

C

Cacioppo, J.T. 61, 62, 63, 84, 118, 124, 128, 159, 166, 189, 192, 198, 201, 202
Calabrese, R. 132, 152
Calabrese, R. J. 19, 35, 132, 152
Campbell, H. 124, 128
Cantril, H. 149, 150, 152
Cappe, R. 127, 128
Carlile, L.W. 92, 103
Carlston, D.E. 135, 136, 147, 148, 150, 154
Carment, D.W. 25, 35
Carpentieri, A.M. 118, 129
Carver, C.A. 41, 44
Carver, C.S. 100, 103, 119, 128
Cervin, V. B. 25, 35
Chaiken, S. 61, 62, 63, 64, 79, 80, 83
Chaikin, A.L. 132, 152
Chan, B. M. 23, 24, 35
Chanowitz, B. 62, 84
Chapman, S.B. 57
Chapple, E. D. 21, 35
Cheek, B. 127, 128
Cheek, J.M. 18, 44, 58, 117, 118, 119, 120, 121, 122, 126, 127, 128, 129, 130
Christal, R.E. 174, 186
Christensen, D. 121, 129
Christophel, D.M. 31, 32, 35
Clair, R.P. 105
Clark, D.A. 9, 17, 188, 201
Clark, J.V. 7, 17, 119, 126, 129
Clark, L.A. 173, 174, 175, 178, 179, 180, 182, 183, 186
Clevenger, T. 28, 30, 35, 85, 92, 103
Cohen, J. 162, 165, 165, 169
Cohen, L.J. 106, 114
Collins, T.M. 124, 128
Cooper, H.M. 157, 169
Cooper, P.E. 8, 17

Coovert, M.D. 135, 148, 150
Costa, P.T., Jr. 174, 182, 184, 185
Coyne, J.C. 184, 185
Cozby, P.C. 132, 152
Crowne, D.P. 179, 184
Crozier, W.R. 118, 119, 124, 129
Cummings, J. 57
Cunningham, S.B. 48, 57
Curran J.P. 122, 129
Cutrona, C. 119, 130

D

Dahlstrom, W.G. 185
Daly, J.A. 20, 26, 27, 30, 32, 35, 36, 37, 85, 89, 91, 103, 104, 105, 110, 115, 128, 159, 160, 162, 166, 167, 169, 204, 210
Dance, F.E.X. 169
Daniels, T.C. 159, 161, 169
Daughton, S.M. 160, 166, 169
Daun, A. 31, 32, 36
Davis, D. 118, 129, 135, 153
Davis, K.E. 135, 136, 137, 147, 150, 153
Defares, P.B. 18
Deffenbacher, J.L. 5, 17, 189, 201
Deitrich, J.E. 102, 103
Delia, J.G. 156, 169
Dembowski, J.S. 57
Derlega, V.J. 132, 151, 152
DeSoto, C.B. 147, 149, 150, 152
Devous, M.D. 57
Diehl, C.F. 102, 104
Diener, E. 181, 184
Dimond, S.J. 54, 57
Dodd, C.H. 203, 204, 210
Dodson, J.D. 64, 84
Dodson, M. 184
Dohrenwend, B.P. 184
Dohrenwend, B.S. 184
Dominowski, R.L. 192, 201
Donisi, M. 133, 138, 152
Donnell, A. 57
Douglas, W. 145, 152
Driver, M.J. 159, 160, 171
Dryden, W. 205, 210
Duck, S. 185
Duncan-Jones, P. 184, 185

E

Eagly, A.H. 61, 63, 83
Easterbrook, J.A. 64, 83
Ebbesen, E.B. 99, 104
Edwards, A.L. 173, 179, 184
Edwards, R. 56, 58
Edwin, D. 119, 129
Eiser, J.R. 84
Ekman, P. 59
Ekstrand, B.R. 192, 201
Ellis, A. 204, 210
Emery, G. 2, 17
Emmons, R.A. 181, 184
Epstein, S. 72, 74, 83
Eysenck, H.J. 25, 36, 173, 174, 178, 184
Eysenck, S.B.C. 173, 174, 178, 184

F

Falcione, R.L. 26, 37, 110, 115
Fazio, R.H. 146, 153
Feather, N.T. 107, 114
Fedoravicius, A. 204, 210
Feffer, M. 118, 129
Feld, S. 179, 185
Feldman, R.S. 57
Fenz, W.D. 72, 74, 83
Feshbach, S. 62, 79, 83
Festinger, L. 53, 57
Fichten, C.S. 189, 199, 201
Finitzo, T. 57
Fischetti, M. 122, 129
Fishbein, M. 107, 114
Fishfader, T. 171
Fiske, D.W. 174, 184
Fiske, S.T. 134, 135, 136, 148, 149, 150, 153, 154
Fitzgerald, P.T. 8, 17
Flett, G.L. 187, 188, 189, 199, 201
Fodor, J.A. 47, 57
Forbes, L. 190, 201
Forst, E 105, 110, 114
Fox, J.E. 190, 201
Frankel, M. 115
Franks, C.M. 201
Franzoi, S.L. 127, 129
Freeman, F.J. 56, 57
Fremouw, W. J. 28, 36, 86, 104, 204, 210
Frierson, H.T. Jr. 188, 201

G

Gabay, S. 57
Gaines, B. 59
Galanter, E. 100, 104
Galassi, J.P. 9, 17, 188, 189, 201, 202
Galassi, M.D. 9, 17
Galin, D. 55, 57
Ganzer, V.J. 5, 17
Garamoni, G.I. 7, 18
Garber, J. 153
Gardner, H. 50, 57
Garrison, J.P. 48, 49, 57
Gazzaniga, M.S. 47, 48, 49, 53, 58
Geddes, D. 56, 58
Geen, R.G. 118, 129, 191, 201
Genest, M. 188, 201, 202
Gibbon, J. 115
Gilbert, D.T. 135, 136, 148, 153
Giles, H. 128
Gilmore, J.B. 204, 210
Glaser, S.R. 204, 210
Glass, C.R. 118, 127, 128, 129, 188, 189, 201, 202
Glass, G.V. 157, 158, 170
Goffman, E. 118, 126, 129
Goldfried, M.R. 118, 119, 129
Goldman, R. 62, 84
Goldman-Eisler, F. 21, 36
Gormally, J. 119, 129
Gorsky, J.M. 124, 128
Gorsuch, R.L. 159, 171
Goss, B. 48, 58
Gough, H.G. 119, 127, 129
Gray, C. 54, 57
Greenberg, J. 136, 148, 154
Greenberg, R. 135, 154
Greene, J.O. 56, 58, 100, 101, 104, 110, 115, 124, 129
Greiger, R. 204, 205, 210
Grenell, R.G. 57
Griffin, J.J. 59
Gur, R.C. 199, 202
Gurin, G. 179, 185

H

Hackman, J.R. 185
Halper, A. 57
Hamilton, D.L. 135, 148, 153
Hamilton, M.A. 56, 58
Hammen, C. 188, 201

Hanna, M.S. 171
Hanson, L.R. 135, 136, 148, 149, 150, 153
Haper, R.A. 210
Harris, M.S. 132, 152
Hartman, D.P. 158, 171
Hartman, L.M. 117, 118, 119, 121, 124, 127, 129, 130
Hastie, R. 136, 153
Hathaway, S.R. 173, 185
Hauser, M.F. 171
Hay, D.F. 185
Hayes, B.E. 9, 18, 189, 202
Hayes, D. 20, 36
Hays, W.L. 122, 130
Hazaleus, S.L. 189, 201
Hedges, L.V. 157, 170
Heise, D.R. 136, 137, 149, 151, 152, 153, 154
Henderson, L.S. 159, 161, 169
Henderson, S. 184, 185
Herman, C.P. 83, 84
Herman, E. 135, 154
Herr, P.M. 146, 153
Hickson, M.L. 52, 58
Higgins, E.T. 83, 84, 148, 153
Hill, R.A. 5, 17
Hinde, R.A. 34, 36
Hirsch, B.J. 184, 185
Hobfoll, S.E. 184, 185
Hodgson, R.J. 3, 18
Hoffman, M.L. 64, 83
Hogan, R. 126, 128
Holland, J.L. 127, 130
Hollon, S.D. 187, 202
Holroyd, K.A. 191, 201
Honess, T. 152
Honeycutt, J.M. 56, 58, 132, 149, 154
Hopf, T.S. 102, 103
Horan, J.J. 105, 109, 115
Horenstein, D. 135, 136, 153
Houston, B.K. 190, 201
Hovland, C.I. 62, 83
Huber, G.P. 106, 107, 115
Hulin, C.L. 181, 186
Hunsley, J. 7, 17, 189, 201
Hunt, R.G. 185
Hunter, J.E. 157, 163, 170
Huntley, J.R. 25, 36
Hurwicz, L. 107, 115

Huws, D. 54, 57
Hyerdahl, J. 158, 170

I

Ickes, W. 129, 185
Infante, D.A. 160, 170
Ingram, R.E. 7, 17, 118, 130
Isen, A.M. 64, 83
Ishii, S. 34, 36

J

Jackson, G.B. 157, 163, 170
Jackson, J. 171
Jackson, P. 136, 150, 154
Jaffe, P.E. 132, 153
Janis, I.L. 62, 79, 83, 105, 106, 109, 115, 116
Jepson, C. 61
Johnson, B. 63, 83
Johnson, J. 134, 135, 153
Jones, C.,R. 148, 153
Jones, E.E. 133, 134, 135, 136, 137, 147, 153
Jones, W.H. 18, 58, 119, 127, 128, 129, 130
Jourard, S.M. 132, 153

K

Kabat, L.G. 148, 152
Kahneman, D. 106, 109, 116
Kanouse, D.E. 135, 136, 148, 149, 150, 153
Katz, J. 59
Katz, L. 148, 153
Keefe, D.E. 9, 11, 18, 189, 202
Keith, R.W. 49, 58
Kelley, H.H. 62, 83, 150, 153
Kelly, L. 204, 210
Kendall, L.M. 181, 186
Kendall, P. 186
Kendall, P.C. 7, 17, 18, 187, 201, 202
Kenney, R.L. 116
Keon, T.L. 183, 185
Keuthe, J.L. 147, 149, 150, 152
Klopf, D. W. 34, 36
Knapp, M.L. 34, 36
Knowles, E.S. 129
Kondraske, G. 57
Kornhauser, A.W. 183, 185
Krantz, S.E. 188, 201

INDEX OF NAMES

Krull, D.S. 148, 153
Kumar, P.A. 136, 153

L

Lake, E.A. 126, 128
Langer, E.J. 62, 84
Langs, R. 54, 58
Lazarus, R.S. 133, 135, 149, 153, 184, 185
Lazowski, L.E. 131, 133, 137, 138, 150, 151, 152, 153
Leary, M.R. 1, 7, 17, 21, 30, 36, 39, 40, 41, 44, 99, 100, 104, 117, 118, 119, 124, 126, 130
Leber, W. 201
LeDoux, J.E. 47, 48, 49, 58
Leirer, V.O. 148, 153
Leitenberg, H. 128
Lepper, M.R. 73, 84
Leventhal, H. 52, 58, 62, 84
Levin, I.M. 173, 181, 184, 185
Levine, S. 84
LeVoi, M. 122, 130
Liberman, A. 61, 83
Light, R.L. 157, 170
Lindbergs, K. 170
Lindner, K.C. 14, 18
Logue, A.W. 115
Lord, C.G. 73, 84
Lushene, R.E. 159, 171
Lustig, M. 21, 37

M

Mackie, D.M. 64, 79, 84
MacKinnon, N.J. 136, 153
Mann, L. 106, 109, 115
March, J.G. 106, 115
Marlowe, D. 179, 184
Marshall, W.L. 189, 202
Maslach, C. 99, 104
Mayzner, M.S. 192, 202
McCrae, R.R. 174, 182, 184, 185
McCroskey, J.C. 19, 20, 21, 23, 24, 26, 27, 28, 30, 31, 32, 34, 35, 36, 37, 39, 40, 41, 44, 47, 58, 85, 86, 91, 95, 97, 103, 104, 105, 110, 115, 128, 156, 159, 160, 170, 203, 204, 210
McCroskey, LL. 23, 26, 27, 31, 37
McDonald, B. 183, 185

McDowell, C.E. 158, 159, 162, 170
McDowell, E.E. 158, 159, 162, 170
McGaw, B. 157, 170
McKinley, J.C. 174, 185
McKirnan, D.J. 184, 186
McReynolds, P. 156, 159, 168, 170
Mednick, S.A. 178, 185
Meichenbaum, D.H. 191, 197, 202, 204, 210
Melchior, L.A. 117, 118, 121, 126, 129, 130
Meltzer, L. 20, 36
Mendelschon, D. 57
Merluzzi, T.V. 118, 128, 188, 189, 201, 202
Miell, D. 122, 130
Miles, C.G. 25, 35
Miller, D.W. 106, 108, 115
Miller, G.A. 100, 104
Miller, M.D. 110, 115
Miller, S.M. 66, 67, 81, 84, 132, 135, 149, 153
Mittelman, J. 132, 152
Mogil, S. 57
Montogomery, B. 185
Moos, R.H. 184
Mortensen, D. C. 21, 37
Moscovitch, M. 52, 58
Motley, M.T. 85, 86, 87, 92, 103, 104
Mueller, J.H. 165, 170
Mychielska, K. 8, 18
Myszka, M.T. 189, 202

N

Near, J.P. 183, 185
Nelson, T.L. 189, 201
Nemeth, C.J. 64, 84
Neufeld, R.W.J. 106, 109, 115
Nisbett, R.E. 106, 115, 133, 136, 146, 153
Norman, W.T. 174, 185

O

O'Hair, D. 160, 162, 166, 168, 170
O'Keefe, B.J. 156, 159, 169, 170
O'Keefe, D.J. 156, 169
Ojemann, G. 48, 58
Oldham, G.R. 181, 185
Olkin, I. 157, 170

Olson, J.M. 81, 83, 84
Ostrom, T.M. 135, 153

P

Padawer, W. 118, 129
Park, M.S. 34, 36
Parkes, K.R. 8, 17
Paschall, K.A. 159, 161, 164, 170
Patterson, M. 159, 170
Payne, S.K. 34, 37, 160, 162, 165, 169
Perecman, E. 58
Peterson, C.R. 106, 108, 115
Petty, R.E. 61, 62, 63, 80, 84, 159, 166, 192, 202
Phillips, G.M. 26, 27, 30, 37, 156, 170
Pierce, G.R. 1, 12, 18, 39, 41, 44
Pilkonis, P.A. 119, 30
Pillemer, D.B. 124, 130, 157, 170
Pineo, S. 56, 58
Planalp, S. 132, 149, 154
Platt, J.J. 106, 109, 116
Pliner, P. 199, 201
Plutchik, R. 99, 104
Pool, K.D. 57
Porter, R. E. 34. 37
Predmore, S.C. 59
Preiss, R.W. 155, 156, 159, 160, 161, 162, 165, 167, 171
Pribram, K.H. 100, 104
Pryor, B. 159, 160, 162, 166, 167, 169
Pullan, G. 170
Pyszczynski, T.A. 136, 148, 154

Q

Quast, H. 12, 18

R

Rachlin, H. 106, 115
Rachman, S.J. 3, 18
Raiffa, H. 116
Rancer, A.S. 160, 170
Raphael, R. 119, 129
Rapoport, A. 108, 116
Reason, J.T. 8, 18
Reckman, R.F. 126, 130
Reeder, G.D. 134, 135, 148, 150, 154
Restak, R. 57

Rholes, W.S. 148, 153
Rice, R.W. 183, 185
Richey, H.W. 135, 154
Richey, M.H. 135, 154
Richmond, V.P. 19, 20, 21, 26, 32, 34, 35, 37, 40, 41, 44, 85, 86, 104, 110, 115, 159, 170
Rindo, J. 171
Rippetoe, P.A. 82, 84
Roach, D.A. 159, 161, 164, 171
Roback, A.A. 124, 130
Roberts, C.V. 37, 57, 58, 59, 114, 159, 161, 164, 171
Robillard, K. 189, 201
Robins, C. 118, 129
Robinson, W.P. 128
Rogers, R.W. 63, 82, 84
Rosenberg, M. 178, 185
Rosenthal, R. 158, 171
Ross, L. 73, 84, 106, 115, 133, 134, 136, 141, 143, 145, 146, 148, 152, 153, 154
Rothstein, L. 127, 128
Runge, T.E. 134, 135, 136, 141, 145, 154
Russell, D. 119, 127, 130
Rutherford, D.K. 132, 149, 154

S

Sackeim, H.A. 199, 202
Safer, M.A. 52, 58
Saine, T. 34, 35
Salz, P.H. 102, 104
Samovar, L. A. 34, 37
Sarason, B.R. 1, 9, 11, 13, 14, 18, 39, 41, 44, 54, 55, 58, 184, 185, 189, 202
Sarason, I.G. 1, 2, 3, 5, 9, 11, 13, 14, 15, 18, 39, 40, 41, 42, 43, 44, 54, 55, 58, 110, 116, 118, 130, 184, 185, 189, 190, 191, 197, 200, 202
Scammell, R.E. 54, 57
Schacter, S. 85, 86, 87, 97, 99, 104
Schaefer, C.C. 184, 185
Schaefer, S. 57
Scheier, M.F. 119, 128
Scherer, K.R. 59
Schlenker, B.R. 44, 99, 100, 104, 126, 130

Schmidt, F.L. 157, 163, 170
Schroder, M.J. 159, 160, 171
Schwartz, R.M. 7, 18
Schwarzer, C. 12, 18
Schwarzer, R. 12, 18, 129
Scott, M.D. 156, 157, 158, 159, 160, 161, 171, 204, 210
Sears, D. O. 63, 83
Segal, Z.V. 189, 202
Segalowitz, S.J. 51, 58
Seligman, M.E.P. 153
Sellers, D.E. 45, 48, 49, 51, 56, 56, 58, 59
Shea, C.A. 127, 129
Sheahan, M.E. 160, 162, 166, 168, 171
Shearin, E.N. 9, 11,18, 184, 185, 189, 202
Shedletsky, L.J. 51, 53, 58
Sherman, S.J. 146, 153
Shipley, W.C. 179, 185
Shrout, P.E. 184
Shure, M.B. 106, 109, 116
Siegel, R.G. 188, 201
Simon, H.A. 42, 44, 106, 115, 116
Singer, J.F. 85, 86, 87, 99, 104
Sipps, G. 119, 129
Skowronski, J.J. 135, 136, 147, 148, 150, 154
Sloan, R.D. 5, 17
Smith, M.L. 157, 170
Smith, P. 128
Smith, P.C. 181, 186
Smith, R.E. 110, 116
Smith, R.J. 188, 190, 200
Smith, S.H. 118, 126, 128
Smith, T.W. 118, 130
Smith-Lovin, L 137, 149, 151, 153, 154
Snyder, M. 137, 154
Sobocinski, D. 119, 129
Sorensen, G.A. 105, 110, 115, 204, 210
Sorrentino, R. 83
Sparks, G.S. 100, 101, 104, 110, 115, 126
Sperry, R.W. 50, 58
Spielberger, C.D. 1, 18, 72, 74, 84, 153, 170, 171, 202
Spivack, G. 106, 109, 116

Srull, T.K. 83, 136, 154
Stacks, D.W. 45, 46, 47, 48, 49, 50, 51, 52, 53, 54, 56, 58, 59
Stafford, L. 20, 27, 32, 35
Stahl, S.S. 118, 129
Stangor, C. 61, 63, 83
Starr, M.K. 106, 108, 115
Steffen, J.J. 126, 130
Steil, L.K. 158, 170
Stewart, R. 105, 110, 114
Stokes, J.P. 173, 184, 185, 186
Stone, J.D. 48, 57
Stoops, R. 11, 18
Strube, M.J. 158, 171
Struefert, S. 159, 160, 171
Suchotliff, L. 118, 129
Sutton, S.R. 62, 63, 84
Swann, W.B., Jr. 49, 59, 137, 154

T
Tarico, V.S. 189, 198, 202
Taylor, D.A. 132, 133, 135, 136, 151, 152
Taylor, J.A. 173, 178, 186
Taylor, S.E. 136, 149,154
Tellegen, A. 174, 180, 183, 186
TenHouten, W.D. 50, 53, 59
Theiman, G. 135, 154
Thein, R.D. 136, 152
Thoits, P.A. 184, 186
Thorne, A. 129, 119, 127, 130
Tice, D. 42, 44
Tivnan, T. 124, 130
Toner, B.B. 188, 191, 201
Tresselt, M.E. 192, 202
Tupes, E.C. 25, 35, 174, 186
Turk, D.C. 188, 201
Turk, S. 14, 15, 18
Turner, S.M. 127, 130
Tversky, A. 106, 109, 116

U
Uleman, J.S. 83
Ursin, H. 84

V
Valins, S. 153
Van Velzen, D.R. 189, 202
van der Ploeg, H.M. 18
Vangelisti, A.L. 166, 169
Varvil-Weld, D. 119, 129

Veroff, J. 179, 185
Vinson, L.R. 57, 59

W

Wald, A. 106, 116
Wallace, A. 203, 210
Wallace, I. 203, 210
Wallander, J.L. 122, 129
Wallechinsky, D. 203, 210
Ware, W.B. 189, 202
Warr, P. 136, 150, 154
Watson, A.K. 117, 127, 129, 130, 203, 204, 210
Watson, B.C. 57
Watson, D. 173, 174, 175, 178, 179, 180, 182, 183, 186
Watson, K. 159, 171
Watson, K.W. 37, 57, 58, 59, 114
Watson, T.E. 9, 17
Weiner, B. 153
Welsh, G.S. 185
Westbrook, T. 191, 201
Wheeler, D. 106, 119, 116
Wheeler, L. 17
Wheeless, L.R. 155, 156, 157, 158, 159, 160, 161, 164, 171
Whisman, M.A. 5, 17
White, R.C. 102, 104
Whitman, R.F. 159, 161, 169
Wickersham, T. 171
Wigley, C.J., III 160, 162, 165, 167, 171
Williams, B.L. 160, 161, 164, 171
Williams, M. 133, 138, 152
Williford, J. 49, 59
Wilson, G.T. 202
Wine, J.D. 192, 197, 202
Witelson, S.F. 47, 48, 59
Wolf, M. 191, 201
Worth, L.T. 64, 79, 84
Wortman, C.B. 135, 154
Wyer, R.S. 83, 136, 154

Y

Yardley, K. 152
Yates, S. 62, 83
Yee, P.L. 12, 18
Yerkes, R. M. 64, 84

Z

Zagacki, K.S. 56, 58
Zaidel, E. 49, 52, 57, 58, 59
Zajonc, R.B. 49, 59, 64, 84, 132, 154
Zakahi, W. R. 23, 24, 37
Zanna, M.P. 81, 83, 84, 135, 148, 153
Zimbardo, P.G. 30, 37, 99, 104, 119, 127, 130
Zuckerman, M. 170
Zwemer, W.A. 5, 17

SUBJECT INDEX

A
affect 43, 49, 132, 134
affect/mood 180, 178
anxiety 1, 39, 121, 132, 157
  and performance 5
  effects 3
  inhibitory effects 80
  social 6, 11, 30, 40, 205
  speech 205
  symptoms, somatic 118
  test anxiety 2, 5, 9, 40, 187, 189
  trait 77
anxious
  cognitions 43
  self-preoccupation 39, 117
apprehension 1, 54
argument 68
assessing cognition
  endorsement methods 188
  production methods 188
attention 4, 8, 15
  distribution of 118
  distribution of 121
  self-focused 118
atypical information 136
audience anxiety 30, 40
autonomic-nervous-system 86
avoidance 29, 55, 62, 105

B
behavioral
  consequences of shyness 122
  disruption 42, 43
  effects 40
  inhibition 43
beliefs, irrational 204
brain functioning, holistic theory 46
brain hemispheres 46

C
cancer, chronic fear of 68, 75
central route to persuasion 62
chronic fear 65
cognition 20, 49, 174
  assessing 188
cognitions 134
  anxious 43
cognitive
  assessments 200
  disruption 42
  effort 62

cognitive (cont.)
  interference 6, 7, 8, 9, 13, 17, 39, 40, 42, 54, 55, 118
  interference, measurement 8
  interpretation 86
  restructuring 204
communication
  avoidance 45
  competence 26, 46
  disruption 3
  orientation 88
  orientation, pragmatic 91
  skills 41
  strategy selection 109
communication apprehension 27, 40, 45, 105, 109, 203
  behavioral effects 40
  effects of 29
  internal effects 27
  link with communication strategy selection 109
  predisposition 47
  trait 47
competence 12, 45
conceptual differences 41
consequences of disclosure 134
contexts 23
cue-utilization hypothesis 165
cyncism 175

D
decision
  counseling 109
  rule orientation 106, 109
    inconsistency 109
  rules 108
delivery behaviors 93
desensitization 205
dispositional inferences 142, 147
disruption 126
dissonance 53
distribution of attention 118, 121

E
education level 157, 166
effect size 162
emotional
  labels 87
  reactions 75
endorsement methods, of assessing cognitions 188

219

evaluation 7, 89, 190
extraversion 182

F

fear 62
  of negative evaluation 121
fear-arousing persuasive messages 61

G

general anxiety 1

H

happiness 179
hemispheric communication 49
holistic theory of brain functioning 46

I

information processing 61, 109
  anxiety 164
  capacity 168
  complexity 165
  effectiveness 157
  state-like 55
informativeness, perceptions of 144
inhibitory effect, of general anxiety 80
intellectual achievement 180
intelligence 178
interference 64
interpersonal
  attraction 132
  processes 12, 33
  strategy 42
interrupt mechanism 42
intimacy 132
intrapersonal communication 45-46, 52
introversion 25, 110, 178
irrational beliefs 204
issue involvement 63, 79

J

job satisfaction 33, 181
judges' rating 189

L

life satisfaction 179
liking, perceptions of 145
listening effectiveness 157, 164
logical errors of arguments 68

M

maximax rule 107
maximin approach 106
maximum expected utility (MEU) 107
measurement 8, 11, 23, 67, 110, 120, 121, 137, 175, 187
meta-analysis 157
modular
  communication 46, 56
  cooperation 50
  dissonance 50, 53, 54
  functioning 48
  mind 47, 48
motivation 64, 79, 147, 196

N

negative
  affectivity 173, 175
  bias 119
  cognition 2
  disclosures 133
  evaluation, fear of 121
  expectations 109
negativity 119, 143, 148
  effects of self-disclosure 135

O

others' ratings 122

P

patterns of thought 39
perceptions
  of informativeness 144
  of liking 145
performance
  anxiety 5
  orientation 88
personal relevance 63
persuasion 61
physiological arousal 86
predisposition 9, 21, 173
prisoner's dilemma-type games 108
privacy 143
  of the disclosure 138, 151
processing styles 81
production methods of assessing cognition 188
psychological health 174, 184
public speaking 85
  apprehension 105

public speaking (cont.)
    orientations, performance vs. communicating 88

R
ratings of others 122
rational emotive therapy 203, 204
receiver apprehension 155
reciprocity 132
recursive process 43
relationship development 132
repression-sensitization 78
reticence 26
rewards and costs 41, 106

S
Schacterian model 86
self-attention 42
self-disclosure 131
    extremity of 136
    intimacy 144
    negativity effects 135
    privacy of 138
self-esteem 26, 174, 110, 178, 182
self-expectancies 168, 190, 196
self-focus 126, 189
self-focused attention 118
self-perception 133
self-preoccupation 2, 3, 4, 9, 14, 16, 39, 42
    anxious 117
self-presentation 44
self-rating 119, 122, 189
shyness 21, 30, 40, 117, 205
skill training 205
social
    anxiety 6, 11, 30, 40, 205
    comparison 119
    desirability 179, 182
    penetration processes 133
    perception 131, 134, 135, 151
    skill 118
    support 13, 14
    withdrawal 204
somatic anxiety symptoms 118
speech
    anxiety 205
    introduction strategies 110
stage fright 30
state-like information processing 55
state anxiety 105
susceptibility 77, 80
systematic processing 62
    capacity for 79

T
task difficulty 200
tension 174
test anxiety 2, 5, 9, 40, 187, 189
therapy 91
thought lists 68, 75, 188, 192
thought patterns 39
trait 50, 55, 65, 109, 156
    anxiety 77
treatment 86

U
uncertainty 132, 135, 149
unwillingness to communicate 30
utility values 111

V
volition 20, 40

W
willingness to communicate 19, 40
    antecedents 25
    effects of 32
Willingness-to-Communicate Scale (WTC) 22, 42
worry 2, 7, 9, 15, 43

About the Authors

Mike Allen received his Ph.D. from Michigan State University and is an Assistant Professor in the Department of Communication at the University of Wisconsin, Milwaukee. His research interests are in the mathematical summarization of empirical data and is co-editing a book on the use of meta-analysis in persuasion research.

Susan Andersen is an Associate Professor in the Department of Psychology at New York University. She received her Ph.D. from Stanford University and is currently an Associate Editor of the *Journal of Social and Clinical Psychology.*

Michael Beatty is Professor in the Department of Communication at Cleveland State University. He is currently the editor of *Communication Research Reports* and former associate editor of *Communication Education.* He received his Ph.D. from Ohio State University.

Kirk R. Blankstein, who received his Ph.D. from the University of Waterloo, is an Associate Professor of Psychology at Erindale College, University of Toronto, Canada. He is the editor of the Plenum Publishing series titled "Advances in the Study of Communication and Affect."

Melanie Booth-Butterfield is Assistant Professor in the Department of Communication Studies at West Virginia University. Her research includes cognitive and emotional processes in anxiety and interpersonal communication. She received her Ph.D. from the University of Missouri, Columbia.

Shelly Chaiken is a Professor in the Department of Psychology at New York University. She received her Ph.D. from the University of

Massachusetts at Amherst and is currently the Associate Editor of the *Attitudes and Social Cognition* section of the *Journal of Personality and Social Psychology*. She is also the Chair of the Executive Committee of the Society of Experimental Social Psychology. Her research interests focus upon attitudes and social cognition.

Jonathan Cheek is an Associate Professor of Psychology at Wellesley College. He received his Ph.D. in personality psychology from Johns Hopkins University and has co-authored and edited numerous books and articles on shyness research and treatment.

Robyn Clair is an Assistant Professor in the Department of Communication at Cleveland State University. She completed her Ph.D. at Kent State University.

Carly Dodd is Professor and Chair of the Communication Department of Abilene Christian University where he was the Outstanding Professor of the Year in Professional Studies in 1985. He received his Ph.D. from the University of Oklahoma and has co-authored textbooks in the areas of intercultural and professional communication.

Gordon L. Flett is an Assistant Professor in the Department of Psychology, York University, Ontario, Canada. He received his Ph.D. from the University of Toronto and was awarded a Social Sciences and Humanities Research Council of Canada Research Fellowship in 1989.

Christopher Jepson (Ph.D., University of Michigan) is a biostatistician at the University of Pennsylvania and is associated with the Fox Chase Cancer Center in Cheltenham, PA.

Linda Lazowski is an Assistant Professor in the Department of Sociology at the University of Indiana. She received her Ph.D. from the University of California at Santa Barbara, after which she was awarded a research fellowship in a National Institute of Mental Health-funded program on Identity and Mental Health at Indiana University.

Mark Leary (Ph.D., Florida State University) is an Associate Professor in the Department of Psychology at Wake Forest University. He received the university's Award for Excellence in Faculty Research in 1990. He has published several books and was awarded the Speech Communication Association's Outstanding Book Award for *Under-*

standing Social Anxiety in 1984. He is currently an associate editor of the *Journal of Social and Clinical Psychology.*

Ira Levin is an Organization Development consultant with Kaiser Permanente Medical Care in Oakland, California. He received his Ph.D. from the University of Illinois in Chicago.

James C. McCroskey is Professor and Chair of the Department of Communication Studies at West Virginia University. A fellow of the International Communication Association, he is a former editor of *Human Communication Research* and *Communication Education,* and past president of the Eastern Communication Association. He received his doctorate from Pennsylvania State University.

Lisa Melchior is Vice President and Research Coordinator of The Measurement Group, a management consulting firm specializing in applied psychological assessment. She received her Ph.D. from the University of Michigan where she was a Regent's Fellow.

Michael T. Motley is Professor and Chair of the Department of Communication at the University of California, Davis. He received his Ph.D. from Pennsylvania State University and his research focus is cognition.

Gregory R. Pierce received his Ph.D. from the University of Washington, where he is now a Post-doctoral research associate. He is a co-editor of *Social support: An interactional view* and his research activities include experimental studies of social support and social learning approaches to stimulating altruistic behavior.

Raymond Preiss is a visiting Assistant Professor in the Communication Department at the University of Puget Sound. He received his Ph.D. from the University of Oregon and is co-editing a book on the use of meta-analysis in persuasion research.

Virginia Peck Richmond is Professor and Coordinator of Graduate Study in the Department of Communication Studies at West Virginia University. She is currently the editor of *Communication Quarterly,* a former editor of *Communication Research Reports,* and past president of the Eastern Communication Association. She received her Ph.D. from the University of Nebraska.

Barbara R. Sarason, Ph.D. Indiana University, is a Professor in the Department of Psychology at the University of Washington where she is also a Professor of the Fred Hutchinson Cancer Research Center. She has edited and co-authored numerous books and scholarly articles on social support, stress, and coping.

Irwin Sarason (Ph.D., Indiana University) is a Professor of Psychology at the University of Washington. He has served as Editor of the *Personality Processes and Individual Differences* section of the *Journal of Personality and Social Psychology* and is a Past-President of the Western Psychological Association. He is a Fellow of both the American Psychological Association and the American Association for the Advancement of Science. His current research interests concern anxiety, cognitive interference, and social support.

Don Stacks is an Associate Professor of communication at the University of Miami. He received his Ph.D. from the University of Florida and serves on the editorial boards of several professional journals.

Joseph P. Stokes is a Professor of Psychology at the University of Illinois, Chicago. His Ph.D. is also from the University of Illinois at Chicago.

Daniel Sullivan is a member of the Speech Pathology and Audiology Department at the University of South Alabama, Mobile, Alabama.

Arden Watson is an Associate Professor in the Communication Department at Pennsylvania State University, Deleware County Campus.

Lawrence R. Wheeless is Professor in the Department of Communication Studies at West Virginia University. He received his Ph.D. from Wayne State University. He is a former editor of *Communication Quarterly*, has been chair of several divisions in professional organizations, and a board member of International Communication Association.